The Welsh Language Commissioner in Context

THE WELSH LANGUAGE COMMISSIONER IN CONTEXT
ROLES, METHODS AND RELATIONSHIPS

Diarmait Mac Giolla Chríost

UNIVERSITY OF WALES PRESS
2016

© Diarmait Mac Giolla Chríost, 2016

All rights reserved. No part of this book may be reproduced in any material form (including photocopying or storing it in any medium by electronic means and whether or not transiently or incidentally to some other use of this publication) without the written permission of the copyright owner. Applications for the copyright owner's written permission to reproduce any part of this publication should be addressed to the University of Wales Press, 10 Columbus Walk, Brigantine Place, Cardiff CF10 4UP.

www.uwp.co.uk

British Library CIP Data
A catalogue record for this book is available from the British Library

ISBN   978-1-78316-904-7
eISBN   978-1-78316-905-4

The right of Diarmait Mac Giolla Chríost to be identified as author of this work has been asserted in accordance with sections 77 and 79 of the Copyright, Designs and Patents Act 1988.

Designed by Chris Bell, cbdesign
Printed by CPI Antony Rowe, Melksham

CONTENTS

List of figures	vii
List of key acronyms	ix
Acknowledgements	xi
1 Introduction: research aims and methodology	1
2 Independence, accountability and structure	7
3 Language rights and freedom	41
4 Regulatory standards	71
5 Promotion and complaint-handling	97
6 The Crown, Ministers of the Crown and Crown bodies	133
7 Official language	159
8 Conclusions: too complex a regime?	207
Bibliography	219
Index	241

FIGURES

Figure 1 Location of language complaint-handling and enforcement functions: domestic (UK) and international case studies according to Welsh Policy Paper 3.   9

Figure 2 Timeline for the Welsh Language Commissioner, Standards and Regulations.   19

Figure 3 360° accountability of the independent regulator (adapted from House of Lords, Select Committee on the Constitution, 2004a: 20).   23

Figure 4 The necessary elements of better regulatory outcomes (adapted from OECD, 2013: 4, and OECD, 2014: 22).   24

Figure 5 Molecular structure of a Welsh language right following Hohfeld, 1919.   49

Figure 6 States in which the freedom to use or the 'right to freely use one's own language' is recognised by statute.   54

Figure 7 Comparative schematic for Welsh Language Schemes and Welsh Language Standards as instruments for setting Welsh language regulatory standards.   89

Figure 8 Welsh Language Board: complaints and statutory investigations based upon data derived from the Welsh Language Board, Annual Reports, 1995–2011.   107

Figure 9   Irish Language Commissioner: complaints and investigations based upon data derived from the Irish Language Commissioner, Annual Reports, 2004–2012.   108

Figure 10   Office of the Commissioner of Official Languages, Canada: complaints based upon data derived from OCOL, Annual Reports, 1971–2012.   110

Figure 11   E-mail from a member of the Welsh Language Society to members of the Welsh Language Society on 17 November 2014.   114

Figure 12   Examples of Civil Law jurisdictions.   189

Figure 13   Length of the Welsh language legislation in the context of UK Government primary legislation based upon data derived in part from House of Lords, 2013: 3–4.   208

Figure 14   Identifying excessively complex legislation (source: Office of the Parliamentary Counsel, 2013: 13).   212

Figure 15   From policy to Bill – a summary of upstream causes of excessively complex legislation (source: Office of the Parliamentary Counsel, 2013: 25).   212

Figure 16   Identifying the potential for complexity arising from the main content and purpose of the Measure.   213

Figure 17   Quantifying the potential for complexity in the current Welsh language regulatory regime: pertinent statute and instruments with statutory force.   214

Figure 18   Quantifying the potential for complexity in Welsh Language Schemes: volume and length of Schemes.   215

KEY ACRONYMS

AM	Assembly Member
BIOA	British and Irish Ombudsman Association
ECHR	European Court of Human Rights
FCA	Financial Conduct Authority
HL	House of Lords
HMRC	Her Majesty's Revenue and Customs
ICO	Information Commissioner's Office
LCO	Legislative Competence Order
NMD	Non-Ministerial Department
NS&I	National Savings and Investments
OCOL	Office of the Commissioner of Official Languages
OECD	Organisation for Economic Co-operation and Development
PSOW	Public Services Ombudsman Wales
TAN	Technical Advice Note
WAG	Welsh Assembly Government

ACKNOWLEDGEMENTS

This work arises from the following research project 'The office of language commissioner in Wales, Ireland and Canada', sponsored by the Economic and Social Research Council (ESRC), reference ES/J003093/1. The author would like to recognise two others as involved in aspects of the research relating to this book – Patrick Carlin and Colin H. Williams, both of the School of Welsh, Cardiff University. Carlin in particular was engaged with aspects of the research from which the book generally arises, and as well as commenting upon the draft texts of the book Carlin transcribed the fieldwork interviews. The author is most grateful to the following for their various contributions to various matters pertaining to the research underpinning this book: Linda Cardinal (Ottawa), Fernand de Varennes (Moncton), Rob Dunbar (Edinburgh), Daniel Elmiger (Geneva), Manon George (Cardiff), Dirk Gorter (Basque Country), Cosmo Graham (Leicester), Daniel Greenberg (UK Parliamentary Counsel and Berwin Leighton Paisner), Neil Harris (Cardiff), Meirion Prys Jones (NPLD), Gwion Lewis (Landmark Chambers), Huw Lewis (Aberystwyth), Wilson McLeod (Edinburgh), David Melding AM (National Assembly for Wales), Jacqueline Mowbray (Sydney),[1] Niamh Nic Shuibhne (Edinburgh), Martin Normand (Montréal), Colm Ó Cinneide (UCL), Seán Ó Conaill (Cork), Peadar Ó Flaharta (Dublin City), R. Gwynedd Parry (Swansea), Maite Puigdevall i Serralvo (Open University Catalonia), Vanessa Pupavac (Nottingham), Elin Royles

---

[1] Cardiff University Incoming Fellowship Award 2015.

(Aberystwyth), John Walsh (Galway) and staff at Cardiff Civil Justice Centre. The author is also grateful to the audiences of presentations given on the research results at Aberystwyth University in 2015, the National Eisteddfod 2015 (by invitation of Cwmni Iaith) and Calgary University's annual conference (2015) on *Language Policy and Planning*, as well as at the international colloquium on *Administrative Justice in Wales and Comparative Perspectives* hosted by Bangor University, also during 2015. The author alone is responsible for the content. In addition, the author is very grateful to the OECD for permission to use the figure entitled 'The necessary elements of better regulatory outcomes', as published in *The Governance of Regulators, OECD Best Practice Principles for Regulatory Policy* (OECD Publishing, 2014; http://dx.doi.org/10.1787/9789264209015-en), in adapted form, in the shape of Figure 4 of this book. Figure 3, entitled '360° accountability of the independent regulator', adapted from House of Lords Select Committee on the Constitution (2004a: 20); Figure 14, entitled 'Identifying excessively complex legislation', from Office of the Parliamentary Counsel (2013: 13); and figure 15, entitled 'From policy to Bill – a summary of upstream causes of excessively complex legislation', from Office of the Parliamentary Counsel (2013: 25), are reproduced under Open Government Licence. The author would also like to acknowledge the value of the comments and suggestions noted in the anonymous reviews of the draft version of this book.

1 | INTRODUCTION: RESEARCH AIMS AND METHODOLOGY

This English-language research monograph is the first authoritative work on the office of the Welsh Language Commissioner and the associated Welsh language regulatory and statutory regime. The work that is at the heart of the book arises from a major research project entitled 'The office of language commissioner in Wales, Ireland and Canada'. The project was sponsored by the Economic and Social Research Council (ESRC).[1] The overarching aim of the research underpinning this book was to produce a scholarly output that will contribute to developing a better understanding of the characteristics of (i) a good regulatory environment, (ii) a high-performing regulator, and (iii) regulatory best practice, along with (iv) the means of realising effective regulatory outcomes in relation to offices of Language Commissioner in general and the office of the Welsh Language Commissioner in particular (henceforth, the Commissioner). This, in turn, will inform how the legitimacy of the regulator may be reinforced, so as to secure the effective implementation of public policy while at the same time reinforcing the confidence and trust of both the bodies subject to regulation and also of citizens.[2]

In setting the Commissioner in context, that is in Wales, the UK and internationally, the work draws upon a rich variety of source material arising from fieldwork conducted in a number of jurisdictions. The methodological approach that underpins the research inherent to this book comprises, in the first place, an authoritative review of the relevant research literature in the fields of language planning and policy, public administration, language law and linguistic rights, regulators and regulatory regimes, and political science. The work is therefore multidisciplinary in approach, engaging with the scholarly and professional literature in language policy and planning, socio-legal studies and the politics of language.

The research data underpinning this text includes a rich vein of material arising from fieldwork conducted in Canada, Ireland and Wales. This comprised a set of fieldnotes taken at a range of public events pertinent to the research questions, along with a series of semi-structured interviews conducted with dozens of key actors from the relevant legislatures, governments, regulatory offices, interest groups and civic society representatives in the various jurisdictions. This body of interviewees included ombudsmen, commissioners, regulators, politicians, civil servants, policy advisors, activists and academic experts. The interviews were transcribed and analysed, using the computer-assisted qualitative data software programme NVivo 10 and its associated tools. In order to make full use of the particular architecture of the programme, the data derived from the fieldwork was organised in a series of text-based and audio files, and a deductive coding structure created from the research issues and questions at the core of the project as a whole was applied to them, using an iterative approach. This coding structure was the foundation of the node and framework matrices through which the data was analysed. The coding exercises included the creation of hierarchical structures of nodes, grouping the codes into code families as co-occurring nodes, as well as creating inductive codes and auto-coding. The data was also explored though matrix coding, key-word and key-phrase text search queries; through creating word-clusters, trees and frequencies in context as well as through generating connection maps based upon group queries. The output of this work was a series of semantic networks, and that enabled the capture of the key themes arising from these particular data, along with the relationships between them. Any material from the fieldwork interviews presented in this book has been wholly anonymised.

The pertinent contemporary and archived professional, technical and grey literature in a number of languages in Wales, as well as Canada, Ireland and elsewhere, provided an alternative source of invaluable data. The linguistic coverage of source material for the purposes of this research includes, in particular, English, French,

German, Irish, Spanish and Welsh. This literature included a substantial body of almost one hundred governmental documents arising from a number of Freedom of Information applications in various jurisdictions. The in-depth analysis of this material is wholly unique to this book. In addition to this literature, close attention was paid to the public discourse on the Commissioner and the language issues associated with the office in the broadcast and print news media. The careful analysis of this material has given rise to a number of important insights.

During the course of the project the author wrote a series of detailed internal discussion papers and briefing on a range of key themes, and directed the development and writing of others by Carlin, and these have formed the basis of a several conference and research seminar presentations and other expert academic discussions under the Chatham House Rule leading to the development of this book. The author, together with Carlin, consulted with certain experts based elsewhere in the UK and internationally, both professional and academic, in order to clarify, in an authoritative manner, some very particular aspects of the research. The robustness of the research results, along with the interpretation of them, has been triangulated[3] with regards to the following 'types':[4] data, investigator, theory and methodology.

The content of the book is organised into a set of thematic chapters comprised as follows: independence, accountability and organisational form or structure (chapter 2); language rights and freedom (chapter 3); regulatory standards (chapter 4); promotion and complaint-handling (chapter 5); the Crown, Ministers of the Crown and Crown bodies (chapter 6); Welsh as an official language (chapter 7); and, the complexity of the Welsh language regulatory regime (chapter 8). The research results thereby presented in the book offer a range of insights into the scope and function of the office of the Commissioner, of value to developing a better understanding of various important aspects of the scholarly field of language policy and planning. Some of the work will also be of substantial interest to academics working in the areas of administrative justice and of language law, domains united by the unfolding debate on the idea of linguistic justice.[5] It is likely that some of the results will be of especial interest to policy-makers and practitioners as well as to opinion-formers engaged in language issues.

A number of the research results have immediate relevance to public policy as pertains to the Welsh language and, indeed, may appear to be rather striking to Welsh policy actors. These include, for example, the following conclusions:

1. the current organisational form, or corporate structure of the office of the Commissioner is not fit for purpose;
2. there are insufficient checks and balances on the operation of the office of the Commissioner;
3. ministerial direction is appropriately framed in the Measure and has been appropriately applied;
4. the current mechanics as regards setting the Commissioner's budget are appropriate;
5. there is a conflict of interest between the First Minister and the Welsh Language Tribunal;
6. the legislative cycle in particular was informed by weak and partial evidence on a number of issues, but in particular on the following matters: statutory declarations of official language status, freedom to use a language, the concept of 'active offer', and the independence and accountability of the office of Language Commissioner generally;
7. distinctions between expert and activist evidence were often substantially blurred;
8. Common Law jurisdictions can, and indeed do, accommodate official languages;
9. that the English language is declared an official language under the National Assembly for Wales (Official Languages) Act 2012 is certainly of doubtful vires, as the Assembly has no legal competency with regard to English;
10. Welsh Language Standards, as per the Measure, can be said to create language rights;
11. Welsh Language Standards are no less complex than are Welsh Language Schemes;
12. that both the Commissioner and the Welsh government are responsible for promoting the Welsh language creates duplication;
13. it is constitutionally unsound for the Commissioner, as a regulator, to be under a duty to critique Welsh government policy;

14. the operation of complaint-handling function by the Commissioner is a marked improvement upon the historical performance of the Welsh Language Board;
15. there are clear signs of regulatory activism by the Commissioner and also indications of regulatory capture of the Commissioner by language interest groups. This is manifest in the Commissioner campaigning for changes to Welsh government legislation and in the manipulation of the complaint-handling process by the Commissioner in relation to specific cases regarding the freedom to use Welsh and the Welsh language services of high street banks;
16. the Commissioner misrepresented the legal implications of the result of the judicial review she initiated against National Savings and Investments;
17. the relationship of the Crown, Ministers of the Crown and Crown bodies to the Welsh language regulatory regime is overly complex and ambiguous;
18. there is no single model of commissioners in Wales to which the Commissioner can, or ought to, conform.

Overall, therefore, the evidence is sufficient to conclude that there is good reason to substantially revise aspects of the Welsh language regulatory regime in its totality, including via legislation. These headline results are not, of course, sufficient in and of themselves; for that, it is necessary to work through the detail of each of the issues to hand. In that regard the devil, as ever, is in the detail.

Notes

1   ESRC reference ES/J003093/1.
2   Refer, for example, to R. Baldwin, M. Cave and M. Lodge, *Understanding Regulation. Theory, Strategy, and Practice* (Oxford: Oxford University Press, 2011); R. Baldwin, M. Cave and M. Lodge (eds), *The Oxford Handbook of Regulation* (Oxford: Oxford University Press, 2010); T. Christensen and P. Lægreid (eds), *Autonomy and Regulation: Coping with Agencies in the Modern State* (Cheltenham: Edward Elgar, 2006); Department for Business, Innovation & Skills / Welsh Government, *Mapping the Regulatory Landscape in Wales* (London: Department for Business, Innovation & Skills, 2013); Department for Business, Innovation & Skills,

Regulators' Code (London: Department for Business, Innovation & Skills, 2014); P. Hampton, *Reducing Administrative Burdens: Effective Inspection and Enforcement* (London: HM Treasury, 2005); C. Hood, H. Rothstein and R. Baldwin, *The Government of Risk: Understanding Risk Regulation Regimes* (Oxford: Oxford University Press, 2001); House of Lords, Select Committee on the Constitution, *The Regulatory State: Ensuring its Accountability. Volume 1: Report* (London: The Stationery Office Limited, 2004a); House of Lords, Select Committee on the Constitution, *The Regulatory State: Ensuring its Accountability: The Government's Response. Report* (London: The Stationery Office Limited, 2004b); House of Lords, Select Committee on Regulators, *UK Economic Regulators. Volume I: Report* (London: The Stationery Office Limited, 2007a); House of Lords, Select Committee on Regulators, *UK Economic Regulators. Volume I: The Evidence* (London: The Stationery Office Limited, 2007b); G. Majone, 'The regulatory state and its legitimacy problems', *West European Politics*, 22/1 (1999), 1–24; M. Moran, 'Review article: Understanding the regulatory state', *British Journal of Political Science*, 32/2 (2002), 391–413; OECD, *Principles for the Governance of Regulators. Public Consultation Draft* (OECD Publishing, 2013); OECD, *The Governance of Regulators, OECD Best Practice Principles for Regulatory Policy* (OECD Publishing, 2014), published online at: http://www.oecd-ilibrary.org/governance/the-governance-of-regulators_9789264209015-en; and C. Scott, 'Accountability in the regulatory state', *Journal of Law and Society*, 27/1 (2000), 38–60.

3   P. M. Rothbauer, 'Triangulation', in L. Given (ed.), *The SAGE Encyclopedia of Qualitative Research Methods* (Thousand Oaks, CA: SAGE, 2008), pp. 893–5.

4   N. K. Denzin (ed.), *Sociological Methods* (New Jersey: Aldine Transaction Publishers, 2006).

5   See, for example, J. Mowbray, *Linguistic Justice. International Law and Language Policy* (Oxford: Oxford University Press, 2012).

2 | INDEPENDENCE, ACCOUNTABILITY AND STRUCTURE

Introduction

The purpose of this chapter is, firstly, to highlight a number of key issues with regard to the independence and accountability of the Welsh Language Commissioner and, secondly, to consider the significance of the structure of the office or, more precisely, the manner of its incorporation or legal personality, whether corporation sole or corporation aggregate. The matter of the independence of the office of the Commissioner was subject to sustained debate, both within the Assembly and in the news media. Despite this scrutiny the evidence shows that the notion of independence was only loosely understood by many of the actors, and this remains the case to a considerable degree. There are important nuances to independence and accountability with regard to a public office of the nature of the Commissioner and these are subject to robust examination here, with regard to both policy and scholarly evidence in the Welsh, the UK and international context, as appropriate. The evidence points to certain significant weaknesses as regards structure and accountability which may usefully inform policy development in the future in this area.

Policy cycle discussion, recommendation and instruction (June 2008–April 2009)[1]

Matters regarding the independence of the office of the Language Commissioner were to the fore at the earliest stage in the policy cycle. A policy paper notes that the independence of the office was among the 'key aims in the establishment of a Commission/er', for example: 'In relation to any regulatory functions, the Commission/er should be, and be seen to be, independent and impartial.'[2] This policy paper also presents evidence to suggest that in jurisdictions where the language being attended to 'is in a weaker position overall, or where there is less political commitment, independent Commissioners have been established' (Figure 1).[3] This appears to imply that a Commission, or other corporate body, rather than a Commissioner would be the more appropriate model for the Welsh context.

A substantial part of the policy discussion regarding the independence of the office focused upon the process of selection and appointment. Consideration was given to the impact of the manner of the selection and appointment of the Commissioner in relation to the independence of the office. It was asserted that were the Commissioner to undertake functions of 'complaints handling, enforcement and general advocacy', then 'there would be a strong case for arguing that the appointment should be made by the National Assembly for Wales',[4] thereby ensuring the 'appropriate degree of independence and transparency for the office holder'.[5] It was also noted there that the Select Committee for Welsh Affairs at Westminster 'recommended that they ['Commissioners', that is the Commissioner for Older People and the Children's Commissioner] should be more accountable to the National Assembly, to provide the appropriate degree of independence from the Assembly Government',[6] adding that 'The argument for pursuing such an approach is that it would help to ensure that the general public see the Commissioner as a genuinely independent and impartial voice for the Welsh language and Welsh speakers.'[7]

It was also noted that were the Commissioner to undertake functions wider than complaint-handling, enforcement and general advocacy and including, therefore, 'more general activities in support of the Welsh language', then, it was contended, 'the argument for involving the National Assembly is weakened'.[8] It is then added that 'Given that part of the Commission's functions might therefore be the delivery of Assembly Government policies, as well as undertaking statutory functions, the Assembly Government would want close involvement in the appointment process.'[9] The matter of operational independence is discussed in this paper under the headline of 'accountability'.[10] Here, it is noted that 'the exact functions of a Commission or Commissioner will determine the appropriate amount of operational independence.'[11] That said, a more precise understanding

	Language Commissioner	Commission, government department or wider governmental agency
Basque Autonomous Region	✗	✓
Canada – Federal	✓	✗
Catalonia	✗	✓
New Brunswick	✓	✗
Québec	✗	✓
Republic of Ireland	✓	✗
Scotland	✗	✗

Figure 1. *Location of language complaint-handling and enforcement functions: domestic (UK) and international case studies according to Welsh Policy Paper 3.*

of these exact functions seems to be based only upon an unspecified difference between general functions on the one hand and more tightly focused functions on the other. In the case of the former, 'The more general the functions given to a Commissioner/er, the more appropriate it would be for the individual/organisation to be more directly responsible to the Assembly Government';[12] in the case of the latter, 'Conversely, if the Commissioner has a relatively narrow focus, then it would be more appropriate to give the Commissioner a large degree of operational independence.'[13]

The matter of funding was raised in the context of accountability. It was noted that a funding mechanism whereby the Assembly Government 'directly' sets the budget of the office 'might compromise the operational and perceived independence of the Commissioner',[14] and that, by implication, serious consideration ought to be given to funding the office through the National Assembly from the Consolidated Fund, as with the Auditor General for Wales and the PSOW.[15] At a later stage in the policy cycle, it was determined that the appointment of the Commissioner be a 'WAG [Welsh Assembly Government] selection process', while noting also that 'it would be possible to involve appropriate interest groups in the [appointment] process much in the same way that young people are currently involved in the process to select the Children's Commissioner.'[16] The reason for the former was that 'the Commissioner [will] be given a relatively wide remit, including at times pursuing WAG policy.'[17]

A number of statements are made in the policy instruction with regard to independence and accountability. For example: 'It is proposed that the Commissioner would be independent of Government' and that the Commissioner's functions 'could include [. . .] to hold government to account for the exercise of its responsibilities and duties with regard to the language' and 'with regard to its language policy.'[18] The creation of the post of Commissioner would ensure that 'there continues to be a formal voice outside government able to both advise government on matters in relation to the language and provide [. . .] an independent assessment of government policies in support of the language.'[19] It is also noted that 'Ministers want to establish a robust appointment process to maintain the independence [. . .] of the Commissioner'.[20] However, under the headline of 'accountability' it is noted that 'In exceptional circumstances [. . .] the Measure should allow Ministers to issue directions to the Commissioner in relation to how he / she exercises his / her functions.'[21] In addition, under the heading of 'funding' it is noted that 'The Measure should allow for the Commissioner to be funded by Welsh Ministers to the levels deemed appropriate by Welsh Ministers' and that 'the Commissioner should be required to gain approval from Welsh Ministers in determining the number of staff it employs'.[22]

Turning now to the matter of the legal personality of the office or, much more loosely speaking, its corporate structure, it is clear from the evidence that during the early stage of the policy cycle there was no assumption 'whether there should be a Commissioner or a Commission (led by a Commissioner[s])'.[23] In considering possible models, it was noted that the office of Irish Language Commissioner[24] 'depend[s] heavily on the *personality* of the individual who undertakes the post'.[25] It is worth pointing out here that it could easily be argued that the circumstances surrounding the resignation of the first holder of this post amply demonstrate the inherent risk of the inevitable dependence upon personality with regard to the corporate sole model. In an elaboration of this initial discussion, it was noted an alternative approach might be more stable. For example, it was noted that were the Commissioner 'part of a wider Commission [then] [i]n this scenario, the Commission is less focused on an individual's personality and is probably more consensual in its approach'.[26] In measuring the potential strengths, weaknesses and risks associated with an individual Commissioner against a Commission, it was noted that the former could be '[a] potentially strong, independent voice for the language', but that there were 'risks associated with an individual Commissioner, especially in a politically sensitive area – heavily dependent on their personality' and there was a danger that it was 'likely to be perceived as a lobbyist';[27] whereas a Commission would be 'potentially less dependent on an individual's personality', while being 'more complex presentationally'.[28]

A later stage of the policy cycle directly addressed the question of whether to establish '[a] Commissioner or a Commission'.[29] It was argued that while a Commissioner would have the advantages of being easily identifiable to the public and to organisations and would be in a position to 'take decisions quickly', the weaknesses were significant, in that 'the effectiveness and public perception of the office would be largely dependent on the personality of the incumbent Commissioner'.[30] In contrast, a Commission

> would provide a 'checks and balances' mechanism which would potentially help ensure that the organisation acts in a balanced and proportionate manner. This may help alleviate concerns about impartiality. It would also provide a greater level of expertise in relation to the Welsh language and be a more inclusive model.[31]

The paper makes the recommendation that the Commission option be adopted for purpose of the Measure,[32] given that one of its advantages was that '[a] Commission structure, with the Commissioner at its head, provides an appropriate mechanism to ensure "checks and balances" exist so that the organisation operates effectively.'[33]

This model was rejected by the Minister at a meeting on 18 March 2009,[34] despite the fact that

> discussion had initially focused on the advantages of adopting a multi commissioner model as this might offer suitable checks and balances to address any concerns that a person's highly individual approach may undermine the public's perception of the Commissioner's ability to maintain an unbiased position.[35]

The policy team was asked to look at other examples, including the other examples of 'the single Commissioner model currently operating in Wales',[36] namely the Children's Commissioner and the Older People's Commissioner, even though it was recognised that these offices had no regulatory functions. Other models considered included the Information Commissioner, the Charity Commissioner and the Equality and Human Rights Commission.

The following factors were identified by the policy team as being instrumental in the choice of model:

> the need to meet the *One Wales* commitment of establishing the post of Welsh Language Commissioner; the need for a strong Commissioner that would effectively champion the cause of the Welsh language; sufficient expertise to enable the Commissioner to produce clear standards with which persons will be expected to comply; the need to ensure that a Commissioner may act effectively without having to refer or revisit decisions with a group of commissioners; sufficient checks and balances to address any risks that a person's highly individual approach may undermine the public's perception of the Commissioner's ability to act in an unbiased manner when dealing with complaints, etc.[37]

The paper concludes that the 'Information Commissioner model' offers a 'way forward',[38] given that it is fronted by a single commissioner who is, in turn, supported by a team of non-executive directors or commissioners with various areas of expertise and particular competence. It was added that while this model does not address concerns with regard to checks and balances this would be 'overcome by ensuring adequate checks and balances in the appointments process'.[39] Thus, with the resulting

> removal of concerns about the ability to ensure adequate checks and safeguarding the ability of the Commissioner to act as an advocate for the language whilst still acting and being perceived to act in a thoroughly impartial manner, the appointment of a Commissioner (as indicated in One Wales) becomes a wholly practical option.[40]

It was suggested, but not recommended, that '[t]here could be a requirement to seek expert advice when dealing with complex issues and to consult appropriately as part of the policy development process'.[41] In noting reasons for rejecting the Commission model at this stage, the paper records that it '[d]oes not chime with the One Wales commitment'.[42] At the close of the policy cycle it was stated that

> Ministers have considered a range of options in relation to the office of the Commissioner, including the question of whether the new body should be a single Commissioner or Commission. It was decided to opt for the Commissioner model since it was felt that having a Commissioner as a single figure able to lead the work, whilst being recognisable to citizens and organisations alike was a benefit [...] There was also a risk that establishing a Commission would be seen as 'rebranding' the Welsh Language Board, rather than establishing a new structure. It was also felt that it was important that the Commissioner, in exercising his / her role as regulator, was able to take decisions without having to refer to the Commission.[43]

In addition, the creation of a cadre of Non-Executive Directors and a Management Board,[44] so as to 'ensure that there are appropriate checks and balances in place to ensure that the Commissioner exercises his / her functions and takes decisions in a robust and proportionate manner',[45] does not survive the migration from policy instruction to the Measure as proposed. Instead, it was determined that the Commissioner be supported by an 'Advisory Panel', as per Part 3 of the Welsh Language Measure as proposed.[46]

Legislative cycle discussion and determination (March–December 2010)

The matter of legal personality can be set aside, for the moment, at this point, as there was no significant discussion of that aspect of the office of the Welsh Language Commissioner during the legislative cycle, although there was considerable discussion of the related matter of the appointment of the Commissioner, with regard to the independence and accountability of the office. On the other hand, considerable attention was paid to the issue of independence. The research has shown that during the course of the legislative cycle many actors argued that the Welsh Language Commissioner must be independent of the Welsh government. For them, the nub of this issue lay in the appointment process, ministerial direction, and to the manner of reporting to, or being accountable to, the Welsh government and the Assembly. A few actors raised the matter of the Commissioner being funded directly by the government.[47]

Specifically, certain actors, including experts who also self-identify as activists,[48] argued that 'the right of Welsh Ministers to instruct the Commissioner' ought to be removed;[49] 'As a regulator, I would prefer the commissioner not to be appointed by the First Minister';[50] 'In order to promote objectivity, we believe that the Commissioner and his or her office should be independent of the Welsh Assembly Government', adding that 'The basis of the arrangement should be similar to that which applies to the Welsh Public Service Ombudsman.'[51] The Committee noted that Emyr Lewis and Colin Williams, along with several other contributors, were of the view that the Commissioner 'was closer to that of Auditor General and Public Services Ombudsman rather than Children's Commissioner for Wales or the Commissioner for Older People in Wales'.[52] In its written evidence, the Welsh Language Board questioned whether the Measure allowed for a Commissioner 'who is sufficiently independent of the government of the day'.[53]

During the legislative cycle Williams argued that in order to be assured of the independence of the Commissioner that 'the Commissioner should be accountable to the Assembly and not to a Minister or a group of Ministers',[54] adding that in his opinion, 'One key element of ensuring credibility and independence is cash flow [. . .] therefore it is proposed that the Assembly, and not one policy department or Minister, should be responsible for the finance, staffing levels and the interests of the Commissioner.'[55] In his oral evidence Williams argued that the Commissioner ought to be accountable to the Assembly because of

> the experiences of other countries [. . .] Looking at the situation in Canada over a long period of time, and at the situation in Ireland, you can see several cases of direct political intervention because the language commissioner was, at one time, accountable to a Minister or to a cluster of Ministers. In order to avoid tension of this kind, the commissioner was made accountable to the Parliament in Canada for the proper reasons.[56]

The political intervention alluded to here is described as follows by Williams: 'there were cuts to staff numbers, funding and the capacity of the commissioner to engage in legal work.'[57] In response to further questioning, Williams asserted at one point that the office of Commissioner would be 'in opposition to the Government'.[58] Later again during the session, Williams contends as follows:

> The language commissioner's ability to protect the interests of the French language was curtailed. The Parliament sensed that that was the case [...] So, the responsibility for resourcing and staffing the office of the language commissioner was transferred from Government to Parliament. In practical terms, the funding of Canada's language commissioner is drawn from the Parliamentary library's budget. It has nothing to do with any department or with politics; it comes through the back door of the Parliament's general resources.[59]

After the Measure gained Royal Assent, and upon the occasion of the Commissioner officially taking up her post, Williams further argued the new Commissioner ought to be accountable to the Assembly as a whole and not to the Minister. He noted also that the 'main target' of the Commissioner would be 'Government departments'.[60]

The accountability of the office was little discussed during the legislative cycle, and when it was, it was almost entirely in terms of the degree of independence the office of Commissioner ought to have from the Welsh government. That said, and in contrast to the activist contributors, including the expert-activists, many of the potential regulatees noted that while they had no strong views on the process of appointment, they were concerned that the operation of the office of the Commissioner in practice needed to be seen to be 'appropriate', 'fair' and 'reasonable'.[61] In giving oral evidence to the Committee, the Minister asserted quite simply that he was 'satisfied' with the process for appointing the Commissioner, given that 'he or she will [...] play an important role with regard to delivering the Government's policy aims for the language. I would expect the Commissioner to work closely with the Welsh Assembly Government.'[62] He also noted, when Emyr Lewis's assertion was put to him that the Commissioner needed greater independence from the Welsh government than other 'Welsh Commissioners', due to the greater powers of the Commissioner, 'in that the Language Commissioner will be able to impose sanctions on Welsh Ministers – for example a civil penalty under section 76(3)(e) – or even bring proceedings against Welsh Ministers',[63] that other regulatory bodies have such powers and such relationships with the government elsewhere in the UK.[64]

In its response the Welsh government noted that:

> many stakeholders [. . .] expressed their opinion that the appointment of the Commissioner should be made by the National Assembly, not the First Minister [because were the appointment made by the First Minister] the Commissioner's office would be insufficiently independent from government to allow for effective scrutiny of Welsh Ministers' compliance with Welsh language standards [. . .][65]

It was also noted here that: 'The Presiding Officer has also spoken publicly in relation to the appointment of the Welsh Language Commissioner, stating that all Commissioners should be appointed by the National Assembly as a matter of constitutional principle.'[66] Elsewhere, it is added that he asserted also that 'every Commissioner should be answerable to the Assembly and not the Government'.[67] The intervention by the Presiding Officer appears wholly unconventional in parliamentary terms. Were the Presiding Officer indeed of the view that this was unconstitutional, then it would appear to be the case that the Measure ought to have been withdrawn. A review of the practice of similar such presiding officers elsewhere[68] illustrates that such a statement by the Presiding Officer is not to be considered a matter of opinion but rather a declaration that is binding upon the Legislature. If, on the other hand, it is asserted that the Presiding Officer was expressing his view or opinion on an aspect of the content of the legislation, then that would be a breach of the impartiality which is a fundamental feature of the function of the office. It is difficult to reconcile the requirement that 'In carrying out the functions of the Presiding Officer, the Presiding Officer and Deputy must demonstrate impartiality at all times'[69] with at the same time asserting a very clear and critical, or partisan, position on the content of legislation proposed by the Welsh government. In asserting the view that the content of the Measure was inadequate in relation to the independence and accountability of the Commissioner, the

Presiding Officer became, in effect, a part of the debate rather than presiding over it.

A later policy paper noted that 'some stakeholders [were afraid] that the mechanism for appointing the Commissioner does not provide a guarantee of independence from the executive', noting also that there were concerns that there were 'extensive powers for the Welsh Ministers to influence the Commissioner'.[70] The paper laid out a range of options for addressing these concerns 'regarding the Commissioner's capacity to act independently from inappropriate interference from Welsh Ministers whilst retaining a necessary degree of accountability to government'.[71] While given further consideration by the Welsh government,[72] the Measure as passed stated that the First Minister makes the appointment, although he 'must take into account the recommendations made by the selection panel in relation to the appointment' (Welsh Language (Wales) Measure 2011, Part 11, Schedule 1, Part 2, § 3(1)(b)) and that he 'may take into account' the views of the National Assembly for Wales, its committees and its members (Welsh Language (Wales) Measure 2011, Part 11, Schedule 1, Part 2, § 3(1)(b)). In addition, regulations, which would be subject to the approval of the Assembly, would be presented outlining the appointment process in more detail.

With regard to the principle of independence in relation to ministerial direction,[73] this was modified (Welsh Language (Wales) Measure 2011 Part 2 § 16) so that it could not be applied to the issue of compliance notices (chapter 6 of Part 4), the enforcement of Standards (Part 5) and the freedom to use Welsh (Part 6). The Measure as proposed stated that 'The Welsh Ministers may give direction to the Commissioner' (Welsh Language (Wales) Measure as proposed Part 2, § 15 (1)) and that 'The Commissioner must comply with the directions given by Welsh Ministers' (Welsh Language (Wales) Measure as proposed Part 2, § 15 (2)). More generally, ministerial direction was only to be used in extremis, with 'good cause'.[74] In addition, a duty was placed upon the Commissioner to take into account the principle that the Welsh language is 'an official language / [has] official status [. . .] in Wales'; that there is the 'need to safeguard the rights and interests of Welsh speakers (those rights being the rights to be established by imposing duties on persons [. . .])';[75] along with the principle understood as 'the aim of people in Wales to be able to conduct their lives in Welsh'.[76]

The political opposition in the Assembly remained unconvinced of the Welsh government's position on the independence and the accountability of the Commissioner. At the plenary stage opposition amendments were tabled so as 'to secure the independence of the Commissioner'.[77] The arguments given included that 'the Language Commissioner will have more powers than the other commissioners'[78] and that it would 'take the language out of politics'.[79] The government remained of the view that such appointments 'should be made by the Government'.[80]

Analysis

The matter of the independence and accountability came to the fore almost immediately during the operation of the office of the Commissioner. Ministerial direction was exercised by Leighton Andrews AM in relation to the Commissioner's non-statutory consultation on draft Standards during 2012 and 2013 (Figure 2). This act of ministerial fiat led Heini Gruffudd, the CEO of the newly formed Welsh language lobby group Dyfodol i'r Iaith, to state that the Minister had undermined the Commissioner to the extent that it was pointless engaging with her, rather than simply going directly to the Minister.[81] The Welsh Language Society came out in defence of the Commissioner, arguing that she had put the Minister 'on the spot'.[82] Since then, a member of the statutory Advisory Panel to the office of the Commissioner has argued that this event demonstrated that the Commissioner was not independent, arguing instead for the creation of a wholly new body funded directly by the Assembly in order to hold the Welsh government to account.[83] In response, the government said: 'Mae Comisiynydd y Gymraeg yn gyfan gwbl ac yn gyfansoddiadol annibynnol' ('The Commissioner is wholly, constitutionally independent').[84] This is both an over-assertion and an over-simplification on the part of the government. In fact, evidence from the fieldwork demonstrates that policy actors from across the political spectrum agreed that the intervention of the Minister was necessary (e.g. Fieldwork Interviews 48, 51, 60 and 63).

The melée regarding the independence and accountability of the office of the Commissioner arises from several sources. First of all, there is the confusion regarding the task of the Commissioner, as some put it, of 'pursuing WAG policy' in an inimical sense. According

Date	Event
May / June 2011	Caroline Turner / WG implementation programme for Welsh Language Measure 2011 (Framework Agreement between WG and WLC under development)
5 October 2011	WLC appointed by WG
13 December 2011	WG briefing to Welsh Language Board and WLC elect and staff on Welsh Language Measure 2011
1 April 2012	WLC starts work
16 May 2012	WLC begins non-statutory consultation on draft standards
10 August 2012	Emyr Roberts / WG response to WLC consultation, reminding WLC of key principles
11 August 2012	WLC closes non-statutory consultation on draft standards
19 September 2012	Framework Agreement between WG and WLC signed
28 November 2012	WLC report on consultation presented to WG
17 December 2012	Caroline Turner / WG letter to WLC
25 February 2013	Leighton Andrews / WG letter rejecting WLC proposals for standards
25 June 2013	Leighton Andrews resigns as Minister
21 October 2013	Carwyn Jones / First Minister statement on WLC and standards
6 January 2014	WG publish first set of Standards
27 January 2014	WLC standards investigation begins
18 April 2014	WLC standards investigation closes
2 June 2014	WLC report on standards investigation presented to WG
7 November 2014	WG publish draft regulations
24 March 2015	Welsh Assembly approve regulations

Figure 2. *Timeline for the Welsh Language Commissioner, Standards and Regulations.*
Key: *WG (Welsh Government); WLC (Welsh Language Commissioner)*

to the research literature and the professional regulatory material examined during the project, this is not how regulators function. Rather, it is the case that the Commissioner is in fact designed to be a key player in the implementation of important aspects of Welsh government Welsh language policy and therefore, of necessity, ought to be a Welsh government appointment. Simply, public policy actors cannot be given absolute independence beyond the purview of democratic accountability. Moreover, the Executive, as it is held accountable for the implementation of its own policy by the Legislature and is subject to scrutiny and criticism by the Legislature, must, therefore, have control over appointments to public policy roles such as this. In fact, it would be a significant conflict of interest were the Legislature to have the function of appointment in such circumstances. Despite the incident of ministerial direction, a certain lack of clarity and, indeed, confidence, on the part of the government is manifest with regard to the independence and accountability of the office of the Commissioner. For example, at a recent meeting of the Committee for the Scrutiny of the First Minister, it was neither immediately clear that the Commissioner is understood to be accountable to the Minister, and with the Minister to the Assembly, nor was there agreement that it was appropriate that the Commissioner be appointed by the Minister.[85] This confusion was unfortunately informed and reinforced by Shooter's report (2014) on the office of the Children's Commissioner in Wales.[86] This report is rather misleading, in that it assumes that the various commissioners in Wales have the same functions, albeit in relation to different subject areas. This is simply not the case.

Since her appointment, the Commissioner has raised the matter of her office being directly funded by government. Her view on this, given during an interview to the Welsh Language Society on 13 April 2012, appears to echo the evidence given by Colin Williams, in that she contends that 'y ffaith mai Llywodaeth Cymru sy'n rheoli cyllideb swydd y Comisiynydd yn golygu nad ydi hi'n gwbl annibynnol' ('the fact that the Welsh Government controls the budget of the office of the Commissioner means that she is not totally independent'); she also notes that the fact that the budget 'yn dod o lywodraeth yn eich gwneud chi falle yn fwy nerfus ar adegau' ('comes from government makes you more nervous at times').[87] However, the empirical evidence from Canada as per the budget-setting mechanism of the

Office of the Commissioner of Official Languages does not seem to bear out the interpretation of that as provided to the Assembly by Williams during the passage of the Measure.[88]

Briefly, it is a recognised constitutional principle in Canada that 'all spending must originate with the Crown (i.e. the cabinet)'.[89] Thus, while the funding mechanism for Officers of Parliament in general was modified in 2005, subsequent to Officers other than OCOL raising 'funding concerns'[90] and 'concerns about the potential for interference',[91] OCOL was not set wholly apart from the budget-setting authority of the Executive. With regard to reporting accountability, OCOL reports, variously, to the President of the Treasury Board, who is a Federal Government Minister (Official Languages Act 1969, 1985 Part VIII, § 62.2 and 63.1), to the Governor in Council, being the Governor General, who is the representative of the Queen in Canada, acting on the advice of the federal Cabinet (Official Languages Act 1969, 1985 Part VIII, § 65.1) and the federal Parliament (Official Languages Act 1969, 1985 Part VIII, § 65.3, 66 and 67).

In actual fact, the House of Commons (Canada) Advisory Panel on the Funding and Oversight of Officer of Parliament was created as an ad hoc measure whereby the budgets of offices such as OCOL are set by the following process: (1) the Officer and the Treasury Board (i.e. the government ministry) develop a joint submission to the Panel; (2) agreement tends to be reached before submission to the Panel; (3) the Panel makes recommendations to the Treasury Board. The Treasury Board has set aside recommendations of the Panel 'without inspiring discernible reaction from Parliament'[92] and when there have been disputes the Panel in all cases, but one, found in favour of the Treasury Board.[93] Membership of the Panel comprises a representative cross-section of elected members of both Houses and their Speakers.[94] It remains the case in Canada that 'It is the exclusive prerogative of the Crown to place recommendations for spending before Parliament'[95] and the Treasure Board remains the 'formal authority' in the budgetary process.[96] That said, the Panel provides for a check upon the Executive with regard to the setting of budgets of Officers of Parliament. In any case, one need go no further than the Westminster Parliament and the Scottish Parliament for operational models of 'a budget-setting mechanism institutionally independent of the executive' in relation to a range of clearly defined 'Officers of Parliament'.[97] An additional point is also worth making here with regards Canada. Those advocates whose opinions are held to be informed by the case of OCOL appear to be wholly unaware of the fact that under the Official Languages Act (1985, Part IX, § 55), OCOL may, potentially, be directed by the Canadian government in certain regards.[98]

Many actors cited the office of Ombudsman as a model for the Commissioner, it being defined by its absolute independence from the Executive. But, two points must be made here. The first is that the Ombudsman has no powers other than the power to recommend. Secondly, the office of Ombudsman is not designed to execute government policy in any shape or form whatsoever.[99] Therefore, as it is not an agent of public policy, it is not accountable to the government. In contrast, regulators are agents of public policy and therefore have to be accountable to the Executive. All UK regulators have a very strong element of political, which is to say government, appointment. The constitutional question raised by the Presiding Officer is answered, at least partly, in the UK-wide review of 'Parliamentary watchdogs'.[100] Here, it is clear that the Commissioner does not conform to Thomas's definition of 'core Parliamentary Officer' in the Welsh context, a category to which the PSOW, the Auditor General for Wales and the National Assembly Commissioner for Standards are ascribed.[101] Familiarity with potential international comparators bears this out.[102] Having said that, neither does the Welsh Language Commissioner easily sit with her notion of the 'hybrid Commissioner' along with the Children's Commissioner and the Commissioner for Older People, both of which are advocates and ombudsmanesque rather than regulatory in character,[103] and for which strong arguments have been made for their being appointed by and accountable to the Assembly rather than the government.[104]

However, there is a problem with 'insulating regulatory decision-making from "improper" political and industry influence'.[105] This arises when the regulator is too dependent: the research literature describes this as regulatory capture.[106] As with other regulators, the independence of the Welsh Language Commissioner is realised in the autonomy[107] of the operation of the office and its functions, rather than in any absolute and unconditional independence from government. In this context, a crucial distinction is to be drawn between policy and operations[108] in which it must be understood as a

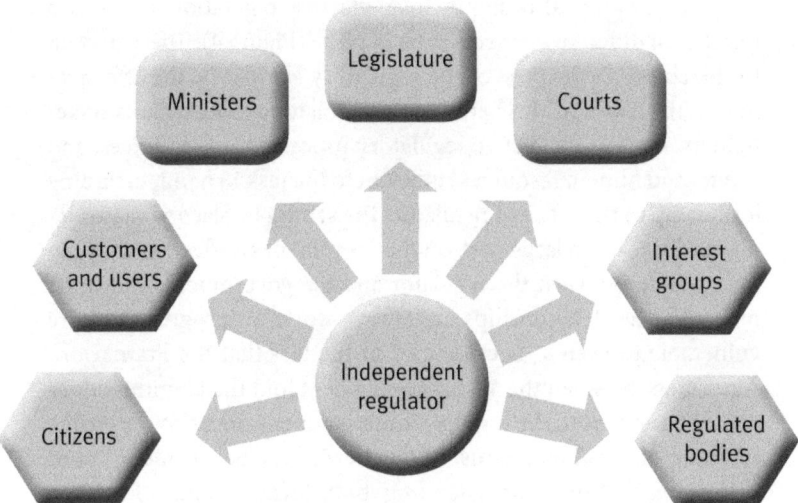

Figure 3. *360° accountability of the independent regulator (adapted from House of Lords, Select Committee on the Constitution, 2004a: 20).*

matter of both principle and practice that, as it was put in the House of Lords review, 'Ministers determine policy and regulators put it into effect', noting at the same time, 'Where that distinction has been recognised, there appear to have been few problems.'[109]

It is a fault of almost all of the critiques of independence and accountability of the Commissioner that these matters are only ever conceived of in relation to the Executive. Government ministers are responsible for appointing independent regulators so as to ensure proper responsibility and appropriate accountability. In addition, the regulator is accountable to the government minister for the independence and effectiveness of the regulation that they have been appointed to implement.[110] It is also important to note that, as a regulator, the accountability of the Commissioner extends beyond the government to a range of other significant stakeholders (Figure 3), of which the government may be said to be *primus inter pares*. The key features of regulatory accountability are: a duty to explain, openness to scrutiny by others, and, the possibility of independent challenge and review of regulatory decisions. Regulators are accountable to government ministers and, in turn, government ministers are, together with regulators, accountable to the Legislature.[111]

The research also shows that effective regulation requires a number of different elements to be in place (Figure 4). These pertain to the clarity of purpose of the regulatory standards, the effectiveness of the relationships between the regulator and its various stakeholders, open and effective regulatory processes and practices, and capital and human resources sufficient to the task in hand, including leadership in the office of regulator. The setting in place of these elements depends, in large part, on the creation of an effective working relationship between the regulator and the government, and in its maintenance. Relationships are always works in progress and are vulnerable to events, as evidenced in the fact that the Framework Agreement between the Welsh government and the Commissioner was not adhered to during the Commissioner's non-statutory consultation on draft Standards, in the view of the government,[112] but cultivating a shared understanding, both formally and informally, of the relationship between the regulator and government is critical

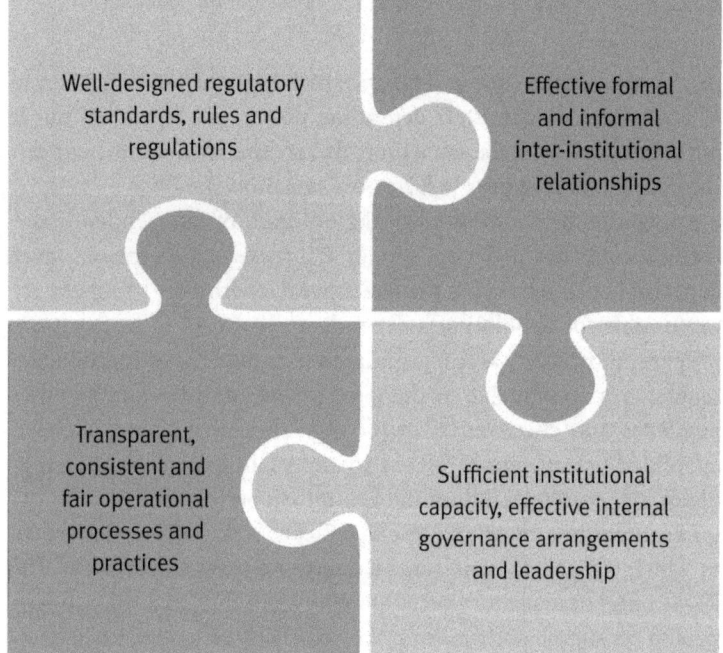

Figure 4. *The necessary elements of better regulatory outcomes (adapted from OECD, 2013: 4 and OECD, 2014: 22).*

to both the effective implementation of public policy and the operation of the related regulatory regime. Formal agreements, in the shape of Memoranda of Understanding, Framework Agreements or Instruction Letters, are an essential part of that relationship. So also is the trust and confidence that only emerges through the informal praxis that is a key feature of the shared task of regulatory governance. It is notable that there is nothing in the Framework Agreement with regard to action in relation to breaching the terms of the agreement. The Framework Agreement between the Ministry of Justice (UK) and the Information Commissioner's Office (ICO), for example, incorporates a section on this subject. This states: 'In the event that any of the requirements in this framework are breached, the ICO or the Department will advise the other immediately in writing and advise on the corrective or preventative action being taken.'[113] Elsewhere in this document the Commissioner and the sponsoring Ministry agree to adhere to 'a culture of no surprises'.[114] The Framework Agreement between the Welsh Language Commissioner and the Welsh government appears to be rather limited with regard to the more expansive documents pertaining to other similar (in the broadest terms only) such relationships, including examples in the Welsh context.[115] That the Welsh Language Commissioner is subject to ministerial direction, and given the political sensitivity of Welsh language policy, would suggest that a statement regarding protocol in response to a breach of the agreement ought to be a part of the document.

As regards the issue of corporate structure, there is evidence that the Commissioner consults with the Advisory Panel, but it is less clear how regular and substantive that consultation is in practice.[116] The Commissioner rightly asserts that she is not accountable to the Panel.[117] By now, the office also has an Audit and Risk Committee, which is associated with the internal management and governance of the office, along with a management team that is

> responsible for leadership and management across the organisation [and] for making executive decisions about operational, resource, communications and other administrative matters [...] The role of the Management Team in decision making carries recognition that on occasion there will be some issues for which the decision-maker is the Commissioner alone.[118]

It is asserted elsewhere that the management team 'manages all of the Commissioner's functions and activities'.[119] Despite this risk assessment machinery, it could be argued that the potential risks associated with the regulator as corporation sole have been realised to some extent in the process of implementing the Measure and in the operation of the office of Commissioner. Issues regarding impartiality, expertise and judgement variously arise in relation to freedom to use Welsh, the judicial review regarding NS&I, TAN 20 and the Planning (Wales) Bill, Standards and Enforcement Policy. The development of Enforcement Policy would appear to have had something of a difficult birth, beginning with the presentation of an Enforcement Policy document by the Commissioner to the Minister on 5 September 2012, including a public consultation on a draft Enforcement Policy[120] in 2014, during which it was pointed out that the policy appeared to run counter to the Measure itself,[121] and eventually arriving at a final version in 2015. The Commissioner appears to have accepted that the draft policy was indeed counter to the Measure.[122]

The matter of the legal personality or manner of incorporation has been given considerable attention in the research and professional literature on regulators. It is stated there that boards are favoured over individual regulators. Arguments for the individual regulator are recognised, as follows: 'such an appointment enables the regulator to take the initiative and move quickly – not being held back by collective decision making – and to represent a clear and consistent face of regulation',[123] especially in the 'initial stages of establishing a regulatory framework'.[124] Nonetheless, it is concluded that 'the move towards boards has been motivated by the need to bring in a greater range of skills [. . .] and to avoid the pitfalls that may occur from relying on the judgement of a single regulator' while adding that 'the board structure also enables the burdens of regulation to be borne by several people'.[125] The evidence strongly suggests that a board provides a wider view, enables greater stability and tends towards more consistency in decision-making. In short, a board is better able to manage risk. The conclusions of the House of Lords review of 2004 are very clearly in favour of the shift from corporation sole to corporation aggregate, or, more loosely speaking, board. For example:

We believe that it is appropriate on the whole that regulators appointed as individuals give way to the appointment of boards [. . .] We welcome the move towards more collective board structures, rather than sole regulators, as one of the principal mechanisms for improving the quality and consistency of regulatory decision-making, and urge that this should be the norm for regulatory regimes.[126]

Let us now, briefly, turn to another, most recent feature of the Welsh language regulatory landscape, namely the Welsh Language Tribunal. While the Welsh Language Tribunal forms an integral part of the infrastructure of accountability with regard to the Welsh language regulatory regime, it has been subject to limited analysis at this point as it has yet to be operated in practice.[127] That said, it is worth making one point. During the course of the legislative cycle for the Measure, the relative independence of the Tribunal from the government was the subject of three policy papers, namely Welsh Policy Papers 27, 32 and 37. In the earliest of these papers it was proposed that 'the Lord Chancellor' make the appointments.[128] Clearly, it was decided otherwise. Under the 2013 regulations, and in line with the Welsh government's policy statement on the appointment process,[129] the First Minister appointed the President of the Tribunal following the recommendations of an independent appointment panel and consultation with the Lord Chief Justice for England and Wales and Lord Justice Richards.[130] This process is very much in line with that of other Welsh tribunals[131] and the recommendations of the report of this Welsh Committee,[132] and followed concerns raised by the Welsh Committee after that.[133]

However, among the recommendations made by the Welsh Committee was that a 'central administrative justice focal point' dealing with the policy and administration of Welsh tribunals ('devolved tribunals') be established within the Welsh government and, moreover, that this focal point should, 'Be separate from subject specific policy departments' so as to, among other things, 'ensure tribunal independence'.[134] It is specifically recommended that this focal point be established, 'in the Department for the First Minister and Cabinet'.[135] The reason for this was explained as follows:

> That in order to ensure that tribunals are seen to be properly independent and impartial, the Welsh Assembly Government transfer policy and administrative responsibility for tribunals to this focal point in the Department for the First Minister and Cabinet, which has no specific responsibility for any of the government decisions under dispute.[136]

Evidence from other sources strongly supports this separation. For example, the UK government concluded, as regards the independence of tribunals, that

> the only way in which customers could be truly satisfied that tribunals were truly independent was by developing clear separation between the Ministers and other authorities whose policies and decisions are tested by tribunals, and the Minister who appoints and supports them.[137]

Similarly, Justice Hickinbottom noted in a presentation given in Wales in 2009 that 'members of the public have real and understandable concerns if the tribunal in which they seek to challenge a government decision is administered, controlled and paid for by the very decision-maker whose decision they wish to challenge'.[138] He further explained that 'In Westminster, that issue has been addressed by the transfer of tribunal from "sponsoring departments" into the control of the Ministry of Justice.'[139] While not arguing for the exact same model to be adopted in Wales, he urged the Welsh government at that time to consider how to ensure the independence of the various Welsh tribunals.

In its written evidence to the Silk Commission, the Welsh Committee noted that the Welsh government had accepted their recommendations and that the focal point had been created as the Administrative Justice and Tribunals Unit 'within the office of the Permanent Secretary and began the process of bringing devolved tribunals into its remit'.[140] Since then, however, the First Minister became the holder of the Welsh language policy portfolio (from June 2013 – see above, Figure 2, other than with regard to the area of education, a field which is irrelevant to the Welsh Language Tribunal) while at the same time the office of the Permanent Secretary is directly accountable to the First Minister.[141] This completely undermines the Welsh

Committee's rationale for situating the Administrative Justice and Tribunals Unit in the Department for the First Minister, as there is no separation of the subject specific (Welsh) responsibilities of government and the subject of the given tribunal (Welsh). Specifically, therefore, the Minister with subject responsibility has appointed the President of the Tribunal that will hear cases on that subject, including, possibly, a case involving the government, that is the Minister with subject responsibility. Also, the Minister with subject responsibility was involved, via the Welsh Language Division, in the consultation on setting the Welsh Language Tribunal Rules.[142] Indeed, the legislative record shows that the Rules were 'Made' by the President of the Tribunal and 'Allowed' by the First Minister, in the statutory meaning of these terms, on April 2 and April 8, 2015, respectively.[143] Moreover, at the time of the transfer of the Unit to the office of the Permanent Secretary, the First Minister gave 'assurances' that 'the democratic accountability for the Unit would remain in his hands'.[144] There is a clear conflict of interest here in relation to the Welsh Language Tribunal, as understood by the Welsh Committee. In addition, such a conflict is widely understood to be incompatible with Article 6 of the European Convention on Human Rights.[145] With regard to ministerial powers of appointment in particular, it is problematic that the First Minister appoints both the Welsh Language Commissioner and the President of the Welsh Language Tribunal, given the conflict of interest identified by the Welsh Committee and confirmed by Justice Hickinbottom. Thus, while the Welsh Language Commissioner ought to be a Welsh government appointment, the responsible Minister ought to be the holder of the Welsh language policy portfolio. In addition, that same Minister ought not be the sponsor of the Welsh Language Tribunal; that responsibility ought to rest elsewhere.[146]

Conclusions

The rationale behind creating the office of the Welsh Language Commissioner as corporation sole rather than aggregate appears to be largely driven by political imperative, in the form of a pre-election commitment on the part of Plaid Cymru to establish such a post. The question arising here is the extent to which this commitment was based upon a substantial examination of the potential policy options by the actors engaged in the drafting of the Welsh Assembly election manifesto of the said political party. The decision to create a corporation sole Commissioner was also informed by 'presentational' concerns. It was deemed to be desirable that the new language regulator be easily perceived as being markedly different from the Welsh Language Board. It was also assumed that the public might find a single Commissioner more readily comprehensible than a more 'complex' Commission.

As the matter of the legal personality of the office progressed through the policy cycle and entered the legislative cycle, any, very reasonable, concerns with regard to check and balances in relation to the operation of the office, as opposed to the making of an appointment to the office, were steadily eroded. As a result, the only substantive check on the regulator in post which is now in place is the rather blunt instrument of ministerial direction, as was demonstrated in relation to the Commissioner's non-statutory consultation on draft standards. Employing such an instrument is fraught with risk for both the Minister and the Commissioner, for different reasons. Notwithstanding some of the issues that have challenged the Commissioner since appointment, it can be asserted as a substantive matter of both principle and practice that the office of Welsh Language Commissioner as corporation sole is anomalous in the UK regulatory state. The reasons for that appear to be as a result of apparent political necessity rather than due to the requirements of the design and function of the Welsh language regulatory regime. As regards the Welsh Language Commissioner, therefore, the empirical evidence argues for a shift from corporation sole to corporation aggregate.

With regard to independence and accountability more specifically, the research data shows, unambiguously, that the relationship between the Welsh government and the Welsh Language Commissioner is appropriately framed, in particular given that the Welsh Language Commissioner is a regulator. Ministerial appointment and direction are necessary features of regulatory regimes in general, and the same principle pertains to the Welsh language regulatory regime. It is crucial that the various stakeholders of the office of the Welsh Language Commissioner understand that as a regulatory agency it cannot ever be free of executive direction, as Feaver and Sheehy[147] put it, of such agencies more generally, but it is equally important to recognise that one must also understand the critical difference between the power of the Minister to direct the regulator, which is appropriate, and the power of the Minister to manage the regulator, which is inappropriate. This distinction comes into play in particular where the Commissioner is required to call the government to account, largely with regard to Standards in the delivery of public services, that the office has the operational independence to do so. To paraphrase the House of Lords review, regulators are independent *within* the State, rather than *of* the State.[148] In other words, as agents responsible for the implementation of important aspects of public policy, regulators, of necessity, are subject to appropriate ministerial guidance, intervention and direction so that the Minister may 'provide a fuller picture of the policy context with which the independent regulators work'.[149] In this context, the research demonstrates that there is a critical distinction between the framing of public policy and its operation or implementation. In brief, ministers determine policy and regulators put it into effect. This principle extends to the budget-setting mechanism and the channels and forums for formal reporting, as well as the selection and appointment process of the office-holder. The Welsh Language Commissioner is not set in structural opposition to the Welsh government; rather, it is an agent of government. It is crucial to the effective implementation of key aspects of Welsh language public policy. While its operational independence is essential, the Commissioner's office will be at its most effective when the relationship is one of appropriate collaboration, defined by a culture of 'no surprises'.[150] Creative friction is a necessary feature of any robust relationship, but divergent points of view can only be considered serious when based upon a depth of evidence rather than mere opinion.

Notes

1   Note that this chronology pertains to the Welsh Language (Wales) Measure 2011. There is, of course, an immediate connection between the Measure and the National Assembly for Wales (Legislative Competence) (Welsh Language) Order 2009, and there is some overlap of policy cycle between the two. The policy cycle for the Order ran from June 2008 up until the Proposed Order was laid on 2 February 2009. The legislative cycle of the Order was completed on 10 February 2010, when the Order was Made by Her Majesty in Council.

2   Welsh Policy Paper 3, *Commission / Commissioner* (unpublished paper, July 2008), p. 1.
3   Welsh Policy Paper 3, p. 5.
4   Welsh Policy Paper 3, p. 9.
5   Welsh Policy Paper 3, p. 10.
6   Welsh Policy Paper 3, p. 10.
7   Welsh Policy Paper 3, p. 10.
8   Welsh Policy Paper 3, p. 10.
9   Welsh Policy Paper 3, p. 10.
10 Welsh Policy Paper 3, p. 11.
11 Welsh Policy Paper 3, p. 11.
12 Welsh Policy Paper 3, p. 11.
13 Welsh Policy Paper 3, p. 11.
14 Welsh Policy Paper 3, p. 12.
15 Welsh Policy Paper 3, p. 12.
16 Welsh Policy Paper 12, *Supplementary Paper. Welsh Language Commission/er and Welsh Language Schemes* (unpublished paper, March 2009), p. 4.
17 Welsh Policy Paper 12, p. 4.
18 Welsh Policy Paper 15, *Policy instructions to legal services on the proposed Welsh Language Measure* (unpublished paper, April 2009), p. 7.
19 Welsh Policy Paper 15, p. 8.
20 Welsh Policy Paper 15, p. 13.
21 Welsh Policy Paper 15, p. 16.
22 Welsh Policy Paper 15, p. 16.
23 Welsh Policy Paper 3, p. 2.
24 Other models considered in this paper are: (1) Office of the Commissioner of Official Languages, Canada (federal), (2) Office of the Commissioner of Official Languages, New Brunswick, (3) Children's Commissioner, Wales, (4) Commissioner for Older People, Wales, (5) Public Services Ombudsman, Wales, (6) Commission for Equality and Human Rights, UK, and (7) the Information Commissioner, UK.
25 Welsh Policy Paper 3, p. 4.
26 Welsh Policy Paper 3, p. 5.
27 Welsh Policy Paper 3, p. 8.
28 Welsh Policy Paper 3, p. 8.
29 Welsh Policy Paper 11, *Welsh Language Commission/er and Welsh Language Schemes* (unpublished paper, 2009), p. 10.
30 Welsh Policy Paper 11, p. 10.
31 Welsh Policy Paper 11, p. 10.
32 Welsh Policy Paper 11, pp. 10 and 23–4.
33 Welsh Policy Paper 11, p. 24.

34 Welsh Policy Paper 12, pp. 1–2.
35 Welsh Policy Paper 12, p. 2.
36 Welsh Policy Paper 12, p. 2.
37 Welsh Policy Paper 12, p. 3.
38 Welsh Policy Paper 12, p. 3.
39 Welsh Policy Paper 12, p. 3.
40 Welsh Policy Paper 12, p. 4.
41 Welsh Policy Paper 12, p. 5.
42 Welsh Policy Paper 12, p. 6.
43 Welsh Policy Paper 15, p. 10.
44 Welsh Policy Paper 15, p. 18.
45 Welsh Policy Paper 15, p. 3.
46 Welsh Assembly Government, *The Proposed Welsh Language (Wales) Measure 2010. Explanatory Memorandum to the Proposed Welsh Language Wales Measure 2010 4 March 2010* (Cardiff: Welsh Assembly Government, 2010a).
47 See, for example, National Assembly for Wales, Legislation Committee No. 2, *Proposed Welsh Language (Wales) Measure Stage 1 Committee Report July 2010* (Cardiff: National Assembly for Wales, 2010), pp. 72–90.
48 The conflation of scholarly expertise and activist empathy is not new to language issues in society, and in a number of cases the integrity of the scholarship has been eroded or compromised by this conflation, as Blommaert, for example, has pointed out (2001). Nor indeed is the capture of academic experts by government wholly uncommon, as may be amply demonstrated by the case of the so-called 'Croll–Lee Report' of New Brunswick (see Ombudsman and Child and Youth Advocate, *Report of the Ombudsman into the Minister of Education's decision to modify the French Second Language Curriculum*, n.p., June 2008).
49 Emyr Lewis, *Written Evidence*, The Proposed Welsh Language (Wales) Measure – Evidence Session 22 April 2010, Legislative Committee 2, the National Assembly for Wales.
50 Emyr Lewis, *Oral Evidence*, The Proposed Welsh Language (Wales) Measure – Evidence Session 22 April 2010, Legislative Committee 2, the National Assembly for Wales.
51 Cwmni Iaith, *Written Evidence. Response to the proposed Welsh Language (Wales) Measure 2010, National Assembly for Wales Legislation Committee No. 2*, 7 May 2010, MI 54, p. 2.
52 National Assembly for Wales Legislation Committee No. 2, p. 74.
53 Welsh Language Board, *Written Evidence, Response to the proposed Welsh Language (Wales) Measure 2010, National Assembly for Wales Legislation Committee No. 2. Paper 1, 29 April 2010* (2010b), p. 1.

54   Colin H. Williams, *Written Evidence*, The Proposed Welsh Language (Wales) Measure – Evidence Session 22 April 2010, Legislative Committee 2, the National Assembly for Wales. This written evidence consists of a list of twelve 'basic principles' and 'other considerations', two of which are questions, together with a set of Microsoft PowerPoint slides, in contrast to the written evidence presented by others. As one rather acerbic commentator noted of another case, it appears to be an unfortunate example of having 'brought a Microsoft PowerPoint to a MS Word party'. As reported on 'Greece news live' by the *Daily Telegraph*, 7 July 2015; see the comments at 15.05. Available online at: http://www.telegraph.co.uk/finance/economics/11722511/Fears-that-Greece-has-voted-itself-out-of-the-euro-force-Barack-Obama-to-intervene-in-latest-talks-live.html.
55   Williams, *Written Evidence*.
56   Colin H. Williams, *Oral Evidence*, The Proposed Welsh Language (Wales) Measure – Evidence Session 22 April 2010, Legislative Committee 2, the National Assembly for Wales.
57   Williams, *Oral Evidence*.
58   Williams, *Oral Evidence*.
59   Williams, *Oral Evidence*. Williams has clarified (Fieldwork Interview 68) that he had in mind the Conservative administration formed in 2006 with Stephen Harper as Prime Minister. This evidence, however, is problematic – see also n. 88.
60   http://www.golwg360.com/newyddion/cymru/34149-comisiynydd-iaith-angen-annibyniaeth.
61   National Assembly for Wales Legislation Committee No. 2 (2010), pp. 75–6.
62   Alun Ff. Jones, *Oral Evidence*, The Proposed Welsh Language (Wales) Measure – Evidence Session 17 June 2010, Legislative Committee 2, the National Assembly for Wales.
63   Michael German AM, question to Alun Ff. Jones, *Oral Evidence*.
64   Jones, *Oral Evidence*.
65   Welsh Policy Paper 18, *Welsh Language Commissioner – Appointment* (unpublished paper, 2010), p. 1.
66   Welsh Policy Paper 18, p. 1.
67   http://news.bbc.co.uk/1/hi/wales/8685447.stm; http://www.bbc.co.uk/news/uk-wales-politics-10733159.
68   See, for example: http://www.parl.gc.ca/about/house/speaker/role-e.html; http://www.oireachtas.ie/parliament/tdssenators/officeholders/ceanncomhairlewebsite/role/; http://www.parliament.uk/business/commons/the-speaker/the-role-of-the-speaker/role-of-the-speaker/; http://www.parliament.nz/en-nz/about-parliament/how-parliament-works/speaker/speakers-role/00SpeakAdminSpeakerSpeakersRoleRole1/

role-of-the-speaker; http://www.aph.gov.au/About_Parliament/ House_of_Representatives/Powers_practice_and_procedure/00_-_ Infosheets/Infosheet_3_-_The_Speaker.

69 National Assembly for Wales, *The Record of Proceedings 7 December 2010 Standing Orders of the National Assembly for Wales May 2010* (Cardiff: National Assembly for Wales, 2010a), par. 2.19.
70 Welsh Policy Paper 20, *Welsh Language Commissioner – Independence* (unpublished paper, 2010), p. 1.
71 Welsh Policy Paper 20, p. 1.
72 Welsh Policy Paper 18, pp. 16–19.
73 Welsh Policy Paper 20.
74 Welsh Policy Paper 20, p. 2.
75 Welsh Policy Paper 20.
76 Welsh Policy Paper 20, p. 3.
77 National Assembly for Wales, *The Record of Proceedings 7 December 2010* (Cardiff: National Assembly for Wales, 2010b), p. 36.
78 National Assembly for Wales, T*he Record of Proceedings 7 December 2010*, p. 39.
79 National Assembly for Wales, *The Record of Proceedings 7 December 2010*, p. 39.
80 National Assembly for Wales, *The Record of Proceedings 7 December 2010*, p. 39.
81 http://www.bbc.co.uk/cymrufyw/21690240; http://www.bbc.co.uk/ cymrufyw/21690238.
82 http://www.bbc.co.uk/cymrufyw/21696539.
83 http://www.bbc.co.uk/cymrufyw/30108707.
84 http://www.bbc.co.uk/cymrufyw/30108707.
85 National Assembly for Wales, The Committee for the Scrutiny of the First Minister, Friday 13 March 2015.
86 M. Shooter, *An Independent Review of the Role and Functions of the Children's Commissioner for Wales* (2014).
87 http://www.golwg360.com/newyddion/70324-pryder-am-annibyniaeth-y-comisiynydd-iaith.
88 In fact, the Canadian government cuts of 2006 that Williams has in mind were not to OCOL but rather to the Court Challenges Program – for example, http://www.lawtimesnews.com/ 200610021298/headline-news/tories-chop-two-legal-programs. The Court Challenges Program was not a part of OCOL but was a wholly separate not-for-profit organisation. See pp. 107–8 in L. Kloegman, 'A democratic defence of the Court Challenges Program', *Constitutional Forum constitutionnel*, 16/3 (2007), 107–15. See also, for example, http://www.cccabc.bc.ca/res/pdf/CourtChallengesProgram.pdf.
89 P. G. Thomas, 'The past, present and future of officers of Parliament', *Canadian Public Administration*, 46/3 (2003), 287–314, p. 301.

90   K. Douglas and N. Holmes, 'Funding Officers of Parliament', *Canadian Parliamentary Review*, 28/3 (2010), 38–42, p. 13. Published online at: *http://www.revparl.ca/English/issue.asp?param=171=1152*.
91   J. Stilborn, 'Funding the Officers of Parliament: Canada's experiment', *Canadian Parliamentary Review*, Summer (2010), 38–42, p. 38.
92   Stilborn, 'Funding the Officers of Parliament', p. 42.
93   Stilborn, 'Funding the Officers of Parliament', p. 41.
94   Douglas and Holmes, *Funding Officers of Parliament*.
95   Stilborn, 'Funding the Officers of Parliament', 38.
96   Stilborn, 'Funding the Officers of Parliament', 39.
97   O. Gay and B. K. Winetrobe, *Officers of Parliament – Transforming the Role* (London: UK Study of Parliament Group, the Constitution Unit, UCL, 2003), pp. 7–8. See also O. Gay, *Officers of Parliament – A Comparative Perspective. Research paper 03/77 20 October 2003* (London: House of Commons Library, 2003) and O. Gay, *Officers of Parliament: Recent Developments SN/PC/04720 29 August 2013* (London: House of Commons Library, 2013).
98   C. M. Macmillan, 'Active conscience or administrative vanguard? The Commissioner of Official Languages as an agent of change', *Canadian Public Administration*, 49/2 (2006), 161–79, p. 164. The Act states that 'The Commissioner [...] may carry out or engage in such other related assignments or activities as may be authorized by the Governor in Council.' The Governor in Council means the Governor General acting on the advice of the Federal Cabinet. Orders in Council and Minutes of the Council are signed by the Governor General, giving legal force to cabinet decisions relating to a statutory authority or the Royal prerogative. The Governor General is the representative of the Queen in Canada. See also: *http://www.pco-bcp.gc.ca/index.asp?lang=eng&page=secretariats&sub=oic-ddc&doc=gic-gec-eng.htm*; see also the constitutional term 'Queen-in-Council'.
99   See, for example, T. Buck, R. Kirkham and B. Thompson, *The Ombudsman Enterprise and Administrative Justice* (Farnham: Ashgate Publishing, 2011), and R. Kirkham, B. Thompson and T. Buck, 'Putting the ombudsman in constitutional context', *Parliamentary Affairs*, 62/4 (2009), 600–17.
100 Gay and Winetrobe, *Officers of Parliament*; Gay, *Officers of Parliament*.
101 See pp. 47–50 in A. Thomas, '"Parliamentary Officers" in Wales: Evolving roles', in O. Gay and B. K. Winetrobe (eds), *Parliament's Watchdogs: At the Crossroads* (London: UK Study of Parliament Group, the Constitution Unit, UCL, 2008), pp. 47–57.
102 Gay and Winetrobe, *Officers of Parliament*; Gay, *Officers of Parliament*.
103 Thomas, *Parliamentary Officers*, pp. 53–4.

104 See also the minutes of the meeting of the Committee for the Scrutiny of the First Minister on Friday, 13 March 2015. The Committee as a body seems rather confused on the fundamental differences between the various commissioners in Wales. This confusion is exacerbated by the report by Shooter (2014) on the Children's Commissioner. The evidence base for this report is weak and its advocacy of a common Welsh approach to commissioners is misconceived.

105 See p. 350 in M. Lodge and L. Stirton, 'Accountability in the regulatory state', in R. Baldwin, M. Cave and M. Lodge (eds), *The Oxford Handbook of Regulation* (Oxford: Oxford University Press, 2010), pp. 349–70.

106 House of Lords, The Regulatory State. Volume 1, p. 16, pars 16, 34, 93, 101(b) and 119; M. Lodge and C. Hood, 'Regulation inside government: retro-theory vindicated', in Baldwin, Cave and Lodge (eds), *The Oxford Handbook of Regulation*, pp. 590–612.

107 See, for example, pp. 76–80 in K. Yeung, 'The regulatory state', in Baldwin, Cave and Lodge (eds), *The Oxford Handbook of Regulation*, pp. 64–86.

108 House of Lords, *The Regulatory State. Volume 1*; House of Lords, *The Regulatory State. The Government's Response*; The House of Lords, *UK Economic Regulators. Report*.

109 House of Lords, *UK Economic Regulators. Report*, par. 118.

110 House of Lords, *The Regulatory State. Volume 1*; House of Lords, *The Regulatory State. The Government's Response*; The House of Lords, *UK Economic Regulators. Report*.

111 House of Lords, *The Regulatory State. Volume 1*; House of Lords, *The Regulatory State. The Government's Response*.

112 C. Turner, *Letter to Meri Huws, the Welsh Language Commissioner* (17 December 2012), p. 1.

113 Ministry of Justice and Information Commissioner's Office, *Framework Agreement* (London: Ministry of Justice and Information Commissioner's Office, 2011), p. 18.

114 Ministry of Justice and Information Commissioner's Office, *Framework Agreement*, p. 6.

115 Children's Commissioner for Wales and Welsh Government, *Memorandum of Understanding: Operational working arrangements between the Children's Commissioner for Wales and the Welsh Government* (Children's Commissioner for Wales and Welsh Government, 2012).

116 The panel may meet up to four times a year. See: http://www.comisiynyddgymraeg.org/English/Publications%20List/20120430%20DG%20S%20Remit%20Panel%20Cynghori%20%20%20-%20terf%20(2).pdf.

117 Welsh Language Commissioner, *Governance Statement* (Cardiff: Welsh Language Commissioner, 2013a), 5.2.
118 Welsh Language Commissioner, *Governance Statement*, 8.2.
119 Welsh Language Commissioner, *Remit of Management Team* (Cardiff: Welsh Language Commissioner, 2014a), 1.1.
120 Welsh Language Commissioner, *Polisi Gorfodi Comisiynydd y Gymraeg [drafft]* (Cardiff: Welsh Language Commissioner, n.d.).
121 Cymdeithas yr Iaith Gymraeg [Welsh Language Society], *Polisi gorfodi Comisiynydd y Gymraeg* (Cymdeithas yr Iaith Gymraeg, 2014).
122 Welsh Language Commissioner, *Enforcement Policy. Welsh Language Commissioner. Consultation: Overview of responses* (Cardiff: Welsh Language Commissioner, 2015a).
123 House of Lords, *The Regulatory State. Volume 1*, p. 39, par. 105.
124 House of Lords, *The Regulatory State. Volume 1*, pp. 39–40, par. 108.
125 House of Lords, *The Regulatory State. Volume 1*, p. 39, pars 105, 106.
126 House of Lords, *The Regulatory State. Volume 1*, p. 40, pars 108, 110.
127 See Welsh Language Tribunal (Appointment) Regulations 2013 and the accompanying Explanatory Memorandum.
128 Welsh Policy Paper 27, *Proposed Welsh Language (Wales) Measure: Government Amendments – Doc. 1 Appointment of the Welsh Language Tribunal* (unpublished paper, 2010), p. 4.
129 Welsh Government, Appointment of the President and other members of the Welsh Language Tribunal. Statement of appointment policy and procedure, dated to 10 December 2013 and published online on 19 December 2013. Published online at: http://www.assembly.wales/Ministerial%20Statements%20Documents/Appointment%20of%20the%20President%20and%20other%20members%20of%20the%20Welsh%20Language%20Tribunal%20(PDF,%20117KB)-19122013-252652/dat20131219-e3-English.pdf.
130 http://wales.gov.uk/about/cabinet/cabinetstatements/2014/presidentwelshlangtribunal/?lang=en.
131 Welsh Committee of the Administrative Justice & Tribunals Council, *Review of Tribunals Operating in Wales* (London: HMSO, 2010), pp. 49–50.
132 See also Arfon-Jones, who noted at this time that 'the most pressing issue remains the lack of separation of powers between devolved tribunals and the department or body whose decision is appealed'; E. Arfon-Jones, *The Tribunal System in Wales: Map and Update on Jurisdictions* (2012), p. 8. Published online at: http://www.publiclawproject.org.uk/resources/129/the-tribunal-system-in-wales-map-and-update-on-jurisdictions. See also J. Wotton, 'Jurisdiction and the Practice of Law in Wales' (lecture to the Public Law Project Wales Conference, Cardiff, 4 April 2012).

Published online at: https://www.lawsociety.org.uk/news/speeches/jurisdiction-and-the-practice-of-law-in-wales/.
133 Welsh Committee of the Administrative Justice & Tribunals Council, *Annual Report 2011/2012* (London: HMSO, 2012).
134 Welsh Committee, *Review of Tribunals*, p. 27.
135 Welsh Committee, *Review of Tribunals*, p. 28, Recommendation 1.
136 Welsh Committee, *Review of Tribunals*, p. 28.
137 Secretary of State for Constitutional Affairs and Lord Chancellor, *Transforming Public Services: Complaints, Redress and Tribunals* (London: HMSO, 2004), p. 26.
138 G. Hickinbottom [The Hon. Mr Justice], 'Administrative justice in Wales: a new dawn?' (lecture to Legal Wales Conference, Cardiff, 8 October 2009), p. 4.
139 Hickinbottom, 'Administrative justice in Wales: a new dawn?', p. 4.
140 Welsh Committee of the Administrative Justice & Tribunals Council, *The Silk Commission on Devolution in Wales. Response of the Welsh Committee of the Administrative Justice & Tribunals Council (WCAJTC) to the Commission's second call for evidence* (2013), p. 3. Available online at: http://commissionondevolutioninwales.independent.gov.uk/files/2013/03/Welsh-Committee-of-the-Administrative-Justice-and-Tribunals-Council.pdf.
141 http://wales.gov.uk/docs/hrd/publications/141014-welsh-government-organisation-chart.pdf?lang=en.
142 Welsh Government, Welsh Language Tribunal, Welsh Language Division, *The Welsh Language Tribunal Consultation Document. The Welsh Language Tribunal Rules* (Cardiff: Welsh Government, 2014c).
143 http://www.legislation.gov.uk/wsi/2015/1028/signature/made.
144 Arfon-Jones, *The Tribunal System in Wales*, pp. 8–9.
145 See Hickinbottom, *Administrative Justice in Wales*, on this, in particular p. 4. See also V. Bondy and A. Le Sueur, *Designing Redress: A Study about Grievances against Public Bodies. Queen Mary University of London, School of Law, Legal Studies Research Paper no. 121/2012* (London: Public Law Project, 2012).
146 The author and Carlin briefed the Welsh Government on this issue in December 2014. In response to a public lecture by the author on this matter, on 6 August 2015 the President of the Welsh Language Tribunal asserted publicly that the responsibility for the Welsh Language Tribunal, as regards the Administrative Justice and Tribunals Unit, had now been transferred to the Minister for Public Services, Leighton Andrews AM. According to the news outlet http://golwg360.cymru, he said, 'mae'r Tribiwnlys wedi ei symud wedyn i ofal y Gweinidog Gwasanaethau Cyhoeddus' ('the Welsh

Language Tribunal has since been transferred to the care of the Minister for Public Services') (see *http://golwg360.cymru/newyddion/cymru/195689-iaith-angen-corff-o-bobol-nid-comisiynydd-unigol*). Were that the case, that would resolve the matter of ministerial conflict of interest regarding ongoing democratic accountability, but it would not resolve the problem regarding appointment, dismissal and rule-setting; these are matters framed by statue and they can be solved only by re-framing the law. That said, while it is that case that by now the Minister for Public Services is responsible for the Justice Policy Unit and the First Minister is responsible for the Welsh Tribunals Unit, according to sources in the Welsh government, as of October 2015 (pers. comm. to the author from the Welsh Tribunals Unit and the Justice Unit, the Welsh Government, 13 and 15 October 2015), the Administrative Justice and Tribunals Unit (AJTU) 'was not split' so as to create the Welsh Tribunals Unit (WTU) and the Justice Policy Unit. Instead, the Justice Policy Unit was created *de novo* around April 2014 and it was simply the case that the 'AJTU was renamed the WTU' in October 2014. Thus, this evidence sets out the following – the First Minister has been, and indeed remains, the sponsoring minister for the Welsh Language Tribunal while also being responsible for Welsh language policy, including the Welsh Language Commissioner.

147 D. Feaver and B. Sheehy, 'The political division of regulatory labour: a legal theory of agency selection', *Oxford Journal of Legal Studies*, 35/1 (2015), 153–77.
148 House of Lords, *UK Economic Regulators. Volume 1*, par. 127.
149 House of Lords, *UK Economic Regulators. Volume 1*, par. 127.
150 House of Lords, *UK Economic Regulators. Volume 1*, par. 127.

3 | LANGUAGE RIGHTS AND FREEDOM

Introduction

There has been considerable interest in the Welsh context in the possibility of creating rights for Welsh language speakers and it is argued by the authors of the Welsh Language (Wales) Measure 2011 that this piece of legislation will have the effect of establishing a discrete set of such rights. Others disagree, and indeed made their views known as the Measure progressed during the legislative cycle. This area of contention remains unresolved in the minds of many. The purpose of this chapter is to set the specific content of the Measure in the context of the scholarly and expert literature on language rights, so as to cast some light upon the relative merits of the respective arguments. The chapter includes the careful consideration of the notion of freedom as it is framed in the Measure and, in addition, as it has been interpreted in practice. Here also, some significant matters of conceptual tension are to be discerned which are very likely to be of especial interest to policy practitioners engaged in this particular aspect of the regulatory governance of the Welsh language, along with a range of other stakeholders, including in the private sector. Given the complexity of the issues, this chapter is divided into two sections, the first of which discusses the relationship between Standards as framed in the Measure and rights, while the second examines the matter of language freedom.

Standards (cf. Rights): Policy cycle discussion, recommendation and instruction (June 2008–April 2009)

A starting point for the policy cycle discussion is provided by the commitment agreed on 27 June 2007 between the Welsh Labour Party and Plaid Cymru, as outlined in the One Wales programme for government document, to create 'linguistic rights in the provision of services'.[1]

The policy aim with regard to meeting the *One Wales* commitment on linguistic rights was put as follows: 'the establishment in legislation of basic rights (or duties) in relation to the provision of services through the medium of Welsh'.[2] In the course of the policy cycle, a very substantive part of the problem that the creation of linguistic rights is designed to solve is described as follows:

> Currently, apart from the right to speak Welsh in the Courts, individuals have no means of enforcing rights in relation to the Welsh language [. . .] Under the Welsh Language Act 1993, unless an individual can resolve the matter [complaint] in hand by complaining to the body concerned, he or she is dependent on the WLB [Welsh Language Board] taking the complaint forward on their behalf.[3]

It is recognised in the same policy paper that the notion of rights may be seen as being problematic in the context of UK Common Law: 'legal drafting in the United Kingdom is more comfortable with the concept of duties rather than rights',[4] and also, elsewhere in the same paper:

> The approach of the UK and other common law jurisdictions contrasts with the legislative approach of Civil law jurisdictions. Legislation is the primary source of law in Civil law jurisdictions [. . .] In this respect, Civil law jurisdictions are more comfortable with establishing the general rights to which individuals are entitled as the basis for making judgements.[5]

It would appear that in order to resolve this apparent tension between the One Wales commitment regarding linguistic rights and the norms of Common Law jurisdictions, it is argued in the policy paper that 'linguistic duties on organizations can be considered as the converse of

[...] rights',[6] implying that the creation of a duty, in some sense, creates a right – duty → right ; right → duty. This matter of the converse relationship between duties and rights is understood to be very significant in presentational terms: 'it may be more appropriate to package any potential rights as duties placed on specific organisation'.[7]

It was noted during the policy cycle that enforcement, or remedy, or vindication, is the crux of the matter: 'what is important in both instances [i.e. whether an approach based upon duties as its starting point or upon rights] is the extent to which any right or duty can be enforced in practice, either by an individual or an Enforcing Authority'.[8] As a consequence of establishing such language rights through legislation, one of the policy objectives was to, 'enable individuals to enforce these rights and to secure appropriate remedies [and] also enable an Enforcing Authority, with the consent of a complainant, to enforce these rights'.[9]

The One Wales commitment was central to how the National Assembly for Wales (Legislative Competence) (Welsh Language) Order 2009 was presented by the Welsh government to the UK Parliament in February 2009. It is stated there, for example, that

> Beyond addressing the weaknesses that have emerged in the system established by the 1993 Act, the Welsh Assembly Government's *One Wales* programme of Government included a commitment to seek legislative competence to enable it to bring forward Assembly Measures to confirm official status for both Welsh and English, linguistic rights in the provision of services and the establishment of the post of Language Commissioner.[10]

The Welsh government reiterated the importance of the One Wales commitment with regard to the Draft LCO in October 2009.[11] During the passage of the LCO, Westminster parliamentary advice appears to echo the view that a duty implies, in turn, a right but does so in the context of the Welsh Language Act 1993 and of Welsh Language Schemes:

> The 1993 Act imposes duties on public bodies – the duty to prepare Welsh Language Schemes under section 5 – rather than enshrining 'rights'. Of course, depending on one's perspective, a duty to provide something when required could be viewed by the recipient as a 'right' to receive it.[12]

This contrasts with the policy view in Wales whereby the 'schemes-based approach' contrasted with a 'rights-based approach' and understood, therefore, to be of wholly different conceptual orders.[13]

At a later point in the policy cycle it is argued that Standards would be a very useful vehicle with regard to the creation of rights. In one policy paper it is asserted that

> It is worth noting that adopting a standards approach could lead to a situation where the Commission [-er] could make it clear to public bodies that certain kinds of services need to be made available in Welsh 'without fail' (such as responding in Welsh to letters received in Welsh, or setting up Welsh language help lines). These could form the basis of absolute rights for Welsh speakers in the provision of services.[14]

This line of thought is directly reflected in the policy instruction, where it is clearly explained that the commitment made under One Wales would be met in that 'Some of these legally binding standards will form the backbone of linguistic rights in the provision of services committed to in the One Wales agreement.'[15] It was anticipated that certain Standards may be identified as rights in cases where the service thereby provided was equal to that provided in English, thus, 'Standards leading to linguistic rights should be published only when *meeting* the standard in question will provide a service in Welsh which will be of equal standard to the equivalent service in English.'[16] It was also recognised that while specific rights will be created as a result of the effect of the legislation not all Standards will lead to rights.[17] In other words, it was the policy intention that the 2011 Measure would, through Standards, create specific legal rights for Welsh speakers and the Measure was drafted so as to have that effect.

Standards (cf. Rights): Legislative cycle discussion and determination (March–December 2010)
In the Explanatory Memorandum accompanying the Measure as introduced it is asserted that 'Standards will also lead to the establishment of linguistic rights in the provision of services, meeting the commitments in One Wales.'[18] However, some significant actors

were unconvinced by this view of rights arising from the imposition of standards. For example, Meri Huws, then Chair of the Welsh Language Board and currently the Welsh Language Commissioner, asserted quite simply that Standards do not create rights: 'What we will have is a structure, based on standards, that places responsibilities on the provider, rather than giving rights to the citizen.'[19] She then explained this as follows:

> I am not a solicitor, but from what I understand, and according to the advice that we have received, the one thing does not naturally lead to the other. From reading the proposed Measure, we feel that this creates duties rather than rights for individuals. The word 'right' does not appear anywhere in the legislation and I therefore think that that is a very circuitous route by which to try to achieve rights.[20]

Huws was subsequently questioned further on this matter by Val Lloyd AM, Chair of the committee who asked the following question: 'Therefore, the question arising from that is: in your view do the standards in the proposed Measure satisfy the conception of language rights as set out in your paper?' In response Huws re-asserted her position, along with that of the Board, in the following terms:

> We do not feel that the proposed Measure achieves what we hoped that it would. To reiterate, there is no mention of rights in this legislation. What you have – again, as was the case with the 1993 Act – is the idea of strengthening the element of duties, which do not lead naturally to absolute legal rights.[21]

At a later point during the same session, and in a response to a question from Gareth Jones AM, Huws restated her position on the matter in the most succinct and direct manner: 'I am repeating myself to some extent in saying this, but [the] standards do not lead to those legal rights.'[22]

A range of other actors agreed with the Commissioner on the matter of rights, or expressed similar scepticism, including in the form of a letter by eighty 'prominent' Welsh people, including some lawyers, in which they noted their concern with the 'absence of rights for individuals'.[23] Another lawyer, Emyr Lewis, stated the notion of right is defined as follows: 'I believe that the word "right" means that you have the right to do something that is justiciable in some way and eventually to have some sort of redress', adding that, 'The proposed Measure does not do that.'[24] At another point during the same session he asserted that in order to ensure 'that you provide rights [...] the individual must have suffered and some means of redress must be ensured in that context [...] which would be enforceable through the courts'.[25] He contended quite simply that Standards are not justiciable and do not allow for redress for the individual Welsh speaker. For example, 'in order to establish a right, you need something that is justiciable and that leads to some sort of outcome, for the benefit of the holder of that right – some sort of redress or compensation [...] The standards do not achieve that. They fall short.'[26] Colin Williams went as far as to argue that 'It is futile to have such a proposed Measure that does not contain fundamental rights that will be safeguarded by the courts.'[27] Elsewhere during this session he also asserted that 'Even now there is confusion regarding the Welsh Language Act 1993. Many people behave as though the Act confers rights on them. Gwynedd Council, for example, suggests using these rights to safeguard Welsh language interests and to provide services.'[28] Another actor, while unconvinced by Standards, argued that it might be possible instead to 'adopt an evolutionary approach and turn the core elements of Welsh Language Schemes [...] into a set of rights'.[29]

No change was made to the substantive detail of the Measure as a result of these interventions. However, the following text was added to the Preamble of the Measure, in which it is asserted that the function of the Measure is, in part, 'to make provision about standards relating to the Welsh language (including duties to comply with those standards, and rights arising from the enforceability of those duties)'. Also, it is similarly asserted in Part 1.1 (2) (a) of the Measure as passed that rights will arise from duties: 'the official status of the Welsh language is given legal effect by the enactments about – duties on bodies to use the Welsh language, and the rights which arise from the enforceability of those duties'. It remained the case, too, that any power to seek legal remedy or redress, or to vindicate claims, resided with the Commissioner and also that only organisations could challenge decisions of the Commissioner via the Welsh Language Tribunal.

Standards (cf. Rights): Analysis

In the operation of the office of Commissioner, under the stewardship of Meri Huws, the rhetoric of language rights has been adopted, despite the previous misgivings of Huws. For example, the Commissioner's publications explain as follows:

> The principal aim of the Welsh Language Commissioner [...] is to promote and facilitate the use of the Welsh language. This entails raising awareness of the official status of the Welsh language in Wales and imposing standards on organisations. This, in turn, will lead to the establishment of rights for Welsh speakers.[30]

The following year the Commissioner noted that the former Irish Language Commissioner, Seán Ó Cuirreáin, 'was generous in sharing his experiences of how to define language rights'.[31] It is not unreasonable to assume, therefore, that the Welsh Language Commissioner is by now convinced that the imposition of standards will indeed lead to the creation of rights. Also, it would appear that the former Irish Language Commissioner played a role in that task of persuasion. In addition, it would also appear to be the case that these Commissioners understand that the task of determining whether language rights may be said to exist, or not, is a matter which is subject to definition, in some sense, by the Commissioner. This volte-face by Huws was a matter of consternation to some authoritative interviewees (Fieldwork Interview 50).

It is clear from the policy cycle paperwork that the policy position in Wales is that Standards are different to Schemes in that they create rights via duties. But the Westminster position is that Schemes can also be understood to create rights in that sense, too. Thus, rights, loosely understood or in a rhetorical sense, may be read into both the duty negotiated under Schemes, as per Ward in his work of 2009, and also into the duty imposed under Standards, as per Welsh Policy Papers 4, 11 and 15. As we see in chapter 4 of this text, the research demonstrates that, in fact, Standards and Schemes are of the same conceptual order – they are both regulatory standards. They only differ in the manner of their setting, either through imposition or as a result of negotiation, and in the effectiveness of their enforcement. Others are completely unambiguous as to whether the Measure, and Standards in particular, establishes, creates or will lead to language rights. For example, de Varennes asserted in 2012, that is since the Measure gained Royal Assent, that

> neither the Welsh Language Act of 1993, nor the Welsh Language (Wales) Measure 2011 recognises a legal obligation on authorities to use Welsh, nor do they grant the right to individuals to demand such use [. . .] the Welsh legislation is very careful to keep the use of Welsh firmly in the political realm by not recognising a right to use Welsh with authorities. None of the Welsh language legislation includes any references to such an entitlement [. . .] the Welsh legislation in the main deals with the obligations of authorities [. . .] and does not recognise any direct right or entitlement for individuals to the use of the Welsh language.[32]

In order to resolve this issue it is useful to turn, in the first instance, to the Hohfeldian[33] analytical system for describing the form of rights.[34] The Hohfeldian system is 'widely accepted' as the authoritative approach to understanding the meaning of rights in the field of law and moral philosophy.[35] According to Hohfeld there are four basic elements or components to the notion of right. These are also known as the 'Hohfeldian incidents', namely: the claim, the privilege, the power and the immunity. These elements each have a distinctive logical form and they relate to each other in a certain manner as 'complex molecular rights'.[36] The Hohfeldian incidents, or the constituent elements of complex molecular rights, are, very briefly, defined as follows:

> Primary rules – Claim: A has a claim that B φ *if and only if* B has a duty to A to φ. Privilege: A has a privilege to φ *if and only if* A has no duty not to φ.

> Secondary rules, i.e. rules that specify how agents can introduce, change and alter primary rules – Power: A has a power *if and only if* A has the ability within a set of rules to alter her own or another's Hohfeldian incidents. Immunity: B has an immunity *if and only if* A lacks the ability within a set of rules to alter B's Hohfeldian incidents.

With regard to the term 'privilege' in particular, some more recent scholars prefer the term 'liberty' while retaining broadly the same meaning.[37] Thomson, writing in 1990, distinguishes between the two, while identifying four basic types of rights – claims, privileges, powers and immunities.[38] For her, a privilege is understood as a moral permission, the condition of not being under an obligation not to do X. A cluster right is where any two, or more, of these four kinds or rights are combined. Thus, a liberty is a cluster right that includes a privilege.[39] Returning to Hohfeld, it is necessary to add here, given the connection made between the notion of duty, on the one hand, and right, on the other, during both the policy cycle and also the legislative cycle with regard to Standards creating or leading to Welsh language rights, that according to Hohfeld, a 'duty' is the correlative of 'claim', thus if *A* has a claim, then some other person *B* has a corresponding duty. Moreover, and following on from Hohfeld most directly, Ellis answers the question 'what are rights?' quite concisely: 'The answer is simply that there are claims, privileges, powers and immunities. What we call rights may be any one of these, or a mixture.'[40] With regard to using the Welsh language, this may be schematised as follows (Figure 5):

In the Welsh context, therefore, it can be argued that de Varennes and others take the view that in order for a duty and claim

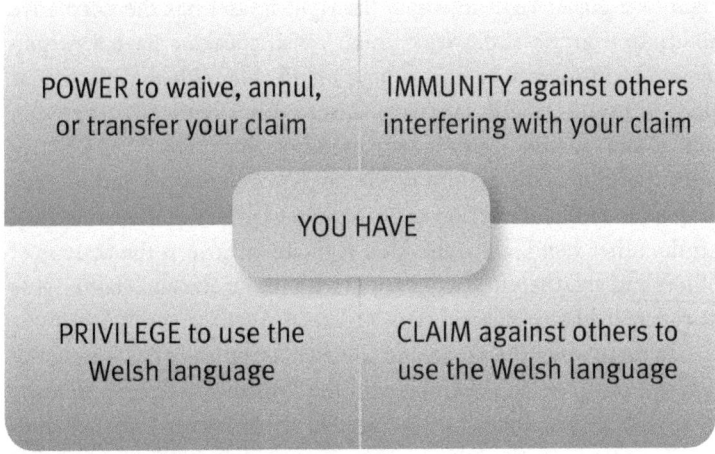

Figure 5. *Molecular structure of a Welsh language right following Hohfeld, 1919.*

to constitute a right then the power, in particular, of the individual to waive, annul or transfer their claim must be held by the individual. Under the Measure the individual Welsh speaker is divested of that power and instead it is invested in the corporate body of the Commissioner. This may be what Huws meant by 'absolute legal rights'. But of course, the Welsh government advisers were at the same time asserting that Standards would be the basis for 'absolute rights'. In that narrow sense Welsh speakers have no rights that arise from the Measure, nor will rights arise from the imposition of Standards. But, in a broader sense Welsh language rights may be said to exist to the extent that the Commissioner is empowered on the part of individual Welsh speakers. Welsh speakers have, indeed, claims against public bodies to use the Welsh language, and those persons are duty-bound to meet those claims. During the course of the fieldwork a number of legal experts familiar with the law in Wales, and in particular the law as pertains to the Welsh language, expressed the view that Standards create rights in that sense.

In addition, Welsh speakers, it may be said, enjoy another kind of right. They have the freedom to use the Welsh language. That is to say, that under the Measure they are entitled to freedom from undesirable actions or interference with their privilege right to use Welsh. This may be conceived of as a 'toleration right',[42] or a 'negative' right (as opposed to a positive right),[43] as opposed to a positive right or a power right in which the right-holder has the normative ability to exercise authority.[44] Thus, Welsh speakers have a certain degree of immunity against others interfering with that particular right to use the Welsh language. Also, Lyons's distinction between 'active' and 'passive' rights is very useful on this point.[45] Here, active rights pertain to the actions of the holder of the rights and thereby map on to Hohfeld's notion of power and of privilege. Passive rights, on the other hand, are rights that regulate or govern the actions of others and are, therefore, concerned with immunity and claim rights as conceived of by Hohfeld.

In these ways, therefore, and somewhat ironically in a number of regards, both Welsh Assembly and the Westminster parliamentary policy advice was correct with regard to rights arising from Schemes and Standards in the broad sense. That said, if it is accepted that Standards do indeed create rights, there may perhaps arise a question as to whether an 'aggrieved person', in other words the individual citizen, ought to have direct access in their own person to a court or tribunal with full jurisdiction as they seek remedy to a complaint, rather than such access being deputed to the Commissioner in order for the regulatory regime, and indeed the Measure itself, to be compatible with the European Convention on Human Rights.[46]

Freedom to use Welsh: Policy cycle discussion, recommendation and instruction (June 2008–April 2009)

Policy paperwork states that ministers, in seeking legislative competence for the National Assembly for Wales with regard to the Welsh language, indicated their desire 'to legislate so as to confirm the freedom which Welsh speakers have to speak the language with one another and to prevent third parties from interfering with that freedom'[47] so as to establish 'a climate where Welsh speakers are not faced with barriers [. . .] to their use of the language.'[48] Rather confusingly, the freedom to use Welsh is also described during the policy cycle as 'the right to speak Welsh', although a large degree of conceptual clarity is arrived at by the close of the policy cycle, insofar as rights entail duties while the exercise of a freedom does not. The case of an employee of Thomas Cook in 2007 was cited as an illustration of such interference.[49]

The policy aim was 'to remove any uncertainty regarding whether third parties can interfere with the freedom which individuals have to choose which language they speak (to each other)'.[50] The policy objectives included 'a clear definition of when that right [to use Welsh] would exist, and what exclusions there might be' and that of the key principles 'there should be clarity regarding the boundaries of such a right'.[51] It is also noted that 'this freedom would not create specific duties or obligations other than a duty not to interfere with a freedom which already exists'.[52] Amongst the possible boundaries of such a 'right', it was noted that 'it might be appropriate to introduce an exemption from the general right to speak Welsh' and that 'possible grounds for exemption' could include 'workplace administration' as 'it might not be appropriate for the right to cover internal meetings within an organisation'.[53]

Evidence from the policy cycle also shows that the freedom to use Welsh would not be 'dependent on placing a duty on anyone'[54] and that 'it is not the intention of Ministers that organisations should have to make any particular arrangements in order to ensure that individuals can exercise the freedom to speak Welsh with one another'[55] and that 'it is not intended to govern dealings between individuals and organisations (public or private) providing services with regard to those services'.[56] In seeking the legislative competence with regard to the Welsh language, the Welsh government explained that under the National Assembly for Wales (Legislative Competence) (Welsh Language) Order 2009 as per the Proposed Order:

> This matter [i.e. Matter 20.2 regarding the freedom to use Welsh, as per the amendment to the Government of Wales Act 2006, S.94(6)(B), 11.2.2010][57] would not require bodies to take positive steps to facilitate the use of the Welsh language between individuals, merely to respect the freedom to use the language.[58]

This is worded at a later stage, as per the Draft Order, as follows:

> The Assembly will be able to consider legislating to require persons to respect the freedom to use the Welsh Language, but Matter 20.2 [i.e. regarding the freedom to use Welsh] will not enable the Assembly to legislate to require them to take positive steps to facilitate the use of the Welsh language between persons wishing to use the Welsh language with one another.[59]

An examination of the material from the policy cycle shows that these particular matters of discussion evolved into recommendation and ultimately policy instruction to legislative drafters with no modification, taking the following form:

> it is not the intention of this policy to place duties or obligations on employers or any other organisation with the intention of ensuring that individuals may exercise the freedom to speak Welsh with one another [. . .] It would not, for example, be our intention that any legislation concerning this freedom could enable an employee or the Commissioner to require aspects of the internal administration of organisations to be in Welsh or to be supported by particular Welsh forms [. . .] Neither is it the intention that employers could be required to make particular arrangements in order to facilitate the exercise of this right.[60]

It was confirmed in the policy instruction for the proposed Welsh Language Measure that the freedom to use Welsh would not be dependent upon duties being placed on organisations and that 'workplace administration' was identified as 'possible grounds for exemption'.[61] More specifically, it is stated that it be recognised

> that there might be circumstances where there needs to be an agreement on a common language [i.e. to the exclusion of Welsh] being spoken to ensure certain outcomes e.g. that certain functions are undertaken in a way that meets particular health and safety requirements.[62]

Freedom to use Welsh: Legislative cycle discussion and determination (March–December 2010)

It was clear during the legislative cycle that the intention of Welsh ministers to enshrine the 'Freedom to use Welsh' was not appreciated by some significant actors, in particular Emyr Lewis and Colin Williams. For example, during the legislative cycle the following assertions were made: 'I fear that these provisions [i.e. Part 6] suggest regulation of the circumstances in which people can speak Welsh together. For that reason, I would prefer to see this Part being dropped from the Measure';[63] 'That [i.e. Part 6] is utter nonsense to me. Freedom to breathe – thanks.'[64] Lewis in particular asserts that current legislation is adequate to the task of preventing interference with the freedom to use the Welsh language.[65] However, that is contrary to the position reached by advisers in the Welsh Assembly[66] and at Westminster.[67] Note that none of the actors in the legislative cycle, nor for that matter actors in the policy cycle, make any reference to or indicate any awareness of the existence in various other jurisdictions of statutory provisions regarding the freedom to use a language.[68] For these, see Ruíz Vieytez's piece from 2004,[69] to which Belgium, China, the Czech Republic, Sri Lanka and Switzerland could be added.[70] See also Paz[71] for a critique on the European Commission of Human Rights and the Court (ECHR) on 'linguistic freedom' and the report of 2011 by the Research Division of the ECHR.[72] One ought also be cognisant of Green, from 1991,[73] and, subsequently, de Varennes, writing in 1993,[74] on understanding 'freedom of expression' as freedom to use a particular language. Their pathfinder, sometimes acknowledged, must be the text by McDougal et al. from 1976.[75] In addition, Schilling[76] and also Schmidt[77] are very useful ports of call. A schematic summary is provided in Figure 6 of the recognition provided in a range of nation-state jurisdictions of the freedom to use a given language. The case of Switzerland may be of particular interest, given that the constitutional principle of 'sprachenfreiheit' has been subject to scholarly scrutiny[78] and, significantly, there is pertinent case law.[79]

Note that Lewis was asked directly by Gareth Jones AM whether he was aware of any similar statutes regarding the freedom to use a language – he confirmed that he was not[80] – and also with regard to the meaning of the freedom to use Welsh on the one hand, as opposed to the right to speak Welsh, on the other[81] – that is to say, the fundamental difference between a freedom and a right. This

State	Recognition of freedom to use or the 'right to freely use one's own language'
Azerbaijan	Constitution, Chapter II, Article 45
Belarus	Constitution, Section II, Article 50
Belgium	Constitution, Title II, Article 30
Croatia	Constitution, Section III, Article 15
Czech Republic	Charter of Fundamental Rights and Freedoms, Chapter III, Article 25 (1)
Georgia	Constitution, Chapter II, Article 38
Hungary	Constitution, Article 68 (2)
Latvia	Constitution, Chapter VIII, Article 114
People's Republic of China	Constitution, Chapter I, Article 4
Poland	Constitution, Chapter II, Article 35
Russian Federation	Constitution, Chapter II, Article 26
Slovenia	Constitution, Part II, Article 61
Sri Lanka	Constitution, Chapter III, Article 14
Switzerland	Constitution, Chapter I, Article 18

Figure 6. *States in which the freedom to use or the 'right to freely use one's own language' is recognised by statute*

exchange could have been usefully informed by the aforementioned material and also by the California Senate Bill SB 242 Civil Rights: Language Restrictions. This Bill was introduced to the Senate on 24 February 2009 with the intention of making it unlawful 'to adopt or enforce a policy that requires, limits, or prohibits the use of any language in or with a business establishment, unless the policy is justified by a business necessity' or that such 'language restriction or requirement is necessary for the safe and efficient operation of the business'.[82] The Bill generated considerable discussion and garnered significant attention in the media during its passage. It was variously described as a law that would 'ban business from language discrimination',[83] protect the freedom of an individual to use their own language through prohibiting unjustifiable 'English-only practices'.[84] While passed by both the Senate and the Assembly, the Bill was vetoed by the Governor on 11 October 2009 on the grounds that it would 'have the unintended effect of increasing frivolous lawsuits against businesses'.[85] Business interests lobbied vigorously against the Bill.[86]

This gap in expert knowledge is also apparent in the closely associated policy and legislative cycle with regard to the National Assembly for Wales (Legislative Competence) (Welsh Language) Order 2009. In this context it is specifically noted that the other pertinent 'legislative frameworks' with 'language rights or freedom' were as follows: the Republic of Ireland, Fryslân (the Netherlands), Finland, Québec (Canada), New Brunswick (Canada), Catalonia (Spain) and the Basque Autonomous Community (Spain).[87] As was remarked upon in Welsh Policy Paper 23, Legislative Committee 2 advised that

> if the Minister accepts our recommendation to include a clear statement regarding the official status of the Welsh language in Part 1 of the proposed Measure, then a subsequent provision to protect a person's freedom would not be necessary. Such a statement would automatically safeguard an individual's freedom to use Welsh in practice. If such changes are made to the proposed Measure, we believe that Part 6 should be removed in its entirety.[88]

This advice takes for granted certain unfounded assumptions about the certainty of legal meaning, the enforceability, or justiciability, of declarative statements on the status of language.[89] This advice was not taken up and Part 6 was retained.

Freedom to use Welsh: Analysis

In the office's first annual report, the Commissioner very much appears to contend that the assertion of the freedom to use Welsh as per the Measure will lead to this freedom becoming a right:

> A new and challenging area where the Commissioner has power is in relation to interference with an individual's freedom to use Welsh. I foresee that interesting cases will arise as a result of complaints of this nature in the future, and that these will force legal questions in relation to the definition of the freedom to use the Welsh language and under which conditions such freedom becomes a right.[90]

This appears to confuse the scholarly and legal literature on this matter. Simply, freedom is a right but it is a negative right; it does not become a right subsequent to legal cases. The Commissioner's assertion appears to imply a confusion of freedom, a negative right, with a positive right. The difference is most significant with regard properly interpreting cases pertaining to freedom to use Welsh. A positive right is asserted through placing a duty upon a body, while a negative right entails no such duty.

During the course of 2013–14 the Welsh Language Commissioner received four complaints of potential relevance to Part 6.[91] Two of these were determined to be 'invalid'.[92] Of the valid applications, one case, pertaining to Swinton Group Limited (henceforth Swinton), resulted in a Statutory Investigation as a result of which the Commissioner found that Swinton had 'interfered with an individual's freedom to use Welsh'.[93] As a result, the Commissioner issued Swinton with the following advice:

> Part 1 of the Measure gives the Welsh language official status in Wales. As an organisation conducting its business in Wales. D [Swinton] should fully recognise this official status by changing its policy of using the English language alone when discussing financial products with its customers in Wales.[94]

In announcing the finding, the Commissioner stated that:

> Tra bod Swinton wedi ei siomi gyda'r costau ychwanegol a'r cymhlethdod o weithredu system fonitro galwadau ar wahân, mae'n cydnabod pwysigrwydd ymchwiliad a chyngor Comisiynydd y Gymraeg.⁹⁵

> ['While Swinton are disappointed with the extra costs and complication of operating a separate monitoring system, they recognise the importance of the investigation and advice of the Welsh Language Commissioner.']

In the Commissioner's report on the case it is noted that:

> As the FCA⁹⁶ has explained that it is acceptable to keep records in another language, and only to reproduce or translate them into English when required (for example, following a request by the FCA), the Commissioner is not of the opinion that the argument about lack of resources justifies the interference.⁹⁷

Swinton had argued that it 'prohibits its staff from using the Welsh language to discuss financial products with its customers' for reasons that included 'a lack of resources to monitor Welsh medium telephone calls and translate records of such conversations into English as required'.⁹⁸

Prima facie, the case of Swinton is quite similar to the application brought by an individual named Gwion Schiavone against Admiral, another financial services company, on 3 May 2013. In this case Schiavone complained that Admiral prevented him discussing financial products in Welsh on the telephone, despite the fact that Admiral has staff that are able to also speak Welsh. The Admiral case was made public by the complainant in July 2013. In the case of Admiral the Commissioner noted that the company was not under any statutory duty to offer services in the Welsh language. At the same time, the First Minister of the Welsh government noted that he was 'happy' to look into the matter and, while noting also that Admiral was under no statutory obligation, added that 'it doesn't make business sense for a company to be seen as one which fails to provide services in Welsh [. . .] I would think that Admiral would want to ensure that services in Welsh are available.'⁹⁹ The Welsh Language Society, noting in particular the case of Schiavone, then sent a letter, which was published online on 24 July 2013, to the Welsh Language Commissioner noting their 'pryderon am y system gwyno' ('concerns about the complaints system').[100] On 24 July 2013 it was reported that the Commissioner promised to 'edrych ar y system gwyno' ('to look at the complaints system').[101] The complaint against Admiral was not pursued by the Commissioner. Admiral subsequently issued an apology on 19 August in which the company noted that 'the First Minister [explained] that there was, in fact, no legal obligation for any company to offer Welsh as an alternative language to clients', but that 'it is likely that Admiral Insurance [...] will be very keen to make sure that their call centre staff and their recording system allows those who wish to speak Welsh to use that language when they contact the company.'[102]

The application against Swinton was made on 13 May 2013. The company appears to have been brought to the attention of the Welsh Language Society during November 2013 when the Society received complaints about the company. It was later noted in the print media that the Society had 'helped the Swinton staff register their complaints'.[103] Subsequent to the case being brought to their attention the Society lobbied the Commissioner on the matter, while the Chairperson of the Society asserted publicly that 'Mae'n rhaid i Gomisiynydd y Gymraeg gynnal ymchwiliad' ('the Welsh Language Commissioner must conduct an investigation').[104] The news report further notes that the Commissioner explained that the office was considering conducting an investigation. The Commissioner decided to pursue a case against Swinton at a meeting of the office's Complaints and Statutory Investigations Panel on 8 January 2014,[105] the matter becoming public knowledge in February 2014.[106] The Welsh government minister who sponsored the Measure made the following intervention at that time: 'If they [Swinton] insist it's their policy to conduct some discussions with the public in English, the customer has a right to walk away and go to a more enlightened company.'[107] The implication of this is that Swinton are not under any duty to facilitate the use of the Welsh language. The Commissioner's publications indicate that the Statutory Investigation was based upon the complaint made on 13 May 2013. There does not appear to be a record of the complaints apparently submitted in November 2013 and facilitated by the Welsh Language Society, either in the relevant Annual Report or in the report on the Statutory Investigation on the Swinton case.[108]

Conclusions

Were one able to safely assume that the Commissioner was fully briefed by the Welsh government on the policy purpose and scope of Part 6 of the Measure, then it could be easily argued that the timetable of events along with the prima facie similarity between the cases of Admiral and Swinton suggest the possibility of regulatory capture.[109] Regulatory capture by special interest groups, which 'value some outcomes and goods [. . .] more than does the public at large',[110] occurs when their influence induces certain regulatory activity or brings about certain regulatory outcomes. Prima facie, the evidence suggests that the Commissioner is vulnerable to the risk of the undue influence of an interest group; the Commissioner, of course, was previously the Chairperson of the Welsh Language Society, between 1981 and 1983.[111] It is a moot point whether the case of Swinton constitutes strong or weak capture, as understood by Carpenter and Moss.[112] Given that it could be argued that the regulatory outcome in this particular case serves the interests of the Welsh language, it could be argued that the capture is weak. Carpenter and Moss characterise weak capture as follows: 'weak capture prevails when the net social benefits of regulation are diminished as a result of special interest influence, but remain positive overall'.[113] However, in this case the regulatee may have a very different position from that of the special interest group on weak capture and its impact upon the regulatory outcome. That said, Part 6 of the Measure and Freedom to Use Welsh is very noticeable by its absence from the Welsh government's preparatory briefing of 13 December 2011 to the office of the Commissioner elect.[114] It could be the case, therefore, that the Commissioner was simply insufficiently briefed on the matter.

A second substantial matter must also be noted and that is with regard to the intended purpose of Part 6, including in particular the intended nature and extent of the impact of its application upon organisations. The crux of the matter here is regulatory activism. This is defined as follows:

> Activist commissions [. . .] impose on utilities requirements and restrictions for the sole purpose of effectuating policies which the regulators believe to be desirable in promoting the general welfare, even though such policies are far removed from the purpose of the regulatory statute.[115]

It is likely to be of particular interest to regulatees, and other potentially relevant organisations, that the additional costs and administrative burdens, as recognised by the Commissioner, to be borne by Swinton as a result of the Commissioner's findings with regard to the freedom to use Welsh run counter to, and indeed beyond, the purpose of the Welsh Language Measure as defined during the policy cycle, including by policy instruction.

According to the Explanatory Memorandum regarding the legislative competence of the National Assembly for Wales in this area, the matter of the freedom to use Welsh 'would not require bodies to take positive steps to facilitate the use of the Welsh language between individuals', in other words the powers of legislative competence 'will not enable the Assembly to legislate to require them [bodies] to take positive steps to facilitate the use of the Welsh language between persons wishing to use the Welsh language with one another', as noted above. According to the policy purpose of the Measure, the application of Part 6 of the Measure does not imply specific duties or obligations 'other than a duty not to interfere', neither is it intended that organisations 'have to make any particular arrangements' in order to allow for the exercise of the freedom to use Welsh, nor is its purpose 'to govern dealings between individuals and organisations (public or private) providing services with regard to those services', and 'workplace administration' was identified as 'possible grounds for exemption'. The determination of the Commissioner, in fact, entails additional costs as well as an additional administrative burden to Swinton so as to cause 'discussing financial products with its customers' in the Welsh language to be possible. In this context, therefore, the matter of Swinton appears to be a demonstrable case of regulatory activism and the regulatory outcome of the case is at odds with the precise legislative intent of the Measure. In addition, there would appear to be a basic confusion on the part of some significant actors with regard to the legal meaning of the freedom to use a language in contrast to the right to use a language.[116]

While the determination of the Commissioner appears to be at odds with the policy purpose behind the Measure, it can only by challenged through judicial review. Some have argued that the powers of the Commissioner in relation to freedom to use Welsh are too limited, being restricted to recommending or advising. While some might balk at granting such powers to the Commissioner, perhaps even in the light of this analysis, providing the office with coercive powers in relation to freedom to use Welsh would also mean, of necessity, providing those persons subject to the determinations of the Commissioner with avenues of appeal that are more readily accessible than judicial review. In addition, binding the sole responsibility for such fine calls of judgement to a single individual may be to place too much of a burden on one set of shoulders; sharing the burden appears useful. On the other hand, given that there have been relatively few cases regarding Freedom to Use Welsh, in other words there is no evidence of a systemic problem, being able to adopt a less formal approach to resolving cases in the form of alternative dispute resolution (ADR)[117] techniques could be of value. That the research team elicited anecdotal evidence suggesting that Swinton were not wholly resistant to the entreaties of the Commissioner lends some weight to this.

As regards the Measure establishing rights for Welsh speakers, Standards do not create or establish language rights in the narrow sense. It can be argued that they do so in a broader sense. Standards and Schemes are both instruments for setting in place regulatory standards. If one is to accept the argument that Standards imply rights in the broader sense, then the same applies to Schemes. Logically, both Standards and Schemes imply claims and duties, and therefore rights in that broad sense. In this case, Standards do not entail the introduction of rights, broadly speaking, any differently than do Schemes. Standards are different to Schemes with regard to the manner in which they are set, but not with regard to claims, duties and, therefore, rights. It was argued that the introduction of Standards would allow the Welsh government to meet the One Wales commitment with regard to language rights and that replacing Schemes was therefore necessary. However, the logic of the case for rights arising from Standards applies equally to Schemes. It is simply a matter of presentation, and whether you define rights in the narrow sense or more broadly. Moreover, it is not in actual fact necessary to couch the moral case for a minority language in terms of rights. Politicians, policy actors, activists and others may feel driven to adopt the rhetoric of language rights as during the second half of the twentieth century, 'almost overnight, international human rights came to provide exclusively the language of political legitimacy for states and international organisations'.[118] Some argue that we fail to see other, equally valid, narratives of legitimacy and to properly understand the 'appeal to rights' as no more and no less than 'one moral language among others'.[119]

Notes

1. Labour Party and Plaid Cymru, *One Wales. A progressive agenda for the government of Wales. An agreement between the Labour and Plaid Cymru Groups in the National Assembly 27 June 2007*, p. 34.
2. Welsh Policy Paper 4, *Linguistic Rights* (unpublished paper, 2008), p. 2.
3. Welsh Policy Paper 4, p. 1.
4. Welsh Policy Paper 4, p. 2.
5. Welsh Policy Paper 4, p. 4.
6. Welsh Policy Paper 4, p. 2.
7. Welsh Policy Paper 4, p. 4.
8. Welsh Policy Paper 4, p. 2.
9. Welsh Policy Paper 4, p. 2.
10. Welsh Assembly Government, *Memorandum from the Welsh Assembly Government. Constitutional Law: Devolution, Wales. The National Assembly for Wales (Legislative Competence) (Welsh Language) Order 2009. Proposal for a Legislative Competence Order on the Welsh Language* (Cardiff: Welsh Assembly Government, 2009a [January]), p. 5.
11. Welsh Assembly Government, *Memorandum from the Welsh Assembly Government. Constitutional Law: Devolution, Wales. The National Assembly for Wales (Legislative Competence) (Welsh Language) Order 2009. Draft Legislative Competence Order on the Welsh Language* (Cardiff: Welsh Assembly Government, 2009b [October]), p. 7.
12. P. Ward, *The proposed Welsh Language Legislative Competence Order. Standard Note SN/HA/4973* (London: House of Commons Library, 11 December 2009), p. 11.
13. Welsh Policy Paper 5, *Language Schemes / Policies* (unpublished paper, 2008), pp. 12–13.
14. Welsh Policy Paper 11, *Welsh Language Commissioner and Welsh Language Schemes* (unpublished paper, 2009), p. 17.
15. Welsh Policy Paper 15, *Policy instructions to legal services on the proposed Welsh Language Measure* (unpublished paper, April 2009), pp. 37, 38.
16. Welsh Policy Paper 15, pp. 37, 38.
17. Welsh Policy Paper 15, pp. 37, 38.
18. Welsh Assembly Government, *The Proposed Welsh Language (Wales) Measure 2010. Explanatory Memorandum to the Proposed Welsh Language Wales Measure 2010 4 March 2010* (Cardiff: Welsh Assembly Government, 2010a), p. 32.
19. Meri Huws, *Oral Evidence*, The Proposed Welsh Language (Wales) Measure – Evidence Session 29 April 2010, Legislative Committee 2, the National Assembly for Wales.

20 Meri Huws, *Oral Evidence*.
21 Meri Huws, *Oral Evidence*.
22 Meri Huws, *Oral Evidence*.
23 http://www.bbc.co.uk/news/uk-wales-11690494; http://cymdeithas.org/2010/11/04/leading_welsh_figures_call_for_language_law_changes.html.
24 Emyr Lewis, *Oral Evidence*, par. 59.
25 Emyr Lewis, *Oral Evidence*, par. 62.
26 Emyr Lewis, *Oral Evidence*, par. 84.
27 Colin H. Williams, *Oral Evidence*, par. 183.
28 Colin H. Williams, *Oral Evidence*, par. 192.
29 Cwmni Iaith, *Written Evidence Response to the proposed Welsh Language (Wales) Measure 2010, National Assembly for Wales Legislation Committee No. 2*, 7 May 2010 MI 54.
30 Welsh Language Commissioner, *Adroddiad Blynyddol 2012-13. Annual Report 2012-13* (Cardiff: Welsh Language Commissioner, 2013b), p. 13.
31 Welsh Language Commissioner, *Adroddiad Blynyddol 2013-14. Annual Report 2013-14* (Cardiff: Welsh Language Commissioner, 2014b), p. 9.
32 F. de Varennes, *International and Comparative Perspectives in the Use of Official Languages. Models and Approaches for South Africa* (Afrikaanse Taalraad, 2012), pp. 52-3.
33 W. Hohfeld, *Fundamental Legal Conceptions* (New Haven: Yale University Press, 1919).
34 The question of whether Standards create rights was the subject of two scholarly papers and subsequent expert discussion at a Chatham House Rule symposium held under the auspices of the ESRC project on the office of Language Commissioner on 28 April 2015: http://www.cardiff.ac.uk/news/view/97404-minority-language-rights-understanding-legislation-law.
35 http://plato.stanford.edu/entries/rights/.
36 http://plato.stanford.edu/entries/rights/.
37 H. Steiner, *An Essay on Rights* (Oxford: Blackwell, 1994).
38 J. Thomson, *The Realm of Rights* (Oxford: Oxford University Press, 1990).
39 See also P. Eleftheriadis, *Legal Rights* (Oxford: Oxford University Press, 2008), see especially pp. 124-8.
40 See p. 200 in A. Ellis, 'Minority rights and the preservation of languages', *Philosophy*, 80/2 (2005), 199-217.
41 Fieldwork Interviews 57 and 67.
42 H. Kloss, 'Language rights of immigrant groups', *International Migration Review*, 5/2 (1971), 250-68; H. Kloss, *The American Bilingual Tradition* (Rowley, MA: Newbury House, 1977); A. Patten,

'Survey article: the justification of minority language rights', *Journal of Political Philosophy*, 17/1 (2009), 102–28.
43 F. Bastiat, *The Law* (Auburn, AL: Ludwig von Mises Institute, 2007 repr.; pub. 1850). Published online at: *https://mises.org/sites/default/files/thelaw.pdf*; S. Holmes and S. Sunstein, *The Costs of Rights* (New York: W. W. Norton, 1990); J. Narveson, *The Libertarian Idea* (Peterborough, Ontario: Broadview, 2001); H. Shue, *Basic Rights: Subsistence, Affluence and U.S. Foreign Policy* (Princeton: Princeton University Press, 1996); K. Vašák, 'Human rights: a 30-year struggle: the sustained efforts to give force of law to the United Nations Declaration of Human Rights', *UNESCO Courier*, 3/11 (1977).
44 L. Sumner, *The Moral Foundations of Rights* (Oxford: Oxford University Press, 1987).
45 D. Lyons, 'The correlativity of rights and duties', *Noûs*, 4 (1970), 45–57.
46 V. Bondy and A. Le Sueur, *Designing Redress: A Study about Grievances against Public Bodies. Queen Mary University of London, School of Law, Legal Studies Research Paper no. 121/2012* (London: Public Law Project, 2012), p. 40.
47 Welsh Policy Paper 7, *The Right to Speak Welsh* (unpublished paper, July 2008), p. 1.
48 Welsh Policy Paper 10, *The Freedom to Speak Welsh* (unpublished paper, June 2008), p. 1.
49 *http://www.walesonline.co.uk/news/wales-news/thomas-cook-welsh-ban-row-2245215* ; *http://news.bbc.co.uk/1/hi/wales/6739121.stm.*
50 Welsh Policy Paper 7, p. 1.
51 Welsh Policy Paper 7, p. 1.
52 Welsh Policy Paper 7, p. 3.
53 Welsh Policy Paper 7, p. 5.
54 Welsh Policy Paper 10, p. 2.
55 Welsh Policy Paper 10, p. 2.
56 Welsh Policy Paper 10, p. 3.
57 *http://www.legislation.gov.uk/ukpga/2006/32/section/94.*
58 Welsh Assembly Government, *Memorandum from the Welsh Assembly Government. Constitutional Law: Devolution, Wales. The National Assembly for Wales (Legislative Competence) (Welsh Language) Order 2009. Proposal for a Legislative Competence Order on the Welsh Language*, (Cardiff: Welsh Assembly Government, 2009a [January]), p. 9.
59 Welsh Assembly Government, *Memorandum from the Welsh Assembly Government. Constitutional Law: Devolution, Wales. The National Assembly for Wales (Legislative Competence) (Welsh Language) Order 2009. Draft Legislative Competence Order on the Welsh Language*, p. 18.

60 Welsh Policy Paper 10, p. 3; Welsh Policy Paper 15, p. 46.
61 Welsh Policy Paper 15, p. 45.
62 Welsh Policy Paper 15, p. 46.
63 Emyr Lewis, *Written Evidence*, The proposed Welsh Language (Wales) Measure – Evidence Session 22 April 2010, Legislative Committee 2, the National Assembly for Wales (2010b).
64 Colin H. Williams, *Oral Evidence*.
65 Emyr Lewis, *Oral Evidence*, pars 116 and 117.
66 Welsh Policy Papers 7, 10 and 15.
67 Ward, *The Proposed Welsh Language Legislative Competence Order*, p. 11.
68 The Wales Office did ask the Welsh government for 'international comparisons' on 17 April 2009 (FOI request published online at: https://www.whatdotheyknow.com/request/18450/response/56740/attach/2/WalesOffice005.PDF.pdf) but were merely referred to a Welsh Language Board publication (2006) which, in fact, contained none.
69 E. J. Ruíz Vieytez, *Official Languages and Minority Languages: Issues about their Legal Status through Comparative Law* (II Simposi Internacional Mercator: Europa 2004: Un nou marc per a totes les llengües? Tarragona – Catalunya, 27–8 February, 2004), in particular 3.1(d)(a) and f.10.
70 http://www.servat.unibe.ch/icl/be00000_.html; http://english.people.com.cn/constitution/constitution.html; http://www.usoud.cz/en/charter-of-fundamental-rights-and-freedoms/; http://www.priu.gov.lk/Cons/1978Constitution/Chapter_03_Amd.htm; http://www.admin.ch/ch/e/rs/101/a18.html.
71 M. Paz, 'The failed promise of language rights: a critique of the international language rights regime', *Harvard International Law Journal*, 54/1 (2013), 195–218.
72 ECHR, Research Division, *Cultural Rights in the Case-law of the European Court of Human Rights* (Strasbourg: Council of Europe, 2011). See in particular pp. 13–16.
73 L. Green, 'Freedom of expression and choice of language', *Law & Policy*, 13/3 (1991), 215–29.
74 F. de Varennes, 'Language and freedom of expression in international law', *Human Rights Quarterly*, 15 (1993), 163–86.
75 M. S. McDougal, L. Chen and H. D. Lasswell, 'Freedom from discrimination in choice of language and international human rights', *Faculty Scholarship Series. Paper 2650* (1976). Published online at: http://digitalcommons.law.yale.edu/fss_papers/2650.
76 T. Schilling, 'Language rights in the European Union', *German Law Journal*, 9 (2008), 1219–42. See especially pp. 1226–30.
77 R. Schmidt, *Language Policy and Identity Politics in the United*

States (Philadelphia: Temple University Press, 2000). See in particular pp. 24–8.

78 G. Biaggini, 'Sprachenfreiheit und Territorialitätsprinzip – Entwicklungstendenzen in der höchstrichterlichen Rechtsprechung zum Sprachenverfassungsrecht', *Recht (Zeitschrift für juristische Ausbildung und Praxis)*, 15/3 (1997), 112–24; T. Fleiner, 'Sprachenfreiheit', in D. Merten and H.-J. Papier (eds), *Handbuch der Grundrechte in Deutschland und Europa* (Heidelberg: Müller, 2007), pp. 405–43; L. Mader, 'Der verfassungsrechtliche Rahmen des Sprachenrechts des Bundes', *Babylonia*, 4/01 (2001), 15–22; D. Richter, *Sprachenordnung und Minderheitenschutz im schweizerischen Bundesstaat. Relativität des Sprachenrechts und Sicherung des Sprachfriedens* (Heidelberg: Springer, 2005), pp. 209–62; D. Thürer and T. Burri, 'Zum Sprachenrecht der Schweiz', in C. Pan and B. S Pfeil (eds), *Zur Entstehung des modernen Minderheitenschutzes in Europa. Handbuch der europäischen Volksgruppen* (Vienna: Springer, 2006), pp. 242–66.

79 For example, 'BGE Urteilskopf 139 / 229: Urteil der II. öffentlich-rechtlichen Abteilung i.S. X. und Mitb. sowie Y. und Mitb. gegen Regierung des Kantons Graubünden (Beschwerde in öffentlich-rechtlichen Angelegenheiten); 2C_806/2012 / 2C_807/2012 vom 12. Juli 2013'. Available online at: *http://www.servat.unibe.ch/dfr/bge/c1139229.html*.

80 Emyr Lewis, *Oral Evidence*, pars 131 and 132.

81 Emyr Lewis, *Oral Evidence*, pars 122 and 128.

82 *http://leginfo.legislature.ca.gov/faces/billNavClient.xhtml?bill_id=200920100SB242*.

83 *http://articles.latimes.com/2009/apr/17/local/me-english17*.

84 *http://www.examiner.com/article/workplace-101-english-only-practices-the-sacramento-workplace*; that is in addition to the protections under the Civil Rights Act 1964 and the California Fair Employment and Housing Act 1959 afforded to employees who speak a language other than English.

85 *http://www.leginfo.ca.gov/pub/09-10/bill/sen/sb_0201-0250/sb_242_vt_20091011.html*.

86 *http://www.sfgate.com/bayarea/article/Language-freedom-law-heads-to-Schwarzenegger-3289376.php*; *http://www.calchamber.com/governmentrelations/businessissues/pages/legalreform.aspx*.

87 National Assembly for Wales, Legislation Committee No. 5, *National Assembly for Wales (Legislative Competence) (Welsh Language) Order 2009. Committee Report. June 2009* (Cardiff: National Assembly for Wales, 2009), pp. 119–20.

88 Welsh Policy Paper 23, *Freedom to Use Welsh* (unpublished paper, 2010), p. 2, par. 459.

89 The legal ambiguity inherent in the term 'official language' was noted by the Westminster legislative drafter Daniel Greenberg in an exchange with the Constitutional Affairs Committee of the National Assembly for Wales on 3 November 2010.
90 Welsh Language Commissioner, *Adroddiad Blynyddol 2012–13. Annual Report 2012–13*, p. 7.
91 Welsh Language Commissioner, *Adroddiad Blynyddol 2013–14. Annual Report 2013–14*, pp. 204–5.
92 Welsh Language Commissioner, *Adroddiad Blynyddol 2013–14. Annual Report 2013–14*, p. 204.
93 *http://www.comisiynyddygymraeg.org/english/news/Pages/Commissioner-determines-that-Swinton-has-interfered-with-an-individual's-freedom-to-use-Welsh.aspx.*
94 Welsh Language Commissioner, *Part 6 of the Welsh Language (Wales) Measure 2011: Freedom to Use Welsh. The Welsh Language Commissioner's determination and report on an investigation into an application under section 111 of the Welsh Language (Wales) Measure 2011* (Cardiff: Welsh Language Commissioner, 2014c), p. 5.
95 *http://www.bbc.co.uk/cymrufyw/27539007.*
96 The Financial Conduct Authority – the relevant regulatory body for companies such as Swinton.
97 Welsh Language Commissioner, *Part 6 of the Welsh Language (Wales) Measure 2011*, p. 5.
98 Welsh Language Commissioner, *Part 6 of the Welsh Language (Wales) Measure 2011*, pp. 3–4.
99 *http://www.bbc.co.uk/news/uk-wales-23334383.*
100 *http://cymdeithas.org/dogfen/llythyr-gomisiynydd-y-gymraeg-pryderon-am-y-system-gwyno.*
101 *http://www.bbc.co.uk/cymrufyw/23434789.*
102 Admiral, *Admiral news update: Admiral apologise for language complaint*, 19 August 2013. Published online at: *http://www.customerservicecontact.co.uk.*
103 *http://www.morningstaronline.co.uk/a-fc5e-Insurance-firm-investigated-after-barring-staff-from-speaking-Welsh/#.VBBW4V6FbfM.*
104 *http://www.golwg360.com/newyddion/cymru/127977-cwmni-yswiriant-yn-gwahardd-y-gymraeg.*
105 Welsh Language Commissioner, *Part 6 of the Welsh Language (Wales) Measure 2011*, p. 1.
106 *http://www.golwg360.com/newyddion/cymru/136988-swinton-comisiynydd-iaith-yn-dechrau-ymchwiliad-statudol.*
107 *http://dailypost.co.uk/news/north-wales-news/welsh-language-commissioner-investigation-ban-6693532.*

108 Welsh Language Commissioner, *Adroddiad Blynyddol 2013–14. Annual Report 2013–14*; Welsh Language Commissioner, *Part 6 of the Welsh Language (Wales) Measure 2011*.

109 G. S. Becker, 'A theory of competition among pressure groups for political influence', *Quarterly Journal of Economics*, 98/3 (1983), 371–400; J. M. Berry, *The Interest Group Society* (Glenview, IL: Addison Wesley Publishing Company, 1989, 2nd edn); E. Dal Bó, 'Regulatory capture: a review', *Oxford Review of Economic Policy*, 22/2 (2006), 203–25; J.-J. Laffont and J. Tirole, *The Politics of Government Decision-Making: A Theory of Regulatory Capture* (Cambridge, MA: MIT, 1988); G. Stigler, 'The theory of economic regulation', *Bell Journal of Economics and Management Science*, 2 (1971), 3–21.

110 D. Carpenter and D. A. Moss, *Preventing Regulatory Capture. Special Interest Influence and How to Limit It* (New York: Cambridge University Press, 2014), p. 13.

111 http://www.comisiynyddygymraeg.org/Cymraeg/Comisiynydd/MeriHuws/Pages/MeriHuws.aspx.

112 Carpenter and Moss, *Preventing Regulatory Capture*.

113 Carpenter and Moss, *Preventing Regulatory Capture*, p. 12.

114 Welsh Government, *Cyflwyniad i'r Bwrdd am y Mesur Iaith 13 Rhagfyr 2011* (Cardiff: Welsh Government, 2011).

115 See p. 449 in W. Pond, 'Restraining regulatory activism: the proper scope of public utility regulation', *Administrative Law Review*, 35/4 (1983), 423–50.

116 More recently again, while the Commissioner, very correctly, intervened in the case of Lidl UK, the subsequent press release rather confuses the issue. There, the Commissioner is noted as saying: 'I am pleased that Lidl have responded to my letter and have made a clear statement of policy that removes any ambiguity about the use of the Welsh language in their shops. The company has confirmed that it considers Welsh as a skill in the workplace' (Welsh Language Commissioner, 2014d). Of course, the nub of the matter is the freedom to use Welsh, irrespective of whether it is a skill or not. The matter of language as a skill pertinent to employment or to the workplace is wholly irrelevant to the issue of freedom to use Welsh as defined by the Measure. For the matter itself see, for example: http://m2.facebook.com/story.php?story_fbid=780178865373267&id=155239327867227&refid=17.
That the issue originated in a ban on the use of the Polish language and the threat to sack employees not using English (see http://www.dailymail.co.uk/news/article-2823575/Polish-workers-Lidl-told-stop-speaking-native-language-sacked.html) strongly indicates that the case is, prima facie, contrary to the Equality

Act 2010 and could easily be subject to a claim at an employment tribunal on that basis (see, for example, Dziedziak v. Future Electronics Ltd 2012 UKEAT/0270/11/ZT (*http://www.bailii.org/uk/cases/UKEAT/2012/0270_11_2802.html*), P F Franco v. Fyffes Group Ltd *c*.2012, or Jurga v. Lavendale Montessori ET/3302379/2012 and ET/3300884/2103).

117 See, for example: *https://www.law.cornell.edu/wex/alternative_dispute_resolution*; *http://guides.library.harvard.edu/adr*; C. Gill, J. Williams, C. Brennan and C. Hirst, *Models of Alternative Dispute Resolution (ADR). A Report for the Legal Ombudsman* (Edinburgh: Queen Margaret University, Consumer Insight Centre, 2014); Ministry of Justice and Attorney General's Office, *The Dispute Resolution Commitment. Guidance for Government Departments and Agencies* (London: Ministry of Justice, 2014).

118 See pp. 393–4 in S. Moyn, 'Review of: *The International Human Rights Movement: A History*, by Aryeh Neier, Princeton University Press, 2012', *Ethics and International Affairs*, 26/3 (2012), 392–5. More generally, see also S. Moyn, *The Last Utopia: Human Rights in History* (Cambridge, MA: Belknap, Harvard University Press, 2010).

119 See p. 161 in R. Beiner, 'National self-determination: some cautionary remarks concerning the rhetoric of rights', in M. Moore (ed.), *National Self-Determination and Secession* (Oxford: Oxford University Press, 1998), pp. 158–80.

4 | REGULATORY STANDARDS

Introduction

The purpose of this chapter is to highlight a number of key issues with regard to Standards, as defined by the Welsh Language (Wales) Measure 2011, as compared to Schemes as defined by the Welsh Language Act 1993. The issues raised are likely to be of especial interest to policy practitioners engaged in the regulatory governance of the Welsh language along with a range of other stakeholders. Amongst the conclusions reached by the research presented in this text is that there was significant confusion during the legislative cycle as to the concept of Standards. Much of this could have been avoided, had there been greater clarity in the manner of their presentation. Difficulties arising from lack of clarity of presentation also arise in relation to the notion of 'active offer', and that matter too will be explored in this chapter. In general terms, Welsh Language Standards are regulatory standards, just as Welsh Language Schemes may be said to comprise or to embody regulatory standards. The key difference is in the imposition of Standards in contrast to the negotiation of Schemes. That said, there was a significant shift during the policy and legislative cycles with regard to how Standards were framed, beginning as 'minimum' Standards to becoming more flexible, multi-layered or complex. As a result, as things now stand one of the Standards, now framed as Regulations, comprises five different levels. Add to that the flexibility inherent to Compliance Notices and one cannot be certain, therefore, that Standards meet the policy goal of being more readily comprehended by the public than Schemes.

Policy cycle discussion, recommendation and instruction (June 2008–April 2009)
Of particular interest in this chapter is the notion of Standards in relation to the delivery of services to the public in Wales as a regulatory concept. It appears to have been implicitly understood that Schemes, in some loose sense, set some sort of standards. For example, in one document dating to July 2008 it is asserted that:

> The following are proposed as the key principles in the development of language schemes/policies: [...] Continuity – any new structure or arrangements should aim to build on the achievements and standards established by Welsh Language Schemes.[1]

At this early stage in the policy cycle the following problematic issue was identified, namely: 'is there a case for a new structure or arrangement to apply consistently to all organisations but that there might be different standards to cover organisations which provide services for the general public in particular geographical areas?'[2]

With regard to the way forward, the introduction of 'Standards' was considered as one possible option[3] – others included 'no change', to continue with 'Welsh Language Schemes' while introducing 'Private Sector Schemes', to develop 'Standard Welsh Language Schemes', or perhaps 'Grouped Schemes (by sector or geographical area)'. The weaknesses with regard to adopting Standards were identified as follows:

> Danger that standards might lower rather than raise standards. How could the best performers be stretched further? Danger of demoralising those furthest from reaching the standards. Risk that standards would not be seen as 'reasonable or practicable'.[4]

Note that in the Annexe of 'Case Studies' there is no reference to any regulatory regime, or statutory or legislative model, based upon or making use of Standards, while there is reference to 'rights-based and scheme-based approaches'.[5]

A later policy paper, from March 2009, asserts that Standards 'was the only option which suggested a way forward which could ensure more focus on outcomes rather than process'.[6] This is put another way, as follows: 'this [Standards option] is the only one that begins to address the concerns [...] with regard to the focus on process – and the time taken to approve Welsh language schemes'.[7] The Welsh Language Board document outlining its 'advice on awarding grants'[8] was offered as an example of how a Standards approach might work, whereby Standards would be 'set out as a range of statutory duties for public bodies to implement' and therefore 'there would be less of a need for the enforcing authority and the public body concerned to agree or negotiate'.[9] Simply, one of the main advantages of Standards would be that 'there would be no need to renegotiate over 500 schemes to ensure compliance'.[10] Other advantages included 'increased consistency' which 'could help the public understand what they can expect in terms of services', noting that 'at present, most of the 500 schemes in existence are the result of individual negotiations between Board [WLB] officials and each public body'.[11] The paper concludes that 'minimum standards' be set, 'which persons placed under a duty need to adhere to'.[12]

It was foreseen that 'initially, these would be in addition to the current Welsh Language Scheme system' and that 'the future of those schemes would depend on the degree to which new standards documents could supersede the equivalent clauses in existing schemes'.[13] A subsequent policy paper from March to April 2009 noted that policy discussion had indicated that that there was 'some common ground' on the Standards approach, but that 'further work needs to be done on the detail of how requirements would be imposed on the bodies in question'.[14] Also, it is noted that an instrumental feature of the new regulatory regime would be to ensure 'sufficient expertise to enable the Commissioner to produce clear standards'.[15]

The policy instruction confirmed that the Standards approach was to be adopted, noting that

> there are some functions where there is more consistency – and, rather than negotiate with each body, clause by clause [as with Welsh Language Schemes], there is an opportunity to legislate to impose requirements on groups or categories of bodies to conform to a range of standards.[16]

Also, a 'key role' is identified for the Welsh Language Commissioner in the 'development of [...] standards'.[17] It is noted that with regard to agreeing Welsh Language Schemes with bodies, the Welsh Language Board was 'often finding itself in a weak negotiating position'.[18]

Legislative cycle discussion and determination (March–December 2010)

The Explanatory Memorandum accompanying the Measure as proposed makes it clear that Standards would 'gradually replace'[19] Welsh Language Schemes. More specifically, it states that

> The policy intention behind the proposed Measure is to establish a rolling programme for the replacement of schemes with a system of standards [. . .] Once standards have been imposed upon the entire range of bodies that currently operate schemes, that Part of the 1993 Act which deals with schemes will be repealed in its entirety.[20]

It is also explained here that 'duties under standards will be capable of being imposed upon individual bodies or on a sector-wide basis so as to provide the recipient of Welsh language services with certainty and clarity as to the level of service they can expect'.[21] That said, it is also clear that Standards would be flexible in some sense, so as to 'enable standards to take into account regional variations as well as to provide for varied timescales for compliance across a sector'.[22] Elsewhere in the document it is explained that

> the introduction of standards will provide greater clarity and consistency for Welsh speakers in terms of the services they can expect to receive in Welsh; reduce the administrative demands placed upon those subject to duties by moving the focus away from the preparation of schemes; establish a system that will ensure that duties imposed on bodies are both reasonable and proportionate; and that there is an appropriate degree of consistency in terms of duties placed on bodies.[23]

One expert actor appears to have expected something rather different in the Measure. In his oral evidence, Colin H. Williams noted that he had anticipated that Standards would be in addition to Schemes, but at a different level to them, as well as being symbolic in sense:

> Before the proposed Measure appeared, I have to admit that I expected the standards to be a symbolic and significant layer – not to replace language schemes, but to protect them so that

national standards would be applied to the education system, the health service, the Government and so on. That is how I still view them, namely as something on a mezzo level, and, underlying them, something similar to the traditional language schemes will continue to operate [...] I viewed these standards as an additional tier that gave some kind of consistency to people's expectations and rights [...] standards [are] to protect and safeguard the minimum service [...] What is not clear from the proposed Measure is the relationship between standards and what we have at present, unless the two are just seen as a tier upon a tier.

In a different exchange during the same session, Rhodri Morgan AM posed the following apparent conundrum to Williams: 'The problem with the proposed Measure as drafted is that it relates to exactly the same aspects as the Welsh Language Board's guidelines to what language schemes can contain.' To which Williams responded: 'I will have to think about that. If you ask that question in writing, I will think about it. I do not wish to give a reply one way or another now because it would be off the top of my head.'[24] During the same evidence session, another expert, when invited to comment upon how the 'mechanism of standards' as laid out in the Measure compares with 'mechanisms' in other language regimes, asserted that 'There is nothing that compares to standards.'[25]

The Minister was in a position to offer some clarity on the relationship between the content of Schemes and likely content of Standards in a letter to the Committee Chair (Val Lloyd AM):

In its simplest form, and reflecting the fact that standards can build on Welsh language schemes, a correspondence standard could see a scheme commitment such as: *Every letter received by the Council in Welsh will receive a signed reply in Welsh whenever a reply is required ... The time targets will be the same when replying to Welsh letters as they are when replying to English letters. (Pembrokeshire County Council)* ... changing to a standard which states: *When someone writes to an organisation in Welsh the organisation must issue a signed reply in Welsh (if a reply is required). The target time for replying will be the same as for replying to letters written in English.* [italics in original][26]

Also, with regard to the apparent confusion as to whether Standards would be at a base or minimum level, the following exchange between the Committee Chair and the Minister provides some insight. To begin with the Committee Chair asked, 'I wish to clarify that. Minister, are you saying that you expect the standards to be set at a higher level that the current arrangements?' The Minister responded as follows: 'That will be a matter for the commissioner to decide initially and for the Assembly to approve'; and then later in the same session the Committee Chair asked,

> I am not quite certain what you were saying there, Minister. Are you considering the imposition of minimum standards, which would apply across the board, to all organisations, subject to the legislation, or are you thinking about the development of more detailed provision in the proposed Measure itself, which would guide the development of core obligations?

To which the Minister responded

> There will not be a single standard that applies to all organisations, otherwise that would be on the face of the proposed Measure. We think that this flexible approach will mean that, within certain sectors, there will be consistency of provision, but where it is needed, there can be greater flexibility [...]

and again that 'The substantive difference between schemes and standards is that standards would be specific duties as opposed to qualified commitments negotiated on an individual basis. This will lead to rights in the provision of services.'[27]

The idea of Standards raised a number of questions for the Welsh Language Board, for whom Standards would either be set at the top, aspirational, level or at the base, minimum, level. Given the expertise of the Board as regards Schemes, it is worth quoting from that organisation's evidence at length here:

> So far as standards are concerned, the first question that must be asked is what precisely is meant by the term 'standards'? Secondly, one has to ask how standards will improve on a process which could have directly built on the current system

of agreeing Welsh Language Schemes? We need more details of how the new system might operate in practice, together with more examples of possible standards, so that we might understand the implications of the new system, which, as it stands, appears to us to be vague. There is a certain ambiguity belonging to the term itself. There are, inter alia, two contrasting meanings of the term 'standard': on the one hand, it can refer to something to which we should all aspire, but, on the other hand, it can refer to the minimum level which everyone must reach.[28]

The Chair of the Board (Meri Huws, now the Commissioner) asserted that: 'Standards are not a concept that we are familiar with in the field of language planning', and that 'uniformity is the essence of standards',[29] while the Chief Executive of the Board stated that 'As far as I am aware, standards are not used anywhere else as a tool for language promotion'; having said that, he saw value in Standards, as follows: 'We believe that setting general principles regarding what we expect on an all-Wales level would also be beneficial.'[30]

Turning now, briefly, to the matter of the notion of 'active offer', this concept was put forward by Colin H. Williams in his written evidence to the Assembly. He stated in this evidence that with regard to 'Standards and/or Schemes' there was a 'need to ensure that an "active offer" underpins any service'.[31] When asked by Lorraine Barrett AM to explain this, Williams asserted that 'Canada insists that those delivering bilingual front-of-house services have to speak basic-level French and English. So, they provide a service, rather than pretend to provide a service. That is a statutory requirement of any federal service provided.'[32] Barrett challenged Williams on the implication of his response that it would be a legal requirement to provide 'any', in other words 'all', services to some degree based upon the premise of the active offer. She said, 'To expand on that, all local authorities in Wales will have to offer a certain level of service through the medium of Welsh. [. . .] How realistic would it be [. . .]?'[33] By way of answer, Williams saluted the question as 'practical, wise and rational' but also evaded it, concluding, rather wanly it would appear, that the active offer, 'is something that evolves over time [. . .] the principle is the important thing. We should not pretend to offer a service.'[34]

Of course, the purpose of Barrett's question was to elicit a precise explanation as to exactly how the notion of active offer worked in practice; she was interested in the implications of its implementation. It was unnecessary of Williams to reiterate the importance he attached to the principle; that was already understood. An authoritative response would have noted that the concept of the active offer varies very considerably across Canada. It may be understood as, 'answering the telephone with "Bonjour," and nametags and or signage identifying French-speaking health care professionals'[35] or it may take the form of the office or facility taking steps to 'clearly indicate that services are available in both official languages' and that the office 'has sufficient bilingual staff on hand to provide its services in both official languages at all times'.[36] Moreover, it is simply not the case that the active offer is a requirement of all federal services; rather, it is subject to a range of conditions at the federal, provincial and territorial levels. At the federal level, for example, while the notion of the active offer is embedded in the Official Languages Act (1969 and 1988), it is only those offices and facilities which are designated bilingual that are required to provide services in both official languages. According to the Treasury Board of Canada, such a service provider is subject to this requirement if it meets one of the following criteria: it is a head or central office; it is located in the National Capital Region; it reports directly to Parliament; there is significant demand for the services of the given provider in both official languages;[37] that the nature of the office justifies that both official languages be used; and, that the office provides services to the travelling public and where there is significant demand.[38] Clearly, many federal offices and facilities do not provide services in both official languages, never mind doing so on the premise of the active offer. Indeed, the Treasury Board of Canada noted in 2014 that around one-third of a total of some 12,000 offices and facilities are 'required to provide bilingual services' and therefore that the overwhelming majority do not.[39]

At the provincial and territorial levels the provision of services in the official languages is similarly managed. In Manitoba, for example, according to the Manitoba Francophone Affairs Secretariat services may only be required to be available in both official languages in certain designated geographical areas and through specifically designated organisations.[40] In Ontario, under the French Language Services Act (FLSA) 1986, individuals have a right to receive government services in French in twenty-five designated geographical areas, and even there not all public services are subject to such a requirement. According to the Ontario Office of Francophone Affairs, for example, 'agencies that are partially funded by the province [...] are not automatically subject to the FLSA. These agencies may ask to be officially designated.'[41] In ascribing designated areas under the Act the following certain criteria have to be met: Francophones must comprise at least 10 per cent of the local population; the number of Francophones must exceed 5,000 in urban centres; there must be demonstrable impartial, transparent and broad-based community support at the local level; and, the proposal must be subject to cost analysis comprising an evaluation of the financial implications of potential designation.[42] As a result, 20 per cent of French speakers in Ontario live outside these designated areas and therefore do not have a legally protected right to avail themselves of services in French. Other provinces and territories take comparable approaches whereby the active offer, to the extent that it exists, is applied only in relation to certain designated services.[43]

Implementation and application

The Welsh Language Commissioner elect (Meri Huws, then Chair of the Welsh Language Board), along with the prospective staff of the office of the Commissioner, were provided with a briefing on the implementation of Standards on 13 December 2011. In that session it was implied that Standards were a straightforward re-articulation of commitments under Schemes:

- Syniad syml?
- Troi 'fe fyddwn yn eich ateb yn Gymraeg' ...
- ... i 'mae angen i chi ateb yn Gymraeg'
- Troi 'fe fyddwn yn dangos arwyddion dwyieithog' ...
- ... i 'mae angen i chi ddangos arwyddion dwyieithog'
- Dyma gychwyn datblygu'r syniad o safonau iaith[44]

['A simple idea? / Turn "we will answer you in Welsh" ... / ... into "you must answer in Welsh" / Turn "we will display bilingual signs" ... / ... into "you must display bilingual signs" / This is the starting point of the development of the idea of language standards']

In other words, the key difference between Schemes and Standards was that the former were negotiated while the latter were imposed. Between May and August 2012 the Welsh Language Commissioner undertook a non-statutory public consultation on a set of draft standards developed through her office. This set was eventually rejected by the Welsh government as being 'too complex' and raising 'significant difficulties' with regard to regulatory impact.[45]

As the approach of the government to Standards became clearer during the course of the year, the Commissioner argued that were Standards introduced per sector this would 'creu dryswch' ('create confusion') and that instead Standards ought to be imposed on all sectors at the same time so that they might plan and adapt together.[46] She articulated her view of Standards as follows: 'Be ddylai'r safonau ei wneud yw sicrhau gwell cysondeb ar draws Cymru' ('What standards ought to do is to create better consistency across Wales').[47] The Welsh ministers presented a new set of draft standards to the Welsh Language Commissioner in January 2014[48] and the Commissioner subsequently presented a report to the Welsh ministers summarising the results of her Standards Investigation in June 2014. According to the Welsh ministers' timetable, the next steps at that point were as follows: draft regulations and associated documentation to be produced by September 2014, followed by a debate and vote on the approval of the regulations in the National Assembly during October/November 2014, and that the regulations would be force by November 2014.[49]

As regards the active offer, the Commissioner took up the concept in her inquiry into the Welsh language in primary health care.[50] There, she argued that the active offer ought to be central to primary health care; while recognising that the Welsh government had laid the foundations, she asserted that this was not enough: 'these steps are not far reaching enough nor provide sufficient guidance to the primary care sector'.[51] In setting out the way forward for Wales, the authors of the report turned to Canada where, in their words, 'the concept has been embedded in the health service' and also to the evidence provided by Williams during the passage of the 2011 Measure through the Assembly, and in particular his assertion 'about the need to ensure that an active offer is a central part of the provision of services in Wales', as it is put in the Commissioners' report.[52] In elaborating upon the active offer as it applies in Canada, it is explained in the report that 'the active offer of services in French or English is a statutory requirement that has been incorporated into Canada's Official Languages Act'.[53] In a section entitled 'what does an active offer mean in practice?', the authors of the report quote directly from a training document created by the Consortium national de formation en santé in explaining that

> the active offer [. . .] represents a global approach to health service delivery [. . .] active offer requires collective accountability from the entire healthcare system [. . .] to ensure the entire Canadian population is treated fairly and equitably in all healthcare matters.[54]

Then, in the description of the constituent elements of an 'effective and systematic active offer', the report lists nine key actions drawn from Cardinal and Sauvé's study of the active offer in the justice sector in Ontario.[55] No further detail is offered and no other material on the application of the active offer to any section of the health sector in Canada is referred to. The Commissioner concludes in the report that she will 'ask Welsh Ministers to take a policy stance in favour of the active offer model to enable it to be implemented systematically and effectively across primary care services'.[56]

Analysis

There are a number of distinct elements with regard to understanding the difficulties in relation to Standards. Firstly, there is a conceptual muddle arising from a failure to understand both Standards and Schemes as regulatory standards.[57] This in turn may explain why none of the expert actors in either the policy or legislative cycle recognised that, in fact, such regulatory standards are a substantive feature of the statutory framework of several, otherwise familiar, language planning regimes. These include, for example, Canada, with regard to the various Federal, Provincial and Territorial jurisdictions, and also the Republic of Ireland. Some actors imply that the policy domains of health, social care and the equalities in the UK informed the development of the notion of Standards in the context of the Measure,[58] although there is no evidence of this in the paperwork with regard to either the policy cycle or in the legislative cycle. That said, standards in this context are formulated as 'national' and 'minimum'.[59]

Welsh Language Schemes may be understood as a type or set of regulatory standards. This is implicit to the Welsh Language Board's guidelines for the drafting of Schemes, where the following assertions are made:

> **Guideline 5** The scheme should specify what standards of quality are to be achieved in the delivery of services in Welsh, including having regard to the principles of the Citizen's Charter presented to Parliament on 22 July 1991.
>
> **Advice** [. . .] The principles of the citizen's Charter also are as applicable to the provision of services in Welsh as in English. Explicit standards relating to the organisation's provision of services and dealings with the public in Welsh should be set, publicised, and regularly monitored. [. . .] Organisations who provide services in different parts of Wales should ensure consistency in the standard of services available in Welsh [. . .].
>
> **Measures** [. . .]
> - A commitment to apply the principles of the Citizen's Charter to the provision of services in Welsh as in English.
> - A commitment to set specific standards as to the use of Welsh relating to the provision of services and dealings with the public.
> - A commitment to monitor these standards, as well as monitoring their implementation.
> - A commitment to ensure consistency in the standard of services in Welsh provided by the organisation in different localities.[60]

The notion of Welsh Language Standards as distinct from Welsh Language Schemes was first proposed by the Welsh Language Society. From around 2000, the Welsh Language Society argued for the introduction of 'Safonau [. . .] Cenedlaethol' ('national [. . .] standards')[61] or 'basic minimum standards', implying also that these would co-exist with Schemes.[62] This view of standards appears to be borrowed by Colin H. Williams in his evidence during the legislative cycle, and elsewhere;[63] it is certainly echoed.

A second crucial feature of the conceptual muddle regarding Standards is the apparent tension between uniformity of coverage and geo-linguistic diversity. It was argued by the government that Standards would be 'sector-wide' and offer 'certainty and clarity', but still facilitate 'regional variations as well as [. . .] varied timescales for compliance'.[64] On the other hand, the Commissioner, when speaking as the Chair of the Welsh Language Board, understood 'uniformity' to be their definitive quality. The Board's understanding of Standards implied that they would be 'general principles [. . .] at an all-Wales level'. This contrasting understanding of the nature of Standards is reflected in the substantive difference that may be easily seen between the two sets of draft Standards, a matter which may be illustrated through reference to service delivery standards.

Under the draft Standards proposed by the Welsh Language Commissioner in 2012, a range of bodies including 'sections of the private sector including gas, water or electricity companies; companies providing postal services or post offices; telecommunications services; bus or railway services; providers of education and training'[65] would be required to implement the following Service Delivery Standard:

> Having established and recorded that the service user chooses to use the Welsh language, it must be ensured, from the date of the record onwards, that the delivery of all services provided by the organisation are supplied through the medium of Welsh.[66]

The draft Standards proposed by the Welsh government are currently limited in their application to local authorities, National Parks and Welsh Ministers, with Standards applicable to other sectors and types of bodies to be proposed at a later point. Also, the range of activities carried out by the bodies to which the Standards are applicable excludes areas that the Commissioner included, such as youth activities, face-to-face provision and care for individuals.[67] The delivery of 'all services' in Welsh envisaged by the Welsh Language Commissioner contrasts, for example, with the Standards proposed by the Welsh government for dealing with direct incoming telephone calls to staff members, as follows: 'the organisation must prepare and implement a plan outlining how employees and workers will deal with incoming calls in Welsh; the organisation must provide a switchboard that will deal with incoming calls in Welsh'.[68] Thus, the set of Standards as proposed by the Commissioner can be broadly characterised as maximalist and that of the government as minimalist or, perhaps, foundational. The implication of foundational is that the approach is gradualist and developmental. That said, there is no statutory mechanism for the periodic review of Standards thereby enabling, indeed causing, such gradualism and development.

More generally, the research literature suggests that there may be a problem with attempting to migrate from a regulatory regime understood in terms of detailed rules (i.e. Schemes) to one characterised by general principles (i.e. as set out in the Measure). For example: 'Whilst the tighter specification of what appear to be broad standards is likely to be fairly routine – through one mechanism or another – there is not generally a route through which very detailed standards can be made more general.'[69] This problem would appear to be a part of the challenge confronting efforts to simplify and generalise the gamut of standards embodied within Schemes in order to arrive at an acceptable set of Standards applicable across Wales as a whole.

The body of scholarly work on regulators shows that legitimacy is a key feature of successful regulatory regimes. According to this literature the notion of negotiated regulation largely derives from the USA. There, regulators and policy-actors and decision-makers became increasingly concerned at the adversarial approach to regulation during the course of the 1980s. In order to set in place a less adversarial and more inclusive approach to regulation, including standard setting, the federal government passed the Negotiated Rule Making Act 1990 (revised 1996). Under this Act the desired approach to regulation is 'characterized by processes in which the various stakeholders are encouraged to discuss proposed regulatory rules in a multilateral setting' thereby enabling 'greater legitimacy and therefore, "buy-in" from participants'.[70] Academic research in this field also shows that a process of negotiating regulatory standards that involves not only the regulator and the regulatee, but also representatives of those whom the regulation is intended to protect or to benefit, can have certain positive outcomes. These include the creation of a form of 'dialogic accountability' for the regulatory standards, on the one hand, and also realise, on the other hand, a set of regulatory standards which are likely to be superior to those merely imposed by legislators.[71]

In this context of Standards, the term 'Standards Investigation' implies consultation,[72] but under the Measure this may or may not include consultation with the public, as was also noted during the government's briefing of the Commissioner elect.[73] Upon publication of their draft Standards on 6 January 2014 the government stated that the consultative material was 'aimed at county borough councils and county councils in Wales, national park authorities and Welsh Ministers', that 'The document will also be of interest to users of services provided by these organisations' and that it would 'form the basis for' a Standards Investigation.[74] The Commissioner confirmed in late January 2014 that Standards Investigation regarding the government's draft Standards would include an element of consultation with the public.[75] However, the process did not include public consultation in the ordinary sense of the term, in that the public was not able to offer comment on the precise content of the Standards as proposed by the government, in complete contrast to the Commissioner's non-statutory consultation on her office's set of draft Standards. The Commissioner confirmed this in a letter published in *Golwg* in March 2014, noting that interested parties ought to: 'cyfeirio unrhyw sylw am gynnwys y safonau at Uned y Gymreg Llywodraeth Cymru' ('refer any comments regarding the contents of the Standards to the Welsh Language Unit of the Welsh Government').[76]

At the completion of the Standards Investigation the Commissioner noted that there had been 'dryswch' ('confusion') during the process, having received a letter from Mudiad Dathlu'r Iaith stating that it was not clear whether it was the government or the Commissioner that was conducting the process and, moreover, that it was unclear whether the content of the Standards themselves were a matter for consultation.[77] The Commissioner noted also, as she reported the results of her Standards Investigation to the government:

> it was not easy for stakeholders to take part in the process and, during the standards investigations, the Commissioner received responses to the proposed standards themselves rather than the subject of the investigation. Responses received by the public and interest groups stated that they were unclear as to whether they could express their views on the Government's proposed standards and respondents chose to present comments on the standards to the Welsh Language Commissioner. The

Commissioner has decided to give advice to Welsh Ministers based on the themes which emerged and respondents' views on the proposed standards. These comments do not endeavour to fulfil a consultation process on the proposed standards.[78]

It was also brought up by some interest groups as a matter of concern.[79] That said, even in the absence of that, such an investigation enables some degree of dialogic accountability to the extent that the process involves the regulator and the regulatee directly. The case could be made that the public more generally may be represented in this process by the ministers of the Welsh government, who have drafted the current version of Standards, along with the elected members of the Assembly, which will approve the Standards and their associated regulations. Considering the relative merits of the discursive and inclusive process inherent to negotiated regulation, it appears to be wholly desirable that some element of public consultation also be a feature of regulatory approaches that are characterised by imposition. Such engagement is important in establishing the legitimacy of the regulatory standards in particular and the regulatory regime in general. Wisely, the government took the advice of the Commissioner on the matter of public consultation and set out a period of consultation on its first set of Standards between 7 November and 5 December 2014.[80] One of the effects of this consultation, along with the fact that the government's set of Standards would be subject to discussion on the floor of the Assembly and to that body's approval, is to reinforce the status of Standards as a 'super-affirmative' statutory instrument.[81] In addition, this addresses the concern expressed by the Wales Governance Centre regarding the Assembly's finding it 'extremely difficult to adequately scrutinise' proposed laws, given the 'imbalance' between primary and delegated legislation, of which the Measure 'is another such example'.[82] Legislatures certainly have adequate opportunity to subject super-affirmative statutory instruments to robust scrutiny.

Turning now to the concept of the active offer, the evidence base upon which the Commissioner made her case in relation to the application of the active offer to the primary health care sector in Wales is very problematic. Specifically, the document of the Consortium national de formation en santé upon which the Commissioner depends in her report does not set the concept of active offer in context. The authors of the Canadian report note that the concept varies across Canada but singularly fail to elaborate upon that.[83] The limitations of Williams's evidence have already been noted and these are echoed in the Commissioner's report. In addition to this failure to recognise and account for the conditionality of the active offer in Canada at the levels of the federal State, the province and the territory, it does not appear to be understood by the authors of the Commissioner's report that while the Official Languages Act in Canada applies to the federal State, provincial and territorial governments are largely responsible for the provision of primary health care in their own jurisdictions and are its 'principal funders'.[84] Given the funding mechanisms, government at these levels have policy leverage in relation to primary care, and as a result 'each jurisdiction takes its own approach', according to the Canadian government,[85] while operating in the context of a federal legislative framework.

Therefore, in order to understand the active offer in the health sector in Canada one has to understand the framework as it pertains at the level of the province or the territory, as well as understanding the relationship between public funding from different sources and private delivery,[86] rather than simply turning to the Official Languages Act. Primary health care in particular is especially complex in this regard[87] and the application of the active offer to that sector reflects that. Thus, in the case of Ontario, for example, organisations such as day-care centres or hospitals are 'not automatically subject to the French Language Services Act' but instead they 'may ask to be officially designated'[88] and thereby be identified by the Government of Ontario as official providers of health services in French as well as English; only then will the notion of the active offer potentially apply. None of this is to deny the potential of the active offer as a policy tool. There is considerable evidence to suggest that the active offer of a service increases the rate of uptake of that service, such as Boileau's report of 2009.[89] The crux of the matter is that its purposeful implementation requires careful planning. To characterise the Canadian active offer as being of 'global' application across a given sector or that it pertains to 'any' federal service, and to criticise the approach taken by the Welsh government on that basis, is to badly misconceive the issue.

That said, the Welsh government's response to the Commissioner's recommendation on the active offer, as set out in a statement by Mark Drakeford, the Minister for Health and Social Services,[90] only goes as far as recognising that further information on the preferred language of health care users needs to be obtained. Indeed, the approach adopted by the government so far allows for progress to be made in a piecemeal manner, whereby discrete parts of the health sector, even small units within large organisations, may achieve notable results.[91] However, while the Commissioner's report is persuasive on a rhetorical, even polemical, level, it falls down on the detail of the active offer. Attention to the Canadian detail is a prerequisite. The evidence from there shows that the realization of the substantive change inherent to the concept of the active offer is best framed by legislation along with the required regulations. Also, that statutory framework sets out the potential scope of the active offer as well as laying out the criteria for identifying the reasonable limitations to its application. That the application of the active offer to primary health care in Wales would have a range of benefits, including health benefits and not simply those of linguistic justice, is in many ways inarguable, but neither the Commissioner's report nor the Welsh government's strategic framework for Welsh language services in the health sector[92] conceives of the active offer in a wholly coherent manner.

Conclusions

Effective regulatory standards in the most general terms are of necessity transparent (easily comprehensible to their audience), accessible (readily applicable to their intended circumstances) and congruent (matches the intentions of the policy-maker). Regulatory standards may be formulated as either general principles or as detailed rules. Schemes can be understood as exemplars of detailed rules. In the Welsh context Schemes have been criticised for being poorly understood by at least a part of their audience, namely the public. They have also been criticised for allowing for unjustifiable variability in the level of service provision between broadly similar linguistic constituencies. In other words, it would appear that the regime suffered from the absence of an overarching set of general principles and a surfeit of detail set out in hundreds of individual Schemes. An effective regulatory regime incorporates both general principles and detailed rules, but the precise relationship between the two is critical to the success of the regime. One of the aims of the Welsh Language (Wales) Measure 2011 was to recalibrate the relationship between general principles and detailed rules with regard to the regulation of Welsh. As yet, the Welsh model is incomplete. Regulations, for example, have yet to be presented to the Assembly for approval. The legitimacy of a regulatory regime depends in part upon the involvement of the regulator, the regulatee and those whom the regulation is intended to protect or benefit in the standard-making process. This dialogic accountability[93] is possible both under a regulatory regime characterised by Schemes, which is generally speaking a regime of negotiation, and by Standards, which is in general terms a regime of imposition. It is a much more obvious feature of the latter, while it is not necessarily a feature of the former at all. The Commissioner conducted a non-statutory public consultation on her version of Standards and has also determined to consult with the public with regard to the Welsh government's version of Standards. Striking the right balance in this regard is crucial to the legitimacy of the regulatory regime in general and the regulatory standards in particular.

Welsh Language Schemes	Welsh Language Standards
Welsh Language Act 1993	Welsh Language Measure 2011
Standards understood as general principles in 1993 Act and detailed rules in Schemes	Standards understood as general principles in 2011 Measure and as detailed rules in subsequent instruments and regulations
Standard setting delegated to agency – Welsh Language Board	Standard setting by Minister and Welsh Assembly
Standards negotiated with individual bodies	Standards imposed, following consultation
Self-regulation, monitoring and reporting by bodies	Self-regulation, monitoring and reporting by bodies
No enforcement pyramid	Enforcement pyramid is inherent
Duties	Rhetoric of rights
No legal remedy	Legal remedy delegated to agency – Welsh Language Commissioner

Figure 7. *Comparative schematic for Welsh Language Schemes and Welsh Language Standards as instruments for setting Welsh language regulatory standards.*

The confusion regarding Standards arises from a shift from their being conceived of as minimum standards during the policy cycle to their being increasingly understood in more variable terms during the legislative cycle. In setting out her own draft Standards, the Commissioner's understanding appears to be much informed by the view of the Board, in that they were either at the highest level – 'aspirational' – or at the minimum level. Inevitably, the former raises problems with regard to regulatory impact. Confusion also arises from the fact that actors in the policy cycle in particular, but also during the legislative cycle, fail to fully conceive of Standards as regulatory standards and are therefore incognisant of pertinent statutory regimes and jurisdictions in which regulatory standards have been set for various languages. This, in turn, appears to cause confusion with regard to differentiating Standards and Schemes. There is common ground, but the important difference relates to regulatory approach – imposition upon regulatees versus negotiation with regulatees (Figure 7). With regard to the confusion about consulting upon Standards, a failure to consult, in the proper meaning of the word, undermines the legitimacy of regulatory standards. In the Welsh context the regulatees were recognised by the government as the 'aim' of the consultation on Standards. In contrast, Welsh-speaking service users were not the 'aim', or one might say 'target audience', but rather were merely identified as a party to whom Standards are 'of interest'. In this particular context the citizen appears to have been allowed much less of a voice than the regulatee.

Notes

1. Welsh Policy Paper 5, *Language Schemes/Policies* (unpublished paper, 2008), p. 3.
2. Welsh Policy Paper 5, p. 3.
3. Welsh Policy Paper 5, p. 11.
4. Welsh Policy Paper 5, p. 11.
5. Welsh Policy Paper 5, pp. 12–13.
6. Welsh Policy Paper 11, *Welsh Language Commissioner and Welsh Language Schemes* (unpublished paper, 2009), p. 13.
7. Welsh Policy Paper 11, p. 13.
8. Welsh Policy Paper 11, p. 13.
9. Welsh Policy Paper 11, p. 14.
10. Welsh Policy Paper 11, p. 14.

11 Welsh Policy Paper 11, p. 15.
12 Welsh Policy Paper 11, p. 17.
13 Welsh Policy Paper 11, p. 17.
14 Welsh Policy Paper 12, p. 3.
15 Welsh Policy Paper 11, pp. 3 and 6.
16 Welsh Policy Paper 15, p. 7.
17 Welsh Policy Paper 15, p. 7.
18 Welsh Policy Paper 15, p. 27.
19 Welsh Assembly Government, *The Proposed Welsh Language (Wales) Measure 2010. Explanatory Memorandum to the Proposed Welsh Language Wales Measure 2010 4 March 2010* (Cardiff: Welsh Assembly Government, 2010a), p. 3.
20 Welsh Assembly Government, *The Proposed Welsh Language (Wales) Measure 2010. Explanatory Memorandum to the Proposed Welsh Language Wales Measure 2010 4 March 2010*, p. 12.
21 Welsh Assembly Government, *The Proposed Welsh Language (Wales) Measure 2010. Explanatory Memorandum to the Proposed Welsh Language Wales Measure 2010 4 March 2010*, p. 13.
22 Welsh Assembly Government, *The Proposed Welsh Language (Wales) Measure 2010. Explanatory Memorandum to the Proposed Welsh Language Wales Measure 2010 4 March 2010*, p. 13.
23 Welsh Assembly Government, *The Proposed Welsh Language (Wales) Measure 2010. Explanatory Memorandum to the Proposed Welsh Language Wales Measure 2010 4 March 2010*, p. 32.
24 Colin H. Williams, *Oral Evidence*.
25 Emyr Lewis, *Oral Evidence*.
26 Alun Ff. Jones, *Letter from Alun Ffred Jones AM, Minister for Heritage to Val Lloyd AM, Chair of Legislation Committee No. 2 National Assembly for Wales, 14 June 2010a*, p. 2; italics in original.
27 Alun Ff. Jones, *Oral Evidence*, The Proposed Welsh Language (Wales) Measure – Evidence Session 17 June 2010, Legislative Committee 2, the National Assembly for Wales.
28 Welsh Language Board, *Oral Session*, Paper 1, The Proposed Welsh Language (Wales) Measure – Evidence Session 29 April 2010, Legislative Committee 2, the National Assembly for Wales.
29 Welsh Language Board, *Oral Session*, Paper 1, The Proposed Welsh Language (Wales) Measure – Evidence Session 29 April 2010, Legislative Committee 2.
30 Welsh Language Board, *Oral Session*, Paper 1, The Proposed Welsh Language (Wales) Measure – Evidence Session 29 April 2010, Legislative Committee 2.
31 Colin H. Williams, *Written Evidence*, The proposed Welsh Language (Wales) Measure – Evidence Session 22 April 2010, Legislative Committee 2, the National Assembly for Wales.

32 Williams, *Oral Evidence*, pp. 49–50.
33 Lorraine Barrett AM, to Williams, *Oral Evidence*, p. 50.
34 Lorraine Barrett AM, to Williams, *Oral Evidence*, p. 51.
35 Health Care Human Resource Sector Council, *Directory of French speaking Primary health care providers in Nova Scotia. Réseau santé. Réseau pour les services de santé en français – Nouvelle-Écosse* (Nova Scotia: Health Care Human Resource Sector Council, 2006), p. 25.
36 http://www.tbs-sct.gc.ca/gui/bob-eng.asp.
37 Significant demand is defined via regulations under the Official Languages Act (§§ 32 and 33, available at: *http://laws-lois.justice.gc.ca/eng/acts/O-3.01/page-8.html#h-12*) in relation to the size and proportion of the given official language minority community.
38 http://www.tbs-sct.gc.ca/gui/bob-eng.asp.
39 http://www.tbs-sct.gc.ca/gui/bob-eng.asp.
40 http:www.gov.mb.ca/fls-slf/activeoffer.html.
41 http://www.ofa.gov.on.ca/en/flsa.html.
42 http://www.ofa.gov.on.ca/en/flsa-designation.html.
43 For example, Northwest Territories Government, *Strategic Plan on French Language Communications and Services* (Government of the Northwest Territories, 2012); Nova Scotia, Public Service Commission, *French Language Services Plan* (Nova Scotia, Public Service Commission, 2013); Yukon Government, French Language Services, *Chronology of Events and Accomplishments* (Yukon Government, French Language Services, 2014).
44 Welsh Government, *Cyflwyniad i'r Bwrdd am y Mesur Iaith 13 Rhagfyr 2011* (Cardiff: Welsh Government, 2011), p. 5.
45 L. Andrews, *Written statement – the Welsh Ministers' response to the Welsh Language Commissioner's proposals for Welsh language standards*, 25 February 2013. Published online at: http://wales.gov.uk/about/cabinet/cabinetstatements/2013/welshlanguagestandards/?lang=en.
46 http://www.bbc.co.uk/newyddion/23579113.
47 http://www.bbc.co.uk/newyddion/23579113.
48 Welsh Government, *Consultation document. Proposed standards relating to the Welsh language* (Cardiff: Welsh Government, 2014a).
49 C. Jones, *Written statement – timetable for the first set of Welsh Language Standards 21 October 2013*. Published online at: http://wales.gov.uk/about/cabinet/cabinetstatements/2013/welshlangstandards/?lang=en.
50 Welsh Language Commissioner, *My language, my health: the Welsh Language Commissioner's inquiry into the Welsh language in primary care* (Cardiff: Welsh Language Commissioner, 2014i).
51 Welsh Language Commissioner, *My language, my health*, p. 83.
52 Welsh Language Commissioner, *My language, my health*, pp. 83, 89.

53 Welsh Language Commissioner, *My language, my health*, p. 90.
54 Welsh Language Commissioner, *My language, my health*, p. 89.
55 Welsh Language Commissioner, *My language, my health*, p. 90–1.
56 Welsh Language Commissioner, *My language, my health*, p. 98, Recommendation 13.
57 C. Diver, 'The optimal precision of administrative rules', *Yale Law Journal*, 93 (1983), 65–109; C. Scott, 'Standard-setting in regulatory regimes', in R. Baldwin, M. Cave and M. Lodge (eds), *The Oxford Handbook of Regulation* (Oxford: Oxford University Press, 2010), pp. 104–19; see ch. 14, 'Standards and principles', in R. Baldwin, M. Cave and M. Lodge, *Understanding Regulation. Theory, Strategy, and Practice* (Oxford: Oxford University Press, 2011), pp. 296–312.
58 Semi-structured interviews comprising the fieldwork in Wales.
59 http://www.cqc.org.uk/public/what-are-standards/national-standards.
60 Welsh Language Board, *Welsh Language Schemes. Their preparation and approval in accordance with the Welsh Language Act 1993* (Cardiff: Welsh Language Board, 1996), pp. 20–1.
61 Welsh Language Society [Cymdeithas yr Iaith Gymraeg], *Y Gymraeg yn goroesi globaleiddio. Maniffesto Cymdeithas yr Iaith Gymraeg 2002* (Aberystwyth: Cymdeithas yr Iaith Gymraeg, 2002), p. 23.
62 Welsh Language Society [Cymdeithas yr Iaith Gymraeg], *Welsh Language Measure 2007* (Tal-y-Bont: Y Lolfa, 2007), pp. 6, 7.
63 P. Ó Flatharta, S. Sandberg and C. H. Williams, *From Act to Action. Implementing Language Legislation in Finland, Ireland and Wales* (2013). Published online at: http://doras.dcu.ie/19655/1/From_Act_to_Action_2014.pdf.
64 Welsh Assembly Government, *The Proposed Welsh Language (Wales) Measure 2010. Explanatory Memorandum to the Proposed Welsh Language Wales Measure 2010 4 March 2010*, p. 13.
65 Welsh Language Commissioner, *Standards and the Welsh language: what are your views?* (Cardiff: Welsh Language Commissioner, 2012a), p. 9.
66 Welsh Language Commissioner, *Standards and the Welsh language*, p. 10.
67 Welsh Government, *Consultation document. Proposed standards relating to the Welsh language* (Cardiff: Welsh Government, 2014a), p. 4; cf. Welsh Language Commissioner, *Standards and the Welsh language: what are your views?*, p. 11.
68 Welsh Government, *Consultation document. Proposed standards relating to the Welsh language*, p. 7.
69 Scott, 'Standard-setting', p. 110.
70 Scott, 'Standard-setting', p. 113. See also J. Freeman and L. I. Langbein, 'Regulatory negotiation and the legitimacy benefit', *New York University Environmental Law Journal*, 9/6 (2000), 543–675.

71 See p. 336 in J. Braithwaite and V. Braithwaite, 'The politics of legalism: rules versus standards in nursing-home regulation', *Social and Legal Studies*, 4 (1995), 307–41; Scott, 'Standard-setting', p. 109.
72 A. Ff. Jones, *Letter from Alun Ffred Jones AM, Minister for Heritage to Val Lloyd AM, Chair of Legislation Committee No. 2 National Assembly for Wales*, 14 June 2010a.
73 Welsh Government, *Cyflwyniad i'r Bwrdd am y Mesur Iaith*.
74 Welsh Government, *Consultation document. Proposed standards relating to the Welsh language*, Preface.
75 http://www.comisiynyddygymraeg.org/english/news/Pages/Welsh-Language-Commissioner-gathers-public-opinion-to-first-standards-investigation.aspx; see also https://twitter.com/ComYGymraeg/statuses/427865069335363585/.
76 M. Huws, 'Comisiynydd y Gymraeg a'r ymgynghoriad', *Golwg*, 6 March (2014a).
77 B. Thomas, '"Dryswch" safonau'r Gymraeg', *Golwg*, 15 May (2014a), 4.
78 Welsh Language Commissioner, *Advice under Section 4, Welsh Language (Wales) Measure 2011. Standards relating to the Welsh language* (Cardiff: Welsh Language Commissioner, 2014e). See also: http://www.comisiynyddygymraeg.org/English/News/Pages/Welsh-Language-Commissioner-presents-standards-reports-and-advice-to-Welsh-Ministers.aspx.
79 Mudiad Dathlu'r Gymraeg, Cymdeithas yr Iaith Gymraeg, UCAC. As reported in the news media on 5 June 2014: http://www.bbc.co.uk/cymrufyw/27708251; see also 'Pigo tyllau yn y safonau', *Golwg*, 5 June (2014), 5.
80 Welsh Government, *Consultation document. Welsh Language Standards: Regulations. Improving services for Welsh speakers* (Cardiff: Welsh Government, 2014b).
81 Hansard Society, *Hansard Society briefing paper. Issues in Law Making. 3: Delegated Legislation* (London: Hansard Society, 2003), p. 2.
82 Wales Governance Centre, *Drafting Welsh Measures: lessons from the first three years evidence presented to the Constitutional Affairs Committee, National Assembly for Wales*, CA DM 5 (2010a). Published online at: http://www.assembly.wales/NAfW%20Documents/ca_5_-_cardiff_law_school.pdf%20-%2028092010/ca_5_-_cardiff_law_school-English.pdf.
83 L. Lortie and A. L. Lalonde, *Consortium national de formation en santé. Reference framework. Training for active offer of French-language services* (Ottawa: Consortium national de formation en santé, 2012), pp. 9–10.

84 B. Hutchison, J.-F. Levesque, E. Strumpf and N. Coyle, 'Primary health care in Canada: systems in motion', *The Millbank Quarterly*, June 89/2 (2011), 256–88. Published online at: *http://www.ncbi.nlm. nih.gov/pmc/articles/PMC3142339/*.

85 *http://healthycanadians.gc.ca/health-system-systeme-sante/services/ primary-primaires/about-apropos-eng.php*; *http://healthycanadians. gc.ca/health-system-systeme-sante/services/hospital-hospitaliers-eng. php*.

86 As variously announced, for example the Canadian government news release of 30 May 2014 entitled 'Harper government invests in healthcare services for minority language communities'. Published online at: *http://news.gc.ca/web/article-en.do?mthd=index=&crtr. page=1&nid=852299*.

87 See, for example, Hutchison, Levesque, Strumpf and Coyle, 'Primary health care in Canada: systems in motion'.

88 *http://www.ofa.gov.on.ca/en/flsa.html*

89 F. Boileau, *Special report on French language health services planning in Ontario* (Toronto: Office of the French Language Services Commissioner, 2009). Published online at: *http://csfontario. ca/wp-content/uploads/2009/05/FLSC_report_french_health_ planning_2009.pdf*. One might also usefully refer to the review of Health Canada by OCOL completed in 2007. Published online at: *http://www.officiallanguages.gc.ca/html/sante_health_2007_e.php*.

90 M. Drakeford, *Written statement – Welsh Government response to My Language, My Health. The Welsh Language Commissioner's inquiry into the Welsh language in primary care*, 10 December 2014. Published online at: *http://gov.wales/about/cabinet/ cabinetstatements/2014/9453684/?lang=en*.

91 *http://www.wales.nhs.uk/sitesplus/866/news/37914*.

92 Welsh Government, *More than just words . . . strategic framework for Welsh language services in health, social services and social care* (Cardiff: Welsh Government, 2012b).

93 Braithwaite and Braithwaite, 'The politics of legalism: rules versus standards in nursing-home regulation', 109.

5 | PROMOTION AND COMPLAINT-HANDLING

Introduction

The purpose of this chapter is to highlight a number of key issues with regard to policy advice and complaint-handling, or grievance-handling, as aspects of the functions of promotion and regulation as per the office of Welsh Language Commissioner. A number of authoritative insights are drawn from the research here. In the first place, there was a significant shift during the policy and legislative cycles with regard to how promotion was framed, beginning with a clear distinction drawn between statutory and non-statutory promotion. This was steadily eroded and, moreover, both the government and the Commissioner are now understood to both have this general function. There is a clear potential for duplication of role here. How this might be resolved could be clarified to a considerable degree via a revised Framework Agreement between the government and the office of the Welsh Language Commissioner. However, there would appear to be a difference of opinion between the Commissioner and the government on this subject; the latter recognises the risk, while the former appears not to.[1] Secondly, while framed as a duty to scrutinise, and understood to mean to challenge or campaign against government policy, the policy advice function places the office of the Welsh Language Commissioner in the invidious position of being duty-bound to offer public criticism of that policy and yet at the same time engage, to varying degrees, in the operation of that policy. That is to ask of the Commissioner to implement, or to ensure that others implement, a policy of which the office has publicly expressed its doubt. It is the function of the regulator to regulate and to report upon its regulatory activities; it is the function of the Assembly to critique government policy and to hold the government to account. Finally, the evidence with regard to complaint-handling in general strongly suggests that, in comparison with the historical performance of the Welsh Language Board, Welsh language regulation is not 'yn y gors' ('in the swamp') as one former Chair of the Board rather colourfully put it.[2] On the contrary, the office of the Welsh Language Commissioner has begun to establish itself as a credible complaint-handling body.

Policy cycle discussion, recommendation and instruction (June 2008–April 2009)

At the earliest stage of the policy cycle promotion was termed as, 'general language promotion'[3] and it was stated that this function could variously be situated within the remit of the Welsh government, the Welsh Language Commissioner or a curtailed Welsh Language Board, were that body to be retained at all. Soon, a more refined definition emerged, described as the 'promotion and education role', in which, 'The Commissioner could have a flexible role to play in terms of commissioning or conducting research, undertaking studies, and conducting public awareness activities.'[4] It is noted in this paper that promotion is one of the roles of the Office of the Commissioner of Official Languages, Canada.[5]

At a late stage of the policy cycle a more refined concept again of promotion was articulated. This conceived of a dual aspect to the function, one of which was set in the context of duties pertaining to statutory regulation duty, and it was understood that this would be the function of the Welsh Language Commissioner. The second aspect to promotion was that pertaining to activity set in non-statutory contexts, and it was anticipated that this would be the function of the Welsh government,[6] unless it were decided that the Welsh Language Board would be retained.[7] This paper therefore sees 'a clear separation between the regulatory functions and the functions to promote and facilitate the use of Welsh', in that the former type of promotion is set in the 'statutory context' and the latter is in the 'non-statutory context'.[8] In Annexe C of this text this conceptual split between 'activities aimed at promoting and facilitating the use of Welsh in a *non-statutory* context' and those set in a '*statutory* context' (original italics and underlining) is quite tidily set out in relation to a range of Welsh Language Board activities for 2008–9.[9]

At the point of policy instruction it was stated that the Commissioner's primary functions were to include 'to develop, publish and promote the Welsh language guidelines, advice and standards',[10] and that the Commissioner should have a role in 'educating organisations and promoting good practice in relation to designing and delivering Welsh language services',[11] and that it would have a duty to 'promote the availability of Welsh language services and advise other organisations how to do so – whether under a duty to do so or otherwise'.[12]

Legislative cycle discussion and determination (March–December 2010)

The first Explanatory Memorandum pertaining to the Measure, dated March 2010, stated that the promotional role for the Commissioner would be as follows: 'The Commissioner will have the general function of promoting and facilitating the use of the Welsh language and to promote equality between the Welsh and English languages.'[13] The significance of this is that the remit was by this point in both the statutory (as per Schemes under the Welsh Language Act 1993 and Standards under the Measure) and in the non-statutory context. It was explained as follows:

> Ministers are clear that it is important that the Commissioner's role should be wider than imposing and enforcing standards. If the Commissioner is to have a positive impact on the Welsh language it is important that he or she can promote and facilitate the use of Welsh outside the regulatory framework which will be established by the proposed Measure.[14]

Indeed, it was asserted that, with regard to the Commissioner's functions under the Measure, 'the Commissioner may do anything that he or she thinks appropriate to promote the use of the Welsh language, facilitate the use of the Welsh language and promote equality between the English and Welsh languages'.[15]

Thus, by this stage the previously very concrete conceptual divide between the statutory and the non-statutory contexts was replaced by an unclear division of labour between the Commissioner and the government in the domain of promotion. While it was foreseen that there would eventually have to be some sort of division of labour, the detail of that was not worked out at this point, either as a matter of principle or as a matter of practice, as is clear from this assertion in the Memorandum that

> some of the Board's [Welsh Language Board] work to promote the use of Welsh will transfer into the Welsh Assembly Government along with some of the Board's staff. Detailed decisions about the distribution of such functions will, however, be a matter to be addressed by the Measure implementation project.[16]

It would appear that there was considerable confusion over the meaning of promotion during discussions in committee. For example, Emyr Lewis explained that he did not want any of the Board's promotional functions to be transferred to government for fear that

> The risk then is that this work could be sidelined, and the expertise lost, as a result of political compromises when determining priorities and resources, which are a part of every government's daily life. In order to avoid this risk, I would like to see clause 134(3) removed from the measure.[17]

Lewis was challenged on this by Rhodri Morgan AM (Labour) and subsequently changed his mind. It is worth quoting from Lewis's explanation at length, as follows:

> I have explained in my written evidence why I think that it is important to keep the promotional functions [. . .] at arm's length from the Government. When giving my oral evidence, I accepted in principle Rhodri Morgan's argument that it would not be appropriate for the Commissioner to undertake this type of function as well as undertaking an auditing and regulatory role [. . .] I still accept Mr Morgan's argument, and now tend to agree that the Commissioner should not have promotional

functions, except to the extent that he/she is promoting good practice in terms of providing services through codes of practice and so on. Language promotion itself should not be the role of the Commissioner.[18]

It appears that Lewis was suggesting that a rump Board be retained, or that a similar such quango be created, so as to undertake promotional work for the following reason, 'I am not convinced that within Government is the most appropriate place for that promotional work to happen.'[19] In his oral evidence, when advocating the value of having a quango, he argued that, 'Being independent of government is valuable. It is neutral.'[20] Of course, the nub of Rhodri Morgan's question also pertains to the danger of overlap or duplication in having two bodies engage in the task of promotion: 'People would [then] ask why there were two units fishing in the same pond, as it were. What is the point of having two bodies doing the work of one?'[21]

In his written evidence Colin H. Williams stated as a 'basic principle', one ought to 'keep policy-making and promotional responsibilities separate from regulating and compliance responsibilities'.[22] He reiterates this in his oral evidence, asserting that

> I noted in my paper that it is necessary to have a clear distinction between the promotion of the Welsh language and the regulation of the Welsh language. In Canada and Ireland, regulation and implementation are the only functions of their language commissioners. They educate by means of pamphlets and public engagement, but the language commissioner's office has no remit in terms of language policy and promotion. Other people do that. The commissioner's role is to stick to regulation.[23]

This contradicts Welsh Policy Paper 3. It is also at odds with the statutory description of the Office of the Commissioner of Official Languages (OCOL) in the Official Languages Act (§ 56, as of 25 August 2013), under which OCOL has a 'mandate to promote the equal status of both official languages',[24] and also with how OCOL self-presents, whereby the promotion of both French and English is described as being one of 'the three main objectives' of the office under the Act.[25] Indeed, Graham Fraser, the current Commissioner, described promotion as 'an integral part of my mandate'.[26] It ought also be noted that in the Irish case the Official Languages Act 2003 is described in its purpose clause as '[a]n Act to promote the use of the Irish language for official purposes in the State [. . .] and for those purposes, to provide for the establishment of Oifig Choimisinéir na dTeangacha Oifigiúla [Irish Language Commissioner]'. All told, what none of the language commissioners do, of course, is to *formulate* language policy, while they are all central to its effective *implementation*.

During the same Committee session Williams agreed with Morgan's assertion that 'the role of policy and the promotional role are a matter of governance'[27] because, in Williams's words, 'it would be difficult for someone in the office of the Language Commissioner, which will have half the responsibility for drafting policy, to have to regulate the policy as well'.[28] In actual fact, it is the case that the functions of policy formulation and promotion are retained by government in many polities, including Québec, the Basque Autonomous Community and Catalonia, along with the regulatory function. There is no overriding principle in the field of governance that the separation of these tasks is functionally necessary. Having said that Williams agreed with Morgan on policy and promotion being a matter for 'governance', when asked whether 'the governance work [. . .] namely promotion, [ought to] be done from within the Government';[29] Williams echoes the evidence given by Lewis advocating the retention of a rump Board or the creation of some other quango, given, in his view, that the nature of promotional work is more 'radical' than the sort of work that would be usual to civil service culture.[30] Williams also stated that the function of promotion could not be usefully taken up by the Commissioner, for a similar reason: 'If the remit to promote the language were given to the language commissioner's office, I doubt that the creative aspect would be given fair play'.[31] That said, Williams stated elsewhere at around the same time that 'it would be advisable were Wales to formalise a division of labour whereby promotional activities are the direct responsibility of a government department'.[32] Although published in 2013, and also in 2014 with minor modifications, Williams notes in his own preface to the document that a 'confidential' version of the report was 'submitted' in 2010. Moreover, he asserts that this was also made available to the Minister and his civil servants at the time of the passage of the Measure through the Assembly, such that it informed the development of the Measure.[33]

The Welsh government's second Explanatory Memorandum, of November 2010, was more assertive again than the first Explanatory Memorandum with regard to the function of promotion, now very broadly defined, as well as being a wholly central function of the Commissioner. Thus:

> The Commissioner's principal aim will be to promote and facilitate the use of the Welsh language and he or she will have the general functions of promoting and facilitating the use of the Welsh language and working towards ensuring that the Welsh language is treated no less favourably than the English language.[34]

The significance of this, in brief, is that between the first and the second Explanatory Memoranda the aim to promote has migrated from being a 'general function' to becoming the 'principal aim' of the office of Commissioner during the course of the legislative cycle.

Implementation

In announcing the advent of the Commissioner, the government announced that the functions of the previous Board had been divided between the Commissioner and the government, as follows:

> The Welsh Language Board was abolished on 1 April 2012 as a result of the Welsh Language (Wales) Measure 2011. The Board's duties have been divided between the Welsh Language Commissioner and the Welsh Government. Under the new arrangements, the Welsh Language Commissioner will: advise the Welsh Government and others on language policy and related issues; provide independent scrutiny of Welsh Government policies and respond to consultation documents.[35]

The implication of this is that there was no clarity of principle on the division of labour on promotion but rather an ad hoc and wholly practical distribution of activities between the Commissioner and the government. In fact, under the statutory instrument pertinent to the distribution of the functions of the Board upon its abolition it is stated that 'The Board's function of promoting and facilitating the use of the Welsh language [. . .] will transfer to the Welsh Ministers *as well as to* the Commissioner' (this author's italics).[36] In the Schedule to the Instrument itself the specific projects to be transferred from the Board to the government alone are clearly listed, but there is no division of labour by principle (Welsh Statutory Instruments 2012 No. 752 (W.102) Welsh language, Wales. The Welsh Language Board (Transfer of Staff, Property, Rights and Liabilities) Order 2012, Part 1). Neither the concept of promotion nor the function of providing policy advice appears to have been a feature of the Welsh government briefing to the prospective Commissioner and her team at the briefing session of December 2011.

There is a brief reference to promotion activities in the Framework Agreement between the government and the Commissioner, signed on 19 September 2012.[37] It is noted there that they will cooperate in the areas of standards, working with the private sector on technology, statistics and research, translation and terminology, and 'hybu a hyrwyddo' ('promotion'), which includes sharing information about campaigns and plans for marketing the Welsh language.[38] The document details the routine schedule of meetings to be held between the Commissioner and the government, and the timetable for sharing information that is likely to 'arwain at sylw cyhoeddus' ('lead to public attention').[39] This means giving notice, in the form of a summary of report or select sections from the report, of two full working days prior to any public announcement. It is also stipulated that any final report regarding the Welsh government itself is to be shared with the government at least five full working days prior to publication.

The Commissioner has taken some practical steps with regard to the task of providing policy advice. The office created a policy 'Observatory' on 31 January 2013,[40] as was also noted in the Commissioner's first Annual Report (5.7). It was also noted that the Commissioner had offered policy recommendations to the Welsh government (5.4) and to Ministers of the Crown (5.5). In the Commissioner's Strategic Plan for 2013–15 the first, no less, listed strategic priority was, 'to influence the consideration given to the Welsh language in policy developments'.[41] In the Annual Report for 2014 the Commissioner noted success in this regard, in that, 'Following regular pressure from my office, the Welsh language was included on the face of the Social Services and Well-being (Wales) Bill.'[42]

Having been presented with the Welsh Language Society's 'black book of complaints' on taking office,[43] the office of the Commissioner has taken several steps with regard to complaint-handling, including developing mechanisms and public guidelines for the submission of complaints[44] and setting up internal processes for the management of complaints, including a Complaints and Statutory Investigations Panel.[45] During the first year of operation, 2012–13, the office received 468 complaints,[46] followed by 375 complaints in the next operating year.[47] In each case, the body of complaints was subjected to analysis.

Analysis: complaint-handling

Regarding effective complaint-handling, the qualities proposed in the scholarly literature are echoed to a great degree in the professional literature, such as the following criteria on best practice in complaint handling as articulated by the British and Irish Ombudsman Association,[48] the National Consumer Council[49] and other scholarly and authoritative professional sources:[50] clarity of purpose; accessibility; flexibility; openness and transparency; proportionality; efficiency; and quality outcomes. In this particular regard the conditions for an effective ombudsman service, as the complaint-handling body par excellence, as set out by the World Bank and quoted in a memorandum by the Northern Ireland Ombudsman to the Constitution Committee of the House of Lords is worth reproducing here. In it, the Ombudsman asserts that the effectiveness of the office as a complaint-handling body rests on the following: political support – from parliament, government, administration, and courts; adequate resources – a proper budget system must provide adequate resources for the job; public perception – the public must be aware of and understand the ombudsman's office and its functions; functional competence – the ombudsman must be effective in receiving, investigating, and resolving complaints against the administration. Functional competence depends on institutional design, administrative capacity and professional expertise, independence from the executive, and procedures for dealing with government, ministers and departments; regulatory value – the ombudsman should fit with existing arrangements for administrative regulation. The regulatory value of an institution depends on the overall system of administrative regulation within a country and on how an ombudsman fits into it. Regulatory value also depends on an institution enduring for a significant period.[51]

Following the new approach to regulation instituted by the Commissioner, certain critics, former Chairs and Chief Executives of the Welsh Language Board, have expressed some nostalgia for the approach to promotion taken by the Board.[52] However, the overall performance of the Board with regard to complaint-handling does not bear up well under scrutiny, in truth. That said, the approach of the Board did evolve considerably between 1996 and 2011, and it eventually took a more robust position with regard to complaint handling and statutory investigations. Drawing upon the Board's annual reports, it is possible to build up an understanding of both the style and the substance of its performance with regard to complaint-handling (Figure 8). Bear in mind, the purpose of this paper is simply to consider the significance of the manner in which the Board set about presenting its approach to complaint-handling in its definitive public statement on its own annual performance, that is in its annual report, and to consider the raw data as presented by the Board. The efficacy of the Board with regard to dealing with specific complaints is not considered here.

Briefly, the year 2008–9 is, clearly, a watershed. Up until 2007–8 the Board did not present data on the body of complaints received on a regular basis, indeed for the period between 2001–2 and 2006–7 inclusive the Board made no reference whatsoever to the body of complaints received. That in itself runs counter to good practice in grievance-handling, as demonstrated by Bondy and Le Sueur, whereby there was no scrutiny of the approach taken by the Board to these issues, or the effectiveness of its practice.[53] Thus, the Board was largely unaccountable to its principal audience in this regard, namely individual Welsh-speaking complainants. In addition, the approach taken by the Board during that period may be characterised as conforming with the 'resolution model', which has been subjected to much criticism in the research literature for 'depriving complainants of the benefits of a fully transparent and accountable public law remedy'.[54] Prior to the reporting year 2008–9, eight investigations had been conducted by the Board during the course of fourteen reporting years. From 2008–9 no fewer than seventeen investigations were

Welsh Language Board: Complaints and statutory investigations		
Year	Complaints	Statutory investigations
1994–5	No reference	
1995–6	Over 250	
1996–7	No reference	
1997–8	No reference	
1998–9	Over 300	1
1999–2000	Over 250	3
2000–1	274	
2001–2	No reference	
2002–3	No reference	
2003–4	No reference	
2004–5	No reference	3
2005–6	No reference	
2006–7	No reference	
2007–8	62	1
2008–9	106	8
2009–10	186	4
2010–11	206	5

Figure 8. *Welsh Language Board: complaints and statutory investigations based upon data derived from the Welsh Language Board, Annual Reports, 1995–2011.*

conducted during the course of three reporting years. That year is also the first occasion on which the Board expresses the view that its regulatory powers are too limited, as 'under the present legislation, those circumstances in which the Board can make recommendations are restricted, as are our powers to enforce change in the light of those recommendations',[55] leading it to the belief that 'the Welsh Language Act 1993 is no longer adequate'.[56] This year also marks the creation by the Welsh Language Board of a Statutory Investigations and Complaints Panel.[57] The Board also finds it a sufficiently noteworthy event to report that in that year also it published 'a booklet that explains the procedure for complaining about the lack of Welsh language services'.[58]

By way of illustrating the point more broadly, the Board suffers in comparison with the Irish Language Commissioner, for example. The office of the Irish Language Commissioner in the Republic of Ireland was created under the Official Languages Act 2003, its first year of operation being completed in 2004. Among the duties of the Commissioner is the monitoring of the provision of services 'as promised by public bodies under the agreed schemes'.[59] The handling of complaints and the power to conduct statutory investigations are important regulatory tools for the Commissioner. From the outset, the Commissioner adopted an approach to its role as a complaint-handling body which reflects the historical practices of Office of the Commissioner of Official Languages in Canada. The influence became quite direct and was formalised in 2006 in the shape of annual staff exchanges between the two offices, so as to 'increase our understanding of each other's work practices as a tool towards establishing norms of best practice'.[60] The office's annual reports present substantial statistical data on the complaints received for each year along with an explanatory narrative and a summary of selected cases felt by the Commissioner to be of particular interest. As a result it is possible to present a complete picture of the level of complaints dealt with by the office (Figure 9). The data indicate that the level has

The Irish Language Commissioner: Complaints and investigations		
Year	Complaints	Investigations
2004	304	
2005	415	
2006	611	
2007	622	12
2008	596	17
2009	687	17
2010	700	11
2011	734	15
2012	756	13

Figure 9. *Irish Language Commissioner: complaints and investigations based upon data derived from the Irish Language Commissioner, Annual Reports, 2004–2012.*

steadily increased since the creation of the office, suggesting that it is increasingly viewed by complainants as a credible complaint-handling body, according to the Commissioner.[61]

The Irish Language Commissioner conducted his first investigations in the reporting year of 2007, as the full provisions of the Official Languages Act 2003 came into effect. The office gave notice to the bodies subject to the pertinent legislation in the annual report of the previous year of his intention to do so, marking a shift from dealing with bodies under the 'spirit of the legislation' as an 'interim strategy' to dealing with bodies 'on the basis of actual obligations'.[62] In each of his annual reports the Commissioner notes the number of new investigations per year while also providing condensed summaries of the investigations conducted, including naming each of the bodies subject to investigation. At the same time he also notes that the authoritative accounts of the investigations are available in the form of official reports issued in accordance with Section 26 of the Official Languages Act 2003.[63] This allows the Commissioner to draw substantive insights from the body of data on complaints. In particular, he is able to identify systemic failings on the basis of empirical evidence, as opposed to simply responding to and resolving a series of discrete and individual complaints.

Turning now to OCOL, in a comprehensive and authoritative overview of the creation and subsequent evolution of its own office published in 2009, it is asserted that from its inception one of the central tasks of that office was to establish itself as a credible complaint-handling body.[64] This is reflected in the manner in which the matter of complaints is dealt with in the office's annual reports. In each of the years since inception the body of complaints received by the office is subject to careful and detailed description and analysis. The retrospective overview of complaints published by OCOL in the annual report of 2005 is an extremely useful starting point with regard to raw empirical data and its interpretation. Drawing upon this and the subsequent annual reports it is possible to construct a picture of the volume of complaints received by OCOL from its beginning up until the present (Figure 10). As with the Irish Language Commissioner, the Board compares equally badly with OCOL as a complaint-handling body.

In contrast to the greater part of the historical practice of the Board, the approach taken by the Welsh Language Commissioner to

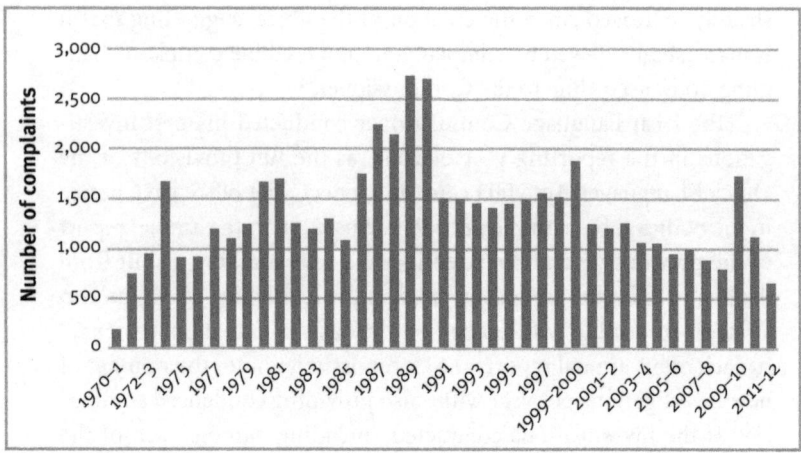

Figure 10. *Office of the Commissioner of Official Languages, Canada: complaints based upon data derived from OCOL, Annual Reports, 1971–2012.*

complaint-handling allows for the robust scrutiny of performance, as is evidenced in the series of annual reports published by the office since its inception. Data is presented in full and analysed in some depth. In short, the working practices of the Commissioner largely replicate the best practice of the language commissioners in Canada and in Ireland. That said, a matter of some ambiguity arises in relation to the action taken by the Commissioner regarding an apparent rise in the numbers of complaints against banks since her work began.

According to the public record, the starting point was an announcement by the Commissioner on 22 December 2014 that material comprising a body of complaints had been brought to her attention indicating a significant, substantial and recent increase in the levels of public dissatisfaction with the Welsh language service provided by banks.[65] In particular, the Commissioner stated as follows,

> over the past weeks and months I have seen a significant increase in complaints about Welsh language services offered by banks. I have also received evidence from voluntary organisations identifying specific concerns about the sector. It is therefore clear that this is a matter of concern to members of the public across Wales.[66]

As a result of this evidence the Commissioner decided, she explained, to conduct a statutory review of the sector. At this point the Commissioner called for evidence to be brought forward and to be submitted by the end of January 2015. In April 2015 the Commissioner published the results of the review.[67] The headline conclusion was that there had been a decline, or backward step, in the level of services, thereby giving rise to the complaints.[68]

Leaving aside the fact that the author of the report mistakenly implies that Welsh and English are 'equal in the eyes of the law'[69] when in fact no such claim is made under the Measure, unlike the Welsh Language Act 1993 which it supplanted, and under which the treatment of Welsh and English on a basis of equality is a basic principle, the most important gap in the report is its failure to present the evidence that was the cause of the statutory review in the first place. In other words, there is no meaningful consideration of the body of complaints said to have been received by the Commissioner's office in the weeks and months leading up to the announcement made in December 2014. Instead, the Commissioner claims in the foreword to the document that 'in recent months and years Welsh language services seem to have degraded. The banks have taken a step backwards'; the Commissioner reinforces this point through reiterating her previous assertion that 'service-users have certainly noticed this, and I have seen a significant increase in complaints from individuals and organisations who are disappointed with the lack of Welsh language provision by banks in Wales'.[70]

An examination of the Commissioner's annual reports leading up to the apparent insight that there was widespread public concern with banks reveals no such evidence either of any such substantial increase in dissatisfaction. For example, in the report for 2012–13 the Commissioner merely noted that 'As Welsh is an official language in Wales,[71] a number of banks are reviewing their policies and renewing them jointly with the Commissioner.'[72] There is no indication of a problem. In actual fact, it is noted in the report that 'discussion between the Commissioner's officers and NatWest led to re-branding the company in Wales as NatWest Cymru'.[73] In the report for the following year the Commissioner implies a strengthening of her office's engagement with the banks where it is noted that 'priority was given [by her office] to developing the use of the Welsh language in banks'.[74] Indeed, the level of complaints recorded in relation to the private sector in terms of absolute numbers and as a proportion of the overall total of complaints received by the Commissioner actually fell between 2012–13 and 2013–14, from 120 (26%) to 93 (25%). It is not possible to identify the data regarding banks alone over this timescale, as the Commissioner did not choose to disaggregate that information for 2012–13.

According to the report for 2013–14 the Commissioner received 21 complaints with regard to banks. Moreover, according to the Commissioner's annual report for 2014–15, her office received a total of 14 complaints about banks in the period between her previous report and the announcement that banks were to be subject to a statutory review, that is from 1 April 2014 until 22 December 2014. In other words, over a period of some eight months the Commissioner received 14 complaints about banks, an average of around 1.75 per month. This compares with the previous reporting period of twelve months, during which a total of 21 complaints about banks were received, also an average of 1.75 per month. Incidentally, the total number of complaints regarding banks for the whole of the reporting year 2014–15 was 17.

Coincidentally, it would seem to be the case that the only new and substantial body of evidence of increased levels of dissatisfaction with high street banks to appear in the time frame identified by the Commissioner in December 2014, that is, in the previous 'weeks and months', is that presented by the Welsh Language Society on its website on 25 November 2014, where it is specifically described as being for the 'attention of the Welsh Language Commissioner'.[75] There is no evidence of any other such material being presented in the public domain at that time, nor is any other alternative body of complaints of that nature identified either in the Commissioner's annual report or in the statutory review itself. In response to the report by the Commissioner, the Welsh Language Society called for banks to be made subject to legislation requiring them to provide services in Welsh.[76] Currently, banks are not obliged by the Measure to provide a service in Welsh, nor indeed were they under any such duty under the Welsh Language Act 1993. The Welsh Language Society had, of course, campaigned for them to be brought within the scope of the Measure.[77]

The extent to which the appearance of the evidence brought forward by the Welsh Language Society is a concurrence seems to be rendered problematic, potentially, by a Welsh Language Society e-mail dated 17 November 2014 in which the following is noted:

'Mae Comisiynydd y Gymraeg eisiau derbyn enghreifftiau o ddiffyg gwasanaeth bancio yn y Gymraeg, gan ei bod yn ystyried gweithredu yn y maes rhyw ffordd' ('The Welsh Language Commissioner wants to receive examples of lack of service in Welsh by the banks, as she is considering taking action in this area somehow') (see Figure 11). The e-mail continues by asking for members of the Society to forward their evidence 'by the end of the week'. Given that no concern with the banking sector was noted in the Commissioner's annual reports prior to the decision to initiate a statutory review, and indeed noting also that the level of complaints received by the Commissioner's office regarding banks remained static, according to the data presented in the pertinent annual reports, this e-mail is most interesting. The public call for evidence by the Commissioner only came on 22 December 2014 as the statutory review itself was announced. The Society published its evidence online on 25 November 2014, just a week after the e-mail was first circulated and a few weeks prior to the Commissioner's public expression of her office's concern.

Thus, the narrative appears to have the following shape:

- 1 April 2012–31 March 2013: no concerns with the banking sector are noted in the Commissioner's Annual Report; banks are reviewing and renewing policies 'jointly with the Commissioner';
- 1 April 2013–31 March 2014: no concerns with the banking sector are noted in the Commissioner's Annual Report; 'developing the use of the Welsh language in banks' is a 'priority' for the Commissioner; 21 complaints regarding banks are presented to the Commissioner (21 in twelve months, 1.75 complaints per month);
- 1 April–18 December 2014: 14 complaints regarding banks are presented to the Commissioner (14 in approximately eight months, 1.75 complaints per month);[78]
- 17 November 2014: the Welsh Language Society e-mail asking for evidence against banks notes that the Commissioner 'wants to receive' such evidence;
- 25 November 2014: the Welsh Language Society publishes its evidence against banks on its website;
- 22 December 2014: the Commissioner initiates the statutory review of banks and announces a public call for evidence.

It is not the statutory review itself that is in question here, of course, but rather the particular passage of events leading up to the review and the nature of the evidence upon which the decision to initiate the review was based. The Welsh Language Society's e-mail seems to problematise any perception of the evidence brought forward by that organisation being an independent concurrence.

---------- Forwarded message ----------
From: **DELETED** <DELETED@cymdeithas.org>
Date: 2014-11-17 15:58 GMT+00:00
Subject: [Deddf Iaith] Bancio - enghreifftiau diffyg Cymraeg
To: deddf-iaith@cymdeithas.org

Annwyl bawb,

Mae Comisiynydd y Gymraeg eisiau derbyn enghreifftiau o ddiffyg gwasanaethau bancio yn Gymraeg, gan ei bod yn ystyried gweithredu yn y maes rhyw ffordd. Mae ddiffyg gwasanaethau lleol / cau banciau cymunedol yn berthnasol fel tystiolaeth nid yn unig oherwydd ei effaith economaidd ond hefyd achos bod tynnu gwasanaethau'r stryd fawr i ffwrdd yn gorfodi pobl i fancio ar-lein - gwasanaethau sy ond ar gael yn uniaith Saesneg.

Os oes unrhyw enghreifftiau gyda chi, allwch chi fy ebostio i gyda'r wybodaeth? Gobeithio y gallwn ni anfon y wybodaeth at y Comisiynydd erbyn diwedd yr wythnos.

DELETED

DELETED

DELETED
DELETED
Cymdeithas yr Iaith Gymraeg
07971 339542 / 02920 486469
cymdeithas.org
@cymdeithas
facebook.com/cymdeithas

Deddf-iaith mailing list
Deddf-iaith@cymdeithas.com
http://lists.cymdeithas.com/mailman/listinfo/deddf-iaith

Figure 11. *E-mail from a member of the Welsh Language Society to members of the Welsh Language Society, 17 November 2014.*

Analysis: policy advice
Regarding the function of providing policy advice more generally speaking, the OECD remarked that

> Some jurisdictions support the principle that independent regulatory agencies should not have primary responsibility for providing policy advice to Ministers, and that this should be the role of the relevant Ministry. However, regulators do undertake important policy functions, by virtue of their familiarity with the regulated sector and responsibility for ultimately carrying out regulatory policy.[79]

In practice, this is not a unique role and many offices of ombudsman, commissioner and regulator fulfil the task of commentating upon or reviewing legislation, or proffering policy advice, as a matter of routine.[80] But, it is argued that the process of agencification,[81] understood as the proliferation of agencies acting on behalf of the Executive in the routine delivery, management or regulation of the administrative tasks of the government, is designed to allow the government to 'specialise' in 'policy-making'.[82] In other words, in this context, regulatory labour is divided between the government, which sets the policy direction, and the regulatory agency, to which is delegated from the Executive the day-to-day tasks of regulatory rule- or standard-setting, enforcement, compliance, complaint-handling, investigation and adjudication.

In general terms, while all sorts of actors attempt to influence policy,[83] the concept of policy adviser is understood as an expert in a particular field who provides advice to government, or to another policy broker. In contrast to the policy adviser, the policy broker is understood to have the power to decide upon and implement policy, or to cause it to be implemented. The key issue here is clarity in differentiating between the roles. In attempting to influence policy, advisers might see value in engaging with other actors, such as interest groups and lobbyists, in a networking approach termed by some as the advocacy coalition framework.[84] The crux of the matter here is the means of gaining access to influence over policy brokers.

According to the research literature, the credibility of policy advisers, however, depends upon the transparency of the policy-advising process or mechanism and upon the regard given to their advice by their expert and scientific peers.[85] The contemporary policy-making context is changing substantially. The intersection of polity, knowledge and intervention is critical to understanding this. This current approach to policy research is termed deliberative policy analysis.[86] There are three central elements to this notion, as follows: (1) 'there are no generally accepted rules and norms according to which politics is to be conducted and policy measures are to be agreed upon'; (2) 'scientific expertise is now negotiated rather than simply accepted'; and, (3) given the weakening of the State, it is 'less obvious that government is the sole actor to intervene in policy making'.[87] The critical issue here is negotiating the 'rules' of policy advising. With regard to this sense of negotiation, the multiple streams approach to understanding policy argues that three streams of 'problems, policies, and politics' must come together to create a 'policy window'.[88] This window is the opportunity for policy actors to bring to bear any influence they might have. In this context the actor must adopt the behaviour of a policy entrepreneur. From this arises a further key issue, namely managing or timing intervention.

In practical terms, the OECD puts the relationship between the regulator as policy adviser and the government as follows, emphasising early and active involvement in policy dialogue and clarity of process or mechanism for doing so:

> if policy set by Ministers is to be well informed, effectively implemented and responsive to changes in the regulatory environment, it is critical that the relevant regulator is *actively involved early in the formulation and subsequent refinement of policy* to support the development process led by the Ministry [...] 'The principal responsibility for assisting the executive to develop government policy should sit with the responsible executive agency and the regulator should have a formal advisory role in this task. In all cases such policy should be advanced in *close dialogue* with affected regulatory and other agencies, and there should be *specified mechanisms* for regulators to contribute to the policy making process.[89] [author's italics]

Turning now to some of the specific cases of policy advice given by the Welsh Language Commissioner, a number of complications arise from some of them.[90] In the case of the creation of a wholly

Welsh language local authority named 'Arfor' in the context of local government re-organisation, as proposed by Adam Price,[91] the Commissioner immediately advised via a television programme that this proposal had to be looked at very quickly.[92] While generating some comment,[93] there is no evidence that the government paid any attention whatsoever. Other cases are more nuanced.[94] For example, taking the Commissioner's claim with regard to her advice resulting in the Welsh language being included on the face of the Social Services and Well-being (Wales) Act 2014, in actual fact the Welsh language is not specified on the face of the Act. Instead, the Act specifies, under the section dealing with other, general, overarching duties that 'The person must – [. . .] have regard to the characteristics, culture and beliefs of the individual (including, for example, language)' (Social Services and Well-being (Wales) Act 2014, Part 2, 6.2.c). In addition, the matter of generic linguistic characteristics that is covered by this clause was already present in the Bill as proposed (Part 6, 62.3.b). In explaining the amendment, the Assembly put it as follows: 'This reflected evidence at Stage 1 about the inclusion of statutory principles on the face of the Bill.'[95] It was also noted in the revised Explanatory Memorandum that the generic terms 'language' and 'linguistic characteristics' were understood to include, of course, the Welsh language, adding that this was 'already a Ministerial intention'.[96] In the Explanatory Memorandum accompanying the Bill as proposed it was stated, with regard to the Welsh language specifically, that 'a Ministerial commitment has been given that the Welsh language will be included within the regulations and Guidance which underpin this Bill'.[97] That remained unchanged.

Perhaps the most fraught case as regards policy advice is that pertaining to the statutory planning system, specifically the Planning (Wales) Bill[98] and Technical Advice Note (TAN) 20.[99] There is considerable background to this issue. This paper confines itself to the role of the Commissioner as opposed to the relative merits or de-merits of the substance of the matter with regard to TAN 20, the Bill and the Welsh language in the planning system generally. Very simply, the starting point is 2011, when Chair of the Welsh Language Board, the current Commissioner, played an active role in the Royal Town Planning Institute (RTPI Cymru) Eisteddfod seminar of 2011, the subject of which was the Welsh government's recent consultation TAN 20.[100]

Since being appointed Commissioner, TAN 20 has re-emerged as an issue of interest. In July 2013 the Commissioner observed that 'The First Minister has today committed to publish a revised TAN 20 in the early autumn. I welcome this commitment, and hope that it will be robust and clear guidance to planning authorities on how to consider the Welsh language.'[101] Shortly after that, at the launch of her first Annual Report at the Eisteddfod, the Commissioner called upon 'Welsh Ministers to amend TAN 20 urgently in order to ensure that the Welsh language is considered in planning decisions'.[102] Subsequent to the Government's statement on TAN 20 in October 2013 the Commissioner said:

> Having a clear and firm process to consider the Welsh Language as part of the planning process is of great importance, and I have called on the Welsh Government on numerous occasions to revise the present Advice Note. The Ministers' statement today raises many questions: for example what will happen until the 'further practical guidelines' are published, and what will happen to local development plans that are under consideration. I will now be arranging an early meeting with the Minister and his officials to seek answers to these and other questions.[103]

A few days later the office of the Commissioner announced the following:

> The Welsh Language Commissioner has written to the Housing and Regeneration Minister asking specific questions about the revised Technical Advice Note (TAN) 20 and considerations relating to the Welsh language in planning decisions. Speaking today, the Welsh Language Commissioner, Meri Huws, said: 'The vitality of the Welsh language as a community language and language considerations in planning decisions are two matters that go together. That's why it is so important that planning authorities have a clear and robust procedure to follow in order to consider the Welsh language in the planning process. In my initial response to the to the [sic] Ministers' [sic] statement regarding the revised TAN last Wednesday I said that it raised many questions. I posed those questions to the Minister in a letter sent on Friday.' In her letter, the Commissioner raised the following questions:

- How will the Government ensure that the revised TAN is implemented by those Authorities who have already adopted a Local Development Plan?
- Local Development Plans are revised every four years, but following the publication of the revised TAN will the Government be asking for revisions before this timescale?
- Will the Government be instructing authorities to delay the adoption of further LDPs until the 'Practical Guide for the consideration of the Welsh language in development plans' is published in 2014?
- How will the Government allow for consideration of the Welsh language in individual applications that (a) arise from LDPs that have already been adopted, or (b) arise from earlier development plans, such as UDPs?
- The revised TAN asks authorities to consider whether the Welsh language is of significance within the planning authority area. Will the 'practical guide' provide guidance on this?

The Commissioner also wrote that she would welcome the opportunity to have a wider discussion with the Minister.[104]

Some commentators perceived something of a stand-off between the government and the Commissioner. For example, in the planning profession journal it was noted that: 'The Welsh government is resisting calls from Welsh language campaigners for its forthcoming Planning Bill to place a statutory responsibility on councils to consider the Welsh language as part of the planning process.'[105] In other sources the views of the Commissioner were juxtaposed so as to cohere with the criticism of TAN 20 by the Welsh Language Society.[106]

More recently, the matter of the place of the Welsh language in the planning system and TAN 20 has arisen once again. On the announcement of the Bill in October 2014, the office of the Commissioner declared that:

The Planning Bill needs to secure the status of the Welsh language. Assembly committees need to ensure that the new planning framework achieves its goal of promoting the use of the Welsh language. That was the Welsh Language Commissioner's

> message today in response to the publication of the Welsh Government's draft Planning Bill. There is one reference to the language in the Bill, namely to enable the proposed Strategic Planning Panels to be liable to be required to comply with standards relating to the Welsh language. When introducing the Bill the Government stated that the new planning framework will promote the use of the Welsh language. The Welsh Language Commissioner, Meri Huws, said: 'The content of the Bill is different to what I recommended in the advice to the Government at the beginning of the year. We advocated that the Government used legislation to secure the status of the Welsh language in the planning system by making it compulsory for planning authorities to consider the Welsh language when reaching decisions. As the democratic process of scrutinising the Bill begins, it is imperative that Assembly Members and others use the committees to ensure that the new planning system secures the status of the Welsh language and reflects the linguistic needs of communities and citizens in Wales.[107]

At the same time, Jamie Bevan, the Chair of the Welsh Language Society, stated that the First Minister ought to yield the policy portfolio for the Welsh language, arguing that 'giving up his responsibilities for the language is the only honourable choice he has'.[108] When later questioned by the Constitutional and Legislative Affairs Committee of the Assembly on the adequacy of the consideration given to the language in legislation, the Commissioner and her office offered the following explanation of how their view was brought to bear on the Planning Bill in particular: '[I]t takes quite a lot of campaigning and lots of responses to persuade them [the government].' In other words, the Commissioner understands her office to have been campaigning against the legislation proposed by the Welsh government and to have aspects of it changed.[109] According to the research literature, it appears to be quite without precedent to have a governmental regulator actively campaigning against the proposed legislation of its own government. Indeed, to tolerate a regulator doing so appears to undermine the distinctive roles of the different branches of government, in particular the Executive and the Legislature, and the regulator could be perceived as attempting to play one off against the other in pursuit of its own agenda; this is regulatory activism writ large. It is one thing for a regulator to provide expert policy advice based upon scientific evidence; it is quite another for a regulator to scrutinise and challenge government policy, never mind actually campaigning against it. To do so is to adopt the behaviour and function of a lobbyist. As noted in chapter 2, this danger, precisely, was identified during the process of drafting the 2011 Measure as one of the substantive weaknesses of adopting the corporation sole at the legal personality of the Commissioner. In addition, the policy advice function as exercised by the Commissioner is undermined by a failure to base her policy advisory interventions on expert evidence. Other regulators that are under a duty to provide expert policy advice to government possess in-house scientific expertise and have amongst their staff, for example, officers dedicated to garnering evidence for the purposes of informing policy advice in an authoritative and scientifically robust manner.[110] To proffer policy advice in the absence of an evidential base is to engage in polemics.

During the consultative process one can see that the substantive concerns of the Commissioner with regard to TAN 20 (as opposed to her remarks with regard to the First Minister) were noted by the minister sponsoring the Bill, Carl Sargeant, the Minister for Housing and Regeneration, who welcomed the fact that the Commissioner, 'has agreed that research she has commissioned can be used to inform this work [i.e. the application of TAN 20 by local planning authorities to their LDPs and their Sustainability Appraisals]'.[111] In the end, the making of the Welsh language a material consideration in planning decisions, along with the environment and sustainability, was amongst the 'few changes' to the Bill during its passage through the Assembly,[112] a matter welcomed by the Commissioner.[113] Leaving that aside, it is another aspect to the Commissioner's contribution to the public debate regarding TAN 20 that is of especial interest. Shortly after the demand made by Jamie Bevan of the Welsh Language Society for the First Minister to resign, the Commissioner appears to echo the call made by Bevan in an interview for a television news programme in suggesting that the First Minister relinquish the Welsh language policy portfolio because 'bod angen darganfod rhywun sy'n gallu rhoi mwy o amser i'r Gymraeg' ('it is necessary to find someone who can give more time to the Welsh language').[114] In the light of the research literature on the relationship between regulators and their sponsors in government, this would appear to be a most remarkable intervention indeed. It would appear to be an exceptional regulator that would survive stating publicly that she or he has no confidence in the sponsoring minister to meet the demands of his or her policy portfolio.

Conclusions

Several concluding remarks can be made here. The first is to assert that any criticism that Welsh language regulation is all at sea must immediately be tempered by the incontrovertible fact that the credibility of the Welsh Language Board as complaint-handling body is hamstrung by its historical performance. Any nostalgia for the Board is completely misplaced in this regard. It would very much appear that the Board prioritised a certain view of promotion over any serious approach to complaint-handling until it was wholly clear that the Welsh government was determined to cause such a regulatory approach to be adopted and to be done with the Board in its bonfire of quangos. The office of the Commissioner as complaint-handling body is wholly necessary and, so far, it retains credibility as a destination for complainants concerned with Welsh language services. However, were the drop in the number of complaints submitted to the Commissioner which occurred between 2013 and 2014 to become a year-on-year trend, then that would be a matter of concern.

Secondly, there is a significant conceptual shift with regard to the function of promotion and how that pertains to the office of the Commissioner during the policy and legislative cycle of the Measure. In the beginning there is a clear distinction between promotion in two types of context, the statutory and the non-statutory, with the Commissioner situated in the former and the government in the latter. This distinction becomes less absolute in the Measure as introduced, in which the Commissioner has a general function to promote the language. There is a further shift again in the Measure as passed, with the promotion of the language in this general sense now becoming a principal aim of the office of the Commissioner. That said, during the course of the Commissioner's appearance before the Communities, Equality and Local Government Committee of the Assembly in November 2013, a senior member of staff of the office asserted to the members of the Committee that '[I]t is the work of the Government's Welsh language unit to undertake promotion work with communities at a grass-roots level; the role of the commissioner is to regulate, make suggestions and to offer advice.'[115] When challenged by Leighton Andrews AM (Labour) as to 'Who owns the role', the Commissioner herself responded that 'every organisation associated with the Welsh language has a responsibility with regard to promotion [...] we all have a responsibility in different ways and we have to collaborate and understand jointly what that means. We should not duplicate, but see this as an opportunity to address gaps.'[116]

Others averred during the legislative cycle that duplication was a risk, and yet both the Commissioner and the government are bound by the current Welsh language regulatory regime to engage in promotion. In addition, while being an agent of the government and a key actor in the implementation of the government's Welsh language policy, the Commissioner is also bound to critique the same policy. The risk here is that the Commissioner may find herself in the unenviable position of voicing opposition to the policy intentions of the government and subsequently finding herself having to implement the very same policy. In addition, when policy advice given, especially if that is given in public, as it were, is not acted upon, this undermines the credibility of the regulator as policy adviser to the government in particular, as the regulator is an agent that is central to the implementation of government policy too – the regulator is an integral part of the policy family and must function as such, and be seen to function as such. In this regard it is useful to turn to certain questions the OECD believe ought to be asked when a regulator has such policy functions, namely: is there an explicit advisory role for regulators in policy development? Are the respective roles of the minister, ministry and regulator in policy development clearly defined and supported by processes to ensure effective collaboration? The research literature is clear: when such a duty falls to the regulator, then policy should be developed with the close involvement of the regulator, and there must be specific mechanisms by which that is to happen. As the OECD puts it,

> The respective roles of the regulator and the Ministry should be clear and agreed. Where the regulator has, for whatever reason, been assigned significant policy activities, their parameters and any channels for communicating advice to the Minister or Ministry should be formally set out.[117]

Policy-making via the media along with role duplication is fraught with numerous dangers. The Framework Agreement between the Commissioner and the government remains underdeveloped in this regard, despite its revision in 2014.[118] In addition, that document does not clearly differentiate between the respective roles of the Commissioner and the government with regard to promotion – to paraphrase one AM, there are two rods fishing in the same pool.

Notes

1. See, for example, the following post on the official blog of the National Assembly for Wales Research Service dated 10 November 2014 and entitled 'Welsh Language Commissioner': *https://assemblyinbrief.wordpress.com/tag/welsh-language-commissioner/*
2. D. Elis-Thomas, 'Dafydd Êl: "rheoleiddio'r Gymraeg yn y gors"', *Golwg*, 30 January (2014), 4–5.
3. Welsh Policy Paper 1, *Potential models and structures* (unpublished paper June 2008), p. 6.
4. Welsh Policy Paper 3, *Commission / Commissioner* (unpublished paper July 2008), p. 6.
5. Welsh Policy Paper 3, p. 16.
6. Welsh Policy Paper 11, *Welsh Language Commissioner and Welsh Language Schemes* (unpublished paper, 2009), pp. 20–4.
7. Welsh Policy Paper 11, p. 20.
8. Welsh Policy Paper 11, p. 20.
9. Welsh Policy Paper 11, pp. 25–6 and 6–7.
10. Welsh Policy Paper 15; *Policy instructions to legal services on the proposed Welsh Language Measure* (unpublished paper, April 2009), p. 7.
11. Welsh Policy Paper 15, p. 11.
12. Welsh Policy Paper 15, p. 12.
13. Welsh Assembly Government, *The Proposed Welsh Language (Wales) Measure 2010. Explanatory Memorandum to the Proposed Welsh Language Wales Measure 2010 4 March 2010* (Cardiff: Welsh Assembly Government, 2010a), pp. 3 and 11.
14. Welsh Assembly Government, *The Proposed Welsh Language (Wales) Measure 2010. Explanatory Memorandum to the Proposed Welsh Language Wales Measure 2010 4 March 2010*, p. 31.
15. Welsh Assembly Government, *The Proposed Welsh Language (Wales) Measure 2010. Explanatory Memorandum to the Proposed Welsh Language Wales Measure 2010 4 March 2010*, p. 46.
16. Welsh Assembly Government, *The Proposed Welsh Language*

(Wales) Measure 2010. Explanatory Memorandum to the Proposed Welsh Language Wales Measure 2010 4 March 2010, p. 39.
17 Emyr Lewis, *Written Evidence*, The proposed Welsh Language (Wales) Measure – Evidence Session 22 April 2010, Legislative Committee 2, the National Assembly for Wales (2010b).
18 Emyr Lewis, *Supplementary Evidence*, The Proposed Welsh Language (Wales) Measure – subsequent to Evidence Session 22 April 2010, Legislative Committee 2, the National Assembly for Wales.
19 Emyr Lewis, *Supplementary Evidence*.
20 Emyr Lewis, *Oral Evidence*, par. 48.
21 Rhodri Morgan, The Proposed Welsh Language (Wales) Measure – Evidence Session 22 April 2010, Legislative Committee 2, the National Assembly for Wales, par. 49.
22 Colin H. Williams, *Written Evidence*, The proposed Welsh Language (Wales) Measure – Evidence Session 22 April 2010, Legislative Committee 2, the National Assembly for Wales.
23 Colin H. Williams, *Oral Evidence*, par. 159.
24 http://www.tbs-sct.gc.ca/pubs_pol/hrpubs/tb_a3/olaannot-eng.asp.
25 http://www.officiallanguages.gc.ca/en/aboutus/mandate.
26 G. Fraser, *Statement to Standing Committee on Official Languages, House of Commons, Parliament of Canada, Evidence Meeting 23, 2nd session, 41st Parliament 8 May 2014.* Published online at: http://openparliament.ca/committees/official-languages/41-2/23/graham-fraser-1/only/. See also OCOL website http://www.officiallanguages.gc.ca/en.
27 Williams, *Oral Evidence*, par. 161.
28 Williams, *Oral Evidence*.
29 Rhodri Morgan, The Proposed Welsh Language (Wales) Measure – Evidence Session 22 April 2010, Legislative Committee 2, the National Assembly for Wales, par. 162.
30 Williams, *Oral Evidence*, par. 163.
31 Williams, *Oral Evidence*, par. 168.
32 P. Ó Flatharta, S. Sandberg and C. H. Williams, *From Act to Action. Implementing Language Legislation in Finland, Ireland and Wales* (2013). Published online at: http//doras.dcu.ie/19655/1/From_Act_to_Action_2014.pdf., p. 59.
33 See Williams's preface in Ó Flatharta, Sandberg and Williams, *From Act to Action*, p. 1.
34 Welsh Assembly Government, *The Proposed Welsh Language (Wales) Measure 2010. Explanatory Memorandum to the Proposed Welsh Language Wales Measure 2010 30 November 2010* (Cardiff: Welsh Assembly Government, 2010b), pp. 3 and 11. See also p. 47.
35 http://wales.gov.uk/topics/welshlanguage/commissioner/?lang=en.

36 Welsh Government, *Welsh Statutory Instruments. 2012 No. 752 (W.102) Welsh language, Wales. The Welsh Language Board (Transfer of Staff, Property, Rights and Liabilities) Order 2012 Explanatory Note* (Cardiff: Welsh Government, 2012a).
37 This was updated on 15 July 2014 with no significant revision regarding the matters to hand here.
38 *Cytundeb fframwaith rhwng Llywodraeth Cymru a Chomisiynydd y Gymraeg* (19 September 2012), p. 4.
39 *Cytundeb fframwaith rhwng Llywodraeth Cymru a Chomisiynydd y Gymraeg* (19 September 2012), p. 1.
40 http://www.comisiynyddygymraeg.org/english/news/Pages/WelshLanguageCommissionertoestablishanObservatorytoconsiderpolicyoptions.aspx.
41 Welsh Language Commissioner, *The Welsh Language Commissioner strategic plan 2013–15* (Cardiff: Welsh Language Commissioner, 2013c), p. 7.
42 Welsh Language Commissioner, *Adroddiad Blynyddol 2013–14. Annual Report 2013–14* (Cardiff: Welsh Language Commissioner, 2014b), p. 7.
43 http://www.golwg360.com/celfyddydau/75643-llyfr-du-yn-dangos-fod-y-gymraeg-yn-dal-i-gael-ei-diystyrru.
44 Welsh Language Commissioner, *Complaints to the Welsh Language Commissioner* (Cardiff: Welsh Language Commissioner, 2012b).
45 Welsh Language Commissioner, *Adroddiad Blynyddol 2012–13. Annual Report 2012–13* (Cardiff: Welsh Language Commissioner, 2013b), p. 47. Note that this activity also included expert training delivered by Queen Mary University, as is noted here: http://ombudsresearch.org.uk/about/375
46 Welsh Language Commissioner, *Adroddiad Blynyddol 2012–13. Annual Report 2012–13*, pp. 47–8.
47 Welsh Language Commissioner, *Adroddiad Blynyddol 2013–14. Annual Report 2013–14* (Cardiff: Welsh Language Commissioner, 2014b), p. 31.
48 British and Irish Ombudsman Association [BIOA], *Guide to Principles of Good Complaint Handling* (Twickenham: BIOA, 2007). Published online at: http://www.ombudsmanassociation.org/docs/BIOAGoodComplaintHandling.pdf.
49 National Consumer Council, *A–Z of Ombudsmen. A Guide to Ombudsman Schemes in Britain and Ireland* (London: National Consumer Council, 1997).
50 J. G. Blodgett, D. J. Hill and S. S. Tax, 'The effects of distributive, procedural and interactional justice on post-complaint behavior', *Journal of Retailing*, 73/2 (1997), 185–210; S. Carl, 'Toward a definition and taxonomy of public sector ombudsmen', *Canadian*

Public Administration, 55/2 (June 2012), 203–22; M. George, C. Graham and L. Lennard, *Complaint Handling: Principles and Best Practice*. Report for energywatch (Centre for Utility Consumer Law, University of Leicester / Gas and Electricity Consumer Council (energywatch), 2007); IFF Research, *NHS Governance of Complaints Handling. Prepared for the Parliamentary and Health Service Ombudsman by IFF Research* (London: IFF Research Ltd, 2013); J. G. Maxham III and R. G. Netemeyer, 'Modeling customer perceptions of complaint handling over time: the effects of perceived justice on satisfaction and intent', *Journal of Retailing*, 78 (2002), 239–52; B. Stauss and W. Seidel, *Complaint Management: The Heart of CRM* (Nashville, TN: South-western Publishing Group, 2004).
51 http://www.publications.parliament.uk/pa/ld200304/ldselect/ldconst/68/68we52htm.
52 J. Elfed Jones, *Dyfroedd dyfnion. Hunangofiant John Elfed* (Talybont: y Lolfa, 2013), p.142; M. Prys Jones, 'Neb yno i hyrwyddo'r iaith', *Golwg*, 14 November (2013), 4; Elis-Thomas, 'Dafydd Êl: "rheoleiddio'r Gymraeg yn y gors"'.
53 V. Bondy and A. Le Sueur, *Designing Redress: A Study about Grievances against Public Bodies. Queen Mary University of London, School of Law, Legal Studies Research Paper no. 121/2012* (London: Public Law Project, 2012), pp. 13, 37 and 44–6.
54 Bondy and Le Sueur, *Designing Redress*, p. 13.
55 Welsh Language Board, *Annual Report 2008–09* (Cardiff: Welsh Language Board, 2009), p. 9.
56 Welsh Language Board, *Annual Report 2008–09*, p. 7.
57 Welsh Language Board, *Annual Report 2008–09*, p. 60.
58 Welsh Language Board, *Annual Report 2008–09*, p. 60.
59 http://www.coimisineir.ie.
60 Irish Language Commissioner, *Annual Report 2005–6* (An Spidéal: An Coimisinéir Teanga, 2006), p. 27.
61 Irish Language Commissioner, *Annual Report 2005–6*, p. 5.
62 Irish Language Commissioner, *Annual Report 2005–6*, p. 36.
63 See, for example, Irish Language Commissioner, *Annual Report 2006–7* (An Spidéal: An Coimisinéir Teanga, 2007), p. 35.
64 OCOL, *Two Official Languages. One Common Space. Annual Report 2008–2009. 40th Anniversary of the Official Languages Act* (Ottawa: Minister of the Public Works and Government Services Canada, 2009).
65 As announced on the Commissioner's website on 22 December 2014: http://www.comisiynyddygymraeg.org/English/News/Pages/Commissioner-to-conduct-a-review-of-Welsh-language-services-by-banks.aspx.

66 *http://www.comisiynyddygymraeg.org/English/News/Pages/Commissioner-to-conduct-a-review-of-Welsh-language-services-by-banks.aspx*. Also, elsewhere the Commissioner is quoted as claiming that this evidence demonstrated that this was a matter of concern to 'a large number of people' ('nifer helaeth o bobl') (*Golwg*, 29 January 2015).

67 Welsh Language Commissioner, *Statutory review of the Welsh language services of high street banks in Wales* (Cardiff: Welsh Language Commissioner, 2015b).

68 See, for example: *http://www.comisiynyddygymraeg.org/english/news/Pages/Following-a-decline,-Commissioner-recommends-a-way-ahead-for-banks.aspx*. This also made the front page headline of the Welsh language press, for example, *Y Cymro*, 1 May 2015.

69 Welsh Language Commissioner, *Statutory review of the Welsh language services of high street banks in Wales*, p. 23.

70 Welsh Language Commissioner, *Statutory review of the Welsh language services of high street banks in Wales*, p. 3.

71 Of course, as we shall see in chapter 7 of this text, the Welsh language is not an official language in Wales; rather, it has official status, an altogether different state of affairs.

72 Welsh Language Commissioner, *Adroddiad Blynyddol 2012–13. Annual Report 2012–13*, p. 51.

73 Welsh Language Commissioner, *Adroddiad Blynyddol 2012–13. Annual Report 2012–13*, p. 51.

74 Welsh Language Commissioner, *Adroddiad Blynyddol 2013-14. Annual Report 2013–14*, p. 49.

75 The material is entitled 'Banks – remarks and evidence for the attention of the Welsh Language Commissioner' ('Banciau – sylwadau a thystiolaeth at sylw Comisiynydd y Gymraeg'). See: *http://cymdeithas.org/dogfen/banciau-sylwadau-thystiolaeth-sylw-comisiynydd-y-gymraeg*.

76 *http://dailywales.net/2015/04/29/banks-should-be-forced-to-provide-welsh-language-services/*; *http://golwg360.cymru/newyddion/cymru/184929-angen-i-fanciau-gael-eu-cynnwys-dan-ddeddfwriaeth-iaith*; *https://cy-gb.facebook.com/cymdeithas/posts/874710339267717*.

77 *http://news.bbc.co.uk/welsh/hi/newsid_9180000/newsid_9186400/9186495.stm*.

78 From 1 April 2014 until the Welsh Language Society's e-mail of 17 November 2014 the Commissioner's office had received 11 complaints about banks. Very crudely speaking, that is an average of around 1.5 complaints per month.

79 OECD, *OECD Best Practice Principles for Regulatory Policy. The Governance of Regulators* (OECD Publishing, 2014), p. 37.

Published online at: http://www.oecd-ilibrary.org/governance/the-governance-of-regulators_9789264209015-en.

80 See, for example, P. Giddings, 'The Parliamentary Ombudsman: A classical watchdog', in O. Gay and B. K. Wintrobe (eds), *Parliament's Watchdogs: At the Crossroads* (London: The Constitution Unit, UCL, 2008), pp. 93–103.

81 K. Verhoest, S. Van Thiel, G. Bouckaert and P. Lægreid (eds), *Government Agencies. Practices and Lessons from 30 Countries* (Houndmills: Palgrave Macmillan, 2012). For the UK in particular see O. James, A. Moseley, N. Petrovsky and G. Goyne, 'United Kingdom', in Verhoest, Van Thiel, Bouckaert and Lægreid (eds), *Government Agencies*, pp. 57–68.

82 See p. 155 in D. Feaver and B. Sheehy, 'The political division of regulatory labour: a legal theory of agency selection', *Oxford Journal of Legal Studies*, 35/1 (2015), 153–77.

83 M. Cahn, 'Institutional and non-institutional actors in the policy process', in S. Z. Theodoulu and M. A. Cahn (eds), *Public Policy: The Essential Readings* (Upper Saddle River, NJ: Pearson, 2012), pp. 199–206.

84 See, for example, P. A. Sabatier and H. C. Jenkins-Smith, *Policy Change and Learning: An Advocacy Coalition Approach* (Westview Press, 1993), and C. M. Weible, P. A. Sabatier, H. C. Jenkins-Smith, D. Nohrstedt, A. D. Henry and P. deLeon, 'A quarter century of the advocacy coalition framework: An introduction to the special issue', *The Policy Studies Journal*, 39/3 (2011), 349–60.

85 See, in particular, the following contributions to N. Verrelli (ed.), *The Role of the Policy Advisor: An Insider's Look* (Kingston: Institute of Intergovernmental Relations, Queen's University, 2008): R. Hrbek, 'The role of expert advisors in the formulation of policy: brief report on the Federal Republic of Germany', pp. 27–33; J. Kincaid, 'Role of expert advisor', pp. 35–8; N. Verrelli, 'The role of experts in policy making', pp. 3–13; and C. Saunders, 'Role of the expert advisor in the formulation of policy, pp. 39–43. See also J. C. Leith, 'The design of policy frameworks and the role of the policy advisor' (conference paper, 'Rationality in public policy: Retrospect and prospect', University of Toronto, November 1998).

86 M. Hajer, 'Policy without polity? Policy analysis and the institutional void', *Policy Sciences*, 36 (2003), 175–95, and P. John, *Local Governance in Western Europe* (London: Sage, 2001).

87 Hajer, 'Policy without polity?', p. 175.

88 J. W. Kingdon, *Agenda, Alternatives and Public Policies* (New York: HarperCollins, 1995).

89 OECD, *Principles for the Governance of Regulators. Public Consultation Draft* (OECD Publishing, 2013), pp. 24 and 28, and OECD, *The Governance of Regulators*, pp. 37 and 30.

90 See, for example, M. Huws, 'Beth wnaeth yr Arsyllfa?', *Golwg*, 1 May (2014b), 15.
91 *http://www.renew.plaidcymru.org/discussion-papers/*.
92 *http://www.bbc.co.uk/programmes/p0174kmh*.
93 See, for example: *http://tafodteifi.blogspot.co.uk/2013/03/sefydlu-ardal-debyg-ir-gaeltacht-yng.html*; *http://glynadda.wordpress.com/2013/04/02/tref-adam-a-gaeltacht-meri/*.
94 The evidence given by the Commissioner to the Silk Commission, while influential with regard to the Births and Deaths Registration Act 1953, the Cremation Regulations 2008 (England and Wales) and the Regulation of Marriages Regulations (Welsh Language) 1999 (Welsh Language Commissioner, 2013c, p. 6; Commission on Devolution in Wales, 2014, pp. 133–4), appears rather confused with regard to the UK government, namely: 'The Welsh Language Commissioner stated that the UK Government had a statutory requirement in relation to the Welsh Language Scheme' (Commission on Devolution in Wales, *Oral Evidence Session*, 5 September 2013, p. 3). A further complication is that the Commissioner gave oral evidence as a part of a 'Commissioners' session', together with the Children's Commissioner, the Older People's Commissioner and the Equality and Human Rights Commission, wrongly implying a similarity of function. The Welsh Language Commissioner is the only regulator amongst them.
95 National Assembly for Wales, Research Service, *Social Services and Well-being (Wales) Bill Summary of Changes at Stage 2* (Cardiff: National Assembly for Wales, 2013), p. 1.
96 Welsh Government, *Social Services and Well-being (Wales) Bill Explanatory Memorandum incorporating the Regulatory Impact Assessment and Explanatory Notes January 2014* (Cardiff: Welsh Government, 2014d), pp. 6–7.
97 Welsh Government, *Social Services and Well-being (Wales) Bill Explanatory Memorandum incorporating the Regulatory Impact Assessment and Explanatory Notes January 2013* (Cardiff: Welsh Government, 2013), p. 89.
98 For the Bill, see: *http://wales.gov.uk/topics/planning/planningresearch/planningreview/billtimeline/?lang=en*.
99 For TAN 20 see: *http://wales.gov.uk/topics/planning/policy/tans/planning-and-the-welsh-language/?lang=en*. For the Bill and TAN 20 in context, as of July 2014, see: *http://wales.gov.uk/topics/planning/policy/ppw/?lang=en*.
100 *http://www.rtpi.org.uk/the-rtpi-near-you/rtpi-cymru/events/previous-events/cynllunio-ar-iaith-gymraeg-planning-and-the-welsh-language/*.
101 *http://www.comisiynyddygymraeg.org/English/News/Pages/The-Welsh-language-at-the-heart-of-policy.aspx*.

102 http://www.comisiynyddygymraeg.org/English/News/Pages/One-year-in-action---launch-of-the-Welsh-Language-Commissioner's-first-Annual-Report.aspx.
103 http://www.comisiynyddygymraeg.org/English/News/Pages/The-Welsh-Language-Commissioner's-response-to-the-TAN-20-announcement.aspx.
104 http://www.comisiynyddygymraeg.org/English/News/Pages/Welsh-Language-Commissioner-asks-further-questions-about-the-Welsh-language-and-planning.aspx.
105 http://www.planningresource.co.uk/article/1216509/welsh-assembly-reveals-language-policy.
106 http://www.golwg360.com/newyddion/cymru/124151-cyhoeddi-canllawiau-newydd-ar-gynllunio-a-r-gymraeg.
107 http://www.comisiynyddygymraeg.org/english/news/Pages/The-Planning-Bill-needs-to-secure-the-status-of-the-Welsh-language.aspx.
108 Jamie Bevan, quoted by R. Misstear, 'Warning that Welsh Government's Planning Bill will only centralise decisions', *Walesonline*, 6 October 2014. Available online at: http://www.walesonline.co.uk/news/wales-news/warning-welsh-governments-planning-bill-7890683.
109 Oral evidence given by Dyfan Sion with Meri Huws to the National Assembly for Wales, Constitutional and Legislative Affairs Committee, 9 February 2015, par. 116. See: http://www.senedd.assembly.wales/ieListDocuments.aspx?CId=219&MId=2595&Ver=4.
110 See, for example, the research and scientific evidence functions of the Environment Agency. This body is a regulator styled as a Non-Departmental Public Body and has as its sponsoring UK government department the Department for Environment, Food and Rural Affairs: https://www.gov.uk/government/organisations/environment-agency/about/research; https://www.gov.uk/government/uploads/system/uploads/attachment_data/file/421578/EA_Organisation_Chart_April_2015.pdf.
111 C. Sargeant, *Written statement – Technical Advice Note 20: Planning and the Welsh Language*, 9 October 2013. Published online at: http://wales.gov.uk/about/cabinet/cabinetstatements/2013/tan20/?lang=en.
112 http://www.planningresource.co.uk/article/1347917/welsh-assembly-passes-new-planning-laws.
113 http://www.comisiynyddygymraeg.org/English/News/Pages/The-Planning-Bill.aspx.
114 http://www.bbc.co.uk/cymrufyw/2985566767.
115 Gwyn Williams, *Meeting 14 November 2013*, the Communities, Equality and Local Government Committee, National Assembly for Wales, par. 62.

116 Meri Huws, *Meeting 14 November 2013*, the Communities, Equality and Local Government Committee, National Assembly for Wales, par. 95.
117 OECD, *The Governance of Regulators*, p. 38.
118 *Cytundeb fframwaith rhwng Llywodraeth Cymru a Chomisiynydd y Gymraeg* (2012), and *Cytundeb fframwaith rhwng Llywodraeth Cymru a Chomisiynydd y Gymraeg* (2014).

6 THE CROWN, MINISTERS OF THE CROWN AND CROWN BODIES

Introduction
The purpose of this chapter is to highlight a number of key issues with regard to the Crown, Ministers of the Crown and Crown bodies,[1] and the current Welsh language regulatory regime. The relationship between two organisations in particular, both of which are broadly understood to be Crown bodies, and the law pertaining to the Welsh language provide the axes around which much of this chapter turns. They are National Savings and Investments (henceforth NS&I) and the National Assembly for Wales Commission. These two cases bring to the fore, in very different ways, a range of complexities and contradictions as regards the implementation of the Welsh Language Act 1993 and the Welsh Language (Wales) Measure 2011 in relation to 'the Crown'. These complexities and contradictions have implications for the current Welsh language legislative framework, the UK ministerial 'veto' and regulatory practice.

Policy cycle discussion, recommendation and instruction (June 2008–April 2009)
During the early stage of the policy cycle it is noted that 'there are issues (for instance, the interaction between Crown Ministers and the framework) which will need more detailed consideration' and 'Particular difficulties might also arise in relation to negotiating with other Crown Ministers.'[2] It is noted in another paper during this stage that the Welsh Language Board perceived there to be problems

regarding enforcement under the Welsh Language Act 1993 in relation to Ministers of the Crown and Crown bodies, leading to the author of that paper to suggest that, in fact, Crown bodies operate under a separate regulatory regime under the 1993 Act.[3] It is also noted in this paper that under the Government of Wales Act 2006, the Welsh Assembly has no power to remove or modify any function of a Minister of the Crown, other than that the Secretary of State consents to it.[4] In addition, the paper differentiates between Ministers of the Crown (e.g. UK government department) and Crown bodies (e.g. HMRC), asserting that the latter term is used in the 1993 Act and, significantly to the mind of the author of the policy paper, concludes that it is the wider term of the two.[5] In actual fact, the 1993 Act uses the terms 'Persons acting on behalf of the Crown' and 'any person acting as the servant or agent of the Crown' in the section entitled 'The Crown' (Welsh Language Act 1993, § 21). Thus, the paper asserts that Ministers of the Crown are more privileged, being exempted from the reach of the Assembly under the Government of Wales Act 2006, than are Crown bodies.[6] Thus, the specific policy advice at this point was that 'Negotiations will need to take place promptly if Ministers wish to pursue the option of ensuring that Ministers of the Crown are subject to the same regulatory framework as other organizations.'[7] It is noted in the Appendix to that paper, by way of informative gloss, that the Equality Act applies to Ministers of the Crown.[8]

In the context of preparing for formal dialogue with Whitehall regarding the LCO it seems to quickly have become clearer that Ministers of the Crown would be protected by the Secretary of State, whose 'consent' would, in all likelihood, be required.[9] It had been agreed that officials would ask the question of Whitehall as to 'whether the LCO could confer competence on the National Assembly to confer or impose new functions or duties on Ministers of the Crown'.[10] Clearly, the answer to that question was 'No, except with the consent of the Secretary of State'. It was determined, therefore, that Ministers of the Crown would be beyond the scope of the LCO:[11] 'Although it is a policy aim to ensure that the provisions within a Measure apply to Ministers of the Crown, these will fall outside the LCO unless agreement is reached with Whitehall regarding their inclusion.'[12] This fact was also noted at that time by Ward in an advice note to MPs at Westminster, where it is stated simply,

> The 1993 Act does not apply to Crown bodies, although UK Government departments and public bodies have schemes on a voluntary basis. The general principle, of course, is that the Welsh Assembly, even when it gains legislative competence in an area hitherto reserved to Westminster, can only make legislation having application in Wales.[13]

Ward then quotes from the Welsh government's Explanatory Memorandum for the LCO: 'The Welsh Ministers intend to require Crown bodies, including Ministers of the Crown, to comply with broadly the same duties as all other public bodies, where the Secretary of State consents.'[14] The Explanatory Memorandum makes it clear, in some detail, that the consent of the Secretary of State will be central to engaging with Ministers of the Crown with the Welsh language regulatory regime.[15]

At a later stage of the policy cycle, in April 2009, it is noted in the policy instruction paperwork, in 'introduction and context' with regard to 'Welsh Language Schemes and Standards', that under the 1993 Act, 'the Board [Welsh Language Board] has no powers to compel Crown bodies to prepare schemes and, as such, often finding itself in a weak negotiating position'.[16] In the section entitled 'detailed instructions – Welsh Language Schemes' of the same policy paper it is noted that provision should be made to enable 'Ministers of the Crown and other persons acting as servant or agents of the Crown to be named and placed under duties [...] to the extent that they fall within the scope of the proposed Welsh Language LCO'.[17] It is noted in this section also that:

> Lawyers will need to consider how Ministers of the Crown should have schemes, or amendments to schemes, imposed on them should they and the Commissioner fail to reach agreement with regard to their preparation. For other persons (including Crown bodies, but excepting Ministers of the Crown), Welsh Ministers will be able to impose schemes on them by following a procedure as set out in section 14 of the Welsh Language Act 1993.[18]

In making this differentiation, it is understood in this paper that Minsters of the Crown are beyond the authoritative reach of the

Assembly, while Crown bodies are not and may indeed, therefore, be imposed upon by Welsh Ministers.

It is noted elsewhere in this policy paper, when explaining 'legislative context' in relation to 'enforcement and remedies', that the 1993 Act has 'limited impact on Crown bodies' (including the Assembly Government). In particular, s.20 does not cover Crown bodies. Whilst it is possible to conduct an investigation into a Crown body, it is not possible to pursue provisions under s.20 of the Act against a Crown body. It could be argued that there are three regulatory regimes in operation under the existing legislation: one for public bodies; another for Crown bodies; and a third for organisations which voluntarily prepare language schemes.[19] Section 20 of the 1993 Act refers to Directions by the Secretary of State – the power of mandamus. This is the case because constitutional theory holds that the Crown cannot be divided against itself. Note that the 1993 Act does not differentiate between Ministers of the Crown and Crown bodies – the section is entitled 'The Crown' and is explained in the marginalia as pertaining to 'Persons acting on behalf of the Crown' (Welsh Language Act 1993, § 21). Having said all of that, it appears to be significant that neither Ministers of the Crown nor Crown bodies are in fact referred to specifically in the 'policy aims' or in the 'detailed instruction' of this policy instruction paper. In other words, the concerns articulated with regard to persons acting on behalf of the Crown pertain to context-setting, as opposed to robustly informing agenda-setting.

Legislative cycle discussion and determination (March–December 2010)

There was no particular, public reference to the Crown, Ministers of the Crown and Crown bodies at Committee stage during the passage of the proposed Measure through the Assembly. That said, there was significant discussion, apparently in camera, as to whether the National Assembly for Wales Commission, as a Crown body, ought to be specifically named in the Measure (Schedule 6) as a person to whom standards may be potentially applicable. There are two whole policy papers on this issue.[20] It is noted in first of these that the civil servants had questioned whether or not the National Assembly for Wales Commission ought to be 'included within a description of person in Schedule 6. Inclusion in Schedules 5 and 6 to the Measure renders the person in question capable of being required to comply with standards.'[21] Significantly, from the point of view of policy, the paper notes that

> The policy intention, when seeking the competence underlying this Measure, was that the categories of person in respect of whom language duties could be subsequently imposed by Measure should be sufficiently widely drawn to capture those persons currently operating schemes under the Welsh Language Act 1993 [. . .] Given that the Commission has had a scheme in place since July 2007, it meets this criterion.[22]

The only recommendation of the paper is as follows:

> It is recommended that a Government amendment be tabled to add the entry 'National Assembly for Wales Commission' to the table in Schedule 6 in order to provide certainty that the policy intention for the Commission to be capable of being required to comply with standards is reflected in the Measure.[23]

This was agreed by the Welsh government and an Amendment (83) was tabled on 5 October 2010. The amendment, however, was withdrawn as it was tabled,[24] and this would seem to have been done so without having been subject to any obvious discussion by the Committee at either of its Stage 2 meetings (14 and 21 October).

This particular issue appears to have snowballed somewhat by November 2010, as it was then subject to a second paper,[25] with a very substantial circulation list at the highest level in Welsh government and crossing key policy domains. The paper was seeking a decision as a matter of urgency (paper dated 18 November, decision needed 23 November) from the Minister and 'members of the Cabinet Committee on Legislation' on the matter, 'as to whether or not the National Assembly for Wales Commission (the Commission) should be added to the table in Schedule 6 to the Proposed Welsh Language (Wales) Measure (the Measure)'.[26] In the paper it is recommended that 'Ministers are invited to agree to table an amendment at

Stage 3 of the National Assembly's scrutiny of the proposed measure in order to add the Commission to the table in Schedule 6.'[27] It is also noted in this second paper that Amendment 83 had been tabled without consulting with the Commission, according to Keith Bush, the Chief Legal Adviser and the Director of Legal Services, adding that as, 'the Commission were going to be introducing its own Measure setting out the Assembly and the Commission's commitment to the Welsh language [. . .] it was inappropriate for the Commission to be included in the Government's Measure.'[28] The Commission asked for the Amendment to be withdrawn and the government did so, 'on the basis that this issue would be discussed with the Commission, with a view to reintroducing the amendments [sic] for consideration at Stage 3'.[29]

It is also noted in the paper that there were arguments for and against and that 'it would be possible to defend either scenario.'[30] The argument of the Commission was that it is not appropriate, 'for a Government appointee to place duties on an elected Assembly, given that the Government is answerable to the Assembly, not vice versa'.[31] The paper draws the arguments together, noting that 'we conclude that the Commission should be added to the table in Schedule 6 to the Government's Measure by Government amendments tabled at Stage 3'.[32] It was also noted that 'Ultimately this is a matter for political judgement but it would clearly be preferable to reach an agreed position on this matter with the Commission,'[33] adding that 'that does not seem possible.'[34] The author of the recommendation anticipates an unwelcoming response on the part of the Commission: 'It seems likely, therefore, that a decision to add the Commission via amendments at Stage 3 will, again, draw a critical response from the Presiding Officer's office.'[35] The government decided against the recommendation.

Implementation and analysis

The Welsh Language Commissioner makes specific reference to Crown bodies in the office's first annual report, where the Commissioner makes the following statement:

> On the last day of March 2013, 39 Welsh language schemes were in operation by Crown bodies. This means that there are

departments in Whitehall which provide services to people in Wales which do not have a Welsh language scheme. The Welsh Language Act 1993 does not make it compulsory for Crown bodies to draw up Welsh language schemes, and it does not give the Commissioner powers to force Crown bodies to comply with Welsh language schemes. In general, the Commissioner's first year of working with Whitehall departments has revealed numerous shortcomings in the Welsh language provisions of Crown bodies. A series of meetings were held between the Welsh Language Commissioner and the Secretary of State for Wales in order to identify opportunities to collaborate to promote the use of Welsh in Whitehall departments. It was agreed in principle to put robust collaboration arrangements in place in the form of a fixed term secondment once the standards had been introduced through Regulations.[36]

The matter of NS&I was highlighted as an unambiguous case in point:

An example of failure to adhere to the core principles of language legislation occurred when one of the Crown agencies, National Savings and Investments, corresponded with the Welsh Language Commissioner in February 2013 noting its intention to terminate its Welsh language scheme on 22 April 2013. The Commissioner replied explaining that there is no provision in the 1993 Welsh Language Act for an organisation to terminate a statutory scheme voluntarily. The Welsh Government wrote to National Savings and Investments noting that Welsh language schemes were to remain in force until standards were introduced.[37]

Also during the first year in office, the Commissioner highlights her concerns, with regard to Crown bodies, in the foreword to her non-statutory consultation on draft standards, that:

It should be noted that Standards can only be imposed on Crown bodies with the consent of the Secretary of State for Wales. Many of the services received by the public in Wales are not devolved. At the time of conducting this consultation, the limitations upon me as Welsh Language Commissioner must be understood with regard to bringing Crown bodies within the remit of Standards. I wish to make my position clear: I am of the view that the Secretary of State for Wales should make arrangements to ensure that anyone in Wales wishing to communicate through the medium of Welsh in their dealings with the UK Government should be able to do so.[38]

The point can be made here, briefly, that it would appear that by this stage the distinction drawn by the policy actors between Crown bodies and Ministers of the Crown is not held to apply; or, at least, it would appear that the Commissioner perceived no such distinction at that time or, perhaps, did not feel it necessary to drawn any such distinction.

Having pursued the case of NS&I via statutory investigation without satisfaction, the Commissioner initiated a judicial review on the matter.[39] Headlines in the popular press at that time, such as 'Comisiynydd y Gymraeg v Llywodraeth Prydain',[40] if taken at face value, would lead one to believe that there was a substantive and complex battle of wills being waged between the Commissioner and 'the Crown'. The Commissioner was clearly of the view that the matter was a high priority, as in her annual report of 2013 she notes that 103 (22%) of complaints received were with regard to Crown bodies. In 2014, 72 complaints (19%) involved Crown bodies[41] (elsewhere in the report (p. 33) the figure given is 88).[42] Having said that, the analysis of the data for 2014 shows that of this body of 'valid' complaints, only 16 met the criteria with regard to breaching the requirements of the pertinent Scheme,[43] basing the action on the following three grounds: (1) 'Having adopted a Welsh Language Scheme under the 1993 Act, NS&I has no legal power to revoke it'; (2) 'NS&I's decision to revoke the Scheme frustrates the legislative purpose of Section 21(5) of the 1993 Act'; (3) 'In the face of NS&I's agreement in the Scheme not to make any changes to it without the approval of the Commissioner, the failure of NS&I to consult with the Commissioner and / or obtain her approval before the decision to withdraw the Scheme was unlawful.'[44] Certain aspects of the case of NS&I are of immediate interest here. The Judgment arrived at by Mr Justice Hickinbottom in relation to the three grounds upon which the Commissioner brought that action was as follows: 'Ground 1 and 2 fail.'[45] The matter of ground 3 is quite nuanced, having several contrastive aspects to it. The Bench found as follows, agreeing with counsel for NS&I (Jones, Lewis being counsel for the Commissioner) on several substantive matters of law:

> NS&I through Mr Jones conceded that the Scheme did give rise to a legitimate expectation that the Commissioner would be consulted before any change to it was made, but he submitted there was no wider legitimate expectation [...] we agree;[46] [...]

> in our judgment, the government's policy upon which the promise not to change the Scheme without the Commissioner's approval was made was not and could not be entrenched: in the light of the statutory provisions, the government was entitled to change it';[47] [...]

> we do not accept Mr Lewis's submission that the Scheme created a legitimate expectation that NS&I would not make any changes to it without obtaining the approval of the Commissioner;[48] [...]

> public bodies, including government departments and Crown bodies, must be able to change policy to fit changing circumstances, including changes in political priorities.[49]

That said, counsel for NS&I conceded that there existed a legitimate expectation in the Commissioner to be consulted, albeit arguing that NS&I had met with this expectation. The Bench found that 'the process fell very far short of proper and lawful consultation'.[50] By process, the Bench means that of consultation regarding Welsh Language Schemes as understood under the Welsh Language Act 1993 and also, in particular, the Pre-Action Protocol for judicial review.[51] Hickinbottom describes this elsewhere in the Judgment as 'the procedural requirements for consultation'.[52] Thus, the Bench notes that 'In conclusion, we have found the decision of NS&I to revoke its Welsh Language Scheme from 22 April 2013 to have been unlawful.'[53]

Following the Judgment, the Commissioner announced to the press that 'Mae hwn yn fuddugoliaeth sylweddol [...] yn ddatganiad bod yna bwer gan y Comisiynydd' ('This is a substantial victory [..

.] a statement that the Commissioner has power').[54] The Commissioner also noted that a member of her office was on secondment at Whitehall in order to

> sicrhau bod adrannau Llywodraeth Prydain yn glynu at eu Cynlluniau Iaith, a fwy na hynny, yn sylweddoli beth fydd yr anghenion i'r dyfodol o dan Mesur y Gymraeg, fydd yn ymestyn y disgwyliadau
>
> ['to ensure that UK Government departments adhere to their Language Schemes, and more than that, realise what future requirements will be under the Measure, which will extend the expectations']

In the second Annual Report the Commissioner asserts that 'the judges declared that National Savings and Investments had acted unlawfully by revoking its Welsh language services'; and also that UK government departments 'cannot revoke Welsh language services on a whim'.[55]

Of course, setting aside the rhetoric, the prosaic reality is that the judicial review confirmed that NS&I has, contrary to the claim of the Commissioner, the legal power to revoke its Welsh Language Scheme. It also confirmed that the Commissioner has no power under the 1993 Act over Ministers of the Crown or Crown bodies. NS&I were found to be at fault in their failure to consult, a substantial breach of statutory protocol, but nothing else. The Commissioner confirmed the right of her office to be consulted when a person acting on behalf of the Crown decides to revoke its Scheme, but she has no power to prevent it. With regard to the matter of 'a whim', Varuhas[56] would seem to be on sure ground when he asserts that it would be an undesirable state of affairs were any court to attempt to scrutinise, as a matter of course, the substantive rationality[57] of a decision of a Minister of the Crown or a Crown body, as opposed to the simple legality of the decision. Given that the first task, with regard to engaging the 'Crown', and Ministers of the Crown certainly, with the Welsh language regulatory regime is one of persuasion, only then to be followed by enforcement, it is not clear that the outcome of the NS&I case will facilitate this persuasion, or whether in fact undermine it. Also, overstating the legal outcome may have the undesirable effect of unreasonably raising the expectations of Welsh speakers while also antagonising the very Ministers of the Crown that the Commissioner must first of all persuade in order to then enforce.

During the course of the judicial review the Welsh Language Board's statutory guidelines on Welsh Language Schemes were subjected to some scrutiny. The pertinent document,[58] published by the Welsh Language Board in 1996, is comprised of two parts. Part 1 of the document is merely advisory, while Part 2 comprises the statutory guidelines themselves. Counsel for NS&I submitted evidence showing that the Board's guidelines ran counter to the 1993 Act in eliding 'Crown organisations' with public bodies in general with regard to changing or amending Schemes. The problem first arises in Part 1 in the sections entitled 'approving schemes' and 'disagreement'. Here, it is simply asserted that Crown organisations will be treated in 'exactly the same way as other public bodies'[59] and, elsewhere in Part 1, that organisations that cannot agree a matter in relation to their Scheme will be subject to the respective powers of the Board and the Secretary of State (now Welsh Ministers) in deciding upon the Scheme.[60] Neither the Board nor the Secretary of State has such powers in relation to Crown organisations under the 1993 Act. With specific regard to the statutory guidelines themselves, the problem relates to the text where it is stated that the, 'organisations may propose amendments under section 16 of the Act [. . .] and The Board will consider each proposal on its merit'.[61] Section 16 of the Act applies only to public bodies – persons acting on behalf of the Crown are explicitly excluded and are subject to completely different terms with regard to making changes. Specifically, in Section 21(4) of the 1993 Act it is clear that Crown bodies do not require the approval of the Board under any circumstances. Simply, the case of NS&I in this regard was that in following guidelines which, although understood to be statutory, were contrary to the 1993 Act, NS&I had been misled.

Noting this, the Bench put this ambiguity to Counsel for the Commissioner so as to ascertain the precise status of the guidelines – in other words, the question was whether the guidelines had been, in fact, approved having been laid before Parliament by the Secretary of State, and also, given the above anomaly, whether they had been subject to challenge. While neither Counsel, in fact, seems to have been in a position to confirm any of this, the Bench took the view in its Judgment that 'That policy guidance must have been approved by the Secretary of State', adding that 'It is still in effect.'[62] In reaching this view, the Bench referred to statements made by the UK government in Parliament that 'Government departments will also submit schemes to the Welsh Language Board just as if the legislation places them under an obligation to do so. These schemes will have regard to the same guidelines as those which apply to all other public bodies.'[63] The Bench asserted that 'The Board took the Government at its word.'[64] Thus, while persons acting on behalf of the Crown were under an obligation to prepare schemes as a result of the UK government's commitment, other public bodies were obliged to do so under the statutory provisions.[65] The result of all of this is that the Bench concluded that NS&I was in a position to take a robust view on the appropriateness of the Board's statutory guidelines itself and, whether it do so or not, NS&I voluntarily bound itself to seeking the approval of the Board (now the Commissioner) prior to making any changes to its Scheme.

Some light can be cast upon the extent to which the Board indeed 'took the Government at its word' by reference to some evidence not presented during the judicial review, as far as the research team can ascertain. Very shortly after the 1993 Act was passed, the Board took legal advice on the interpretation of the 1993 Act with specific regard to 'the significance of ministerial statements made during the passage of the Welsh Language Bill'.[66] Here, legal opinion is given on the weight that might be given to such statements in the light of the case of Pepper v Hart.[67] Counsel stated that a court may take such statements into consideration,

> if genuine uncertainties were to arise as to its interpretation. Otherwise, statements made on behalf of the Government during the passage of the Bill as to the manner in which it was envisaged that the legislation would be implemented are likely to be seen as no more than expressions of intention not having any legal force.[68]

One may conclude from this that in taking the UK government at its word, the Board understood this as an expression of intent 'not having any legal force', but in the event of genuine uncertainty arising, then it could well be a material consideration. This would be consistent with the view expressed recently by Greenberg on the significance of Pepper v Hart.[69]

The developing uncertainty, and indeed unhappiness, of the Board with regard to Crown organisations can be seen in a number of places and the case of NS&I can be seen as the confrontation of the uncertainty. For example, concerns were raised by Jenny Randerson AM, then Minister for Culture, Sport and the Welsh Language,[70] by Alan Pugh AM, Minister for Culture, Sport and the Welsh Language 2003–7,[71] and also by the Board, as follows:

> There is no requirement on Crown bodies (which include government departments and agencies) to prepare a Welsh Language Scheme, although many have already done so voluntarily. The Board is unable to give them a statutory notice to prepare a Scheme, and the Assembly does not have power to direct a Crown body to prepare a Scheme if it rejects the Board's request. In fact, we have to rely on a promise made to Parliament when the Act was introduced, that Crown bodies would prepare Schemes exactly as if the Act made it a requirement. That promise has been supported as a policy by the political parties which have been in power [. . .] It can be seen, therefore, that the Welsh Language Act does not give the Assembly any statutory remit in relation to the Welsh Language Schemes of Crown bodies, and we have to depend on different channels of influence when a problem arises. [. . .] **It now appears inconsistent and insufficient, therefore, that a Crown body 'from outside Wales' cannot be accountable to the Assembly's statutory responsibility for the Welsh language, either under the Welsh Language Act or the Government of Wales Act. We respectfully ask the Commission to consider as part of its review what steps could be taken to correct this anomaly.** Is it possible, for instance, to use powers under Section 22 of the Government of Wales Act to resolve this?[72] [bold in original]

In 2005 Meri Huws, in her first year as Chair of the Board, noted that 'the Board's hold on supervising the preparation and implementation of Language Schemes by Crown bodies is considerably weaker than it is when other public bodies are preparing their Schemes'.[73] Also under her stewardship, the position of Crown bodies was described in a positioning paper by the Board (2006) as a major weakness:

> We need clarity and consistency, and the same expectations and measures should be placed on Crown Bodies as on other public bodies [. . .] **It is important that the Assembly attempts to remedy this unacceptable solution before transferring any powers to the proposed regulator.**[74] [bold in original]

In 2007 Huws noted that 'It is sad to have to report that the Foreign Office has refused to prepare a Language Scheme, in spite of the UK government's undertaking in 1993 that every Crown Body would prepare a Scheme under section 21 of the Welsh Language Act.'[75] It was also noted in later reports that the Board conducted statutory investigations into the HM Courts Service in 2009 and HM Revenue and Customs in 2010, noting in both cases that the bodies did not comply with the recommendations made by the Board and that neither could be compelled to do so, as they are Crown bodies.

Leaving aside the historical concerns, not to say confusion, of the Welsh Language Board on the issue of the Crown, further complexity is also apparent. Clearly the Commissioner now recognises the intention of the architects of the 2011 Measure that Crown bodies other than Minsters of the Crown be brought within the scope of the Measure, given that certain 'government departments', including NS&I, along with a range of persons exercising functions 'on behalf of the Crown', are named in Round 3 of the Standards Investigations to be conducted by the Commissioner from May 2015.[76] Why pursue NS&I if the Commissioner understood that it would be subject to Standards in any case, and have no choice in that matter? The naming of NS&I here raises another issue. In accordance with UK constitutional conventions that the Crown cannot be bound unless such a bind was expressly stated in the Act[77] and where the Crown is bound by legislation, such as under the National Health Service and Community Care Act 1990 (s.60) and the Environmental Protection Act 1990 (s.159), it is expressly so.[78] While it is bound by health and safety legislation, the Crown enjoys the privilege of Crown immunity[79] from the enforcement powers of the HSE.[80] Failure on the part of the Crown to 'comply with standards [. . .] will open it to proceedings for a declaration of non-compliance, rather than criminal prosecution,'[81] and in those particular cases in which Crown immunity does not apply it has been expressly removed.[82]

Intriguingly, the National Assembly for Wales Commission made such a bind in 2007. Very briefly, the Commission, as a body with Crown status (National Assembly for Wales Commission (Crown Status) (No. 2) Order 2007), adopted a Welsh Language Scheme in 2007 in which it was noted that: 'No changes will be made to this Scheme without the approval of the Welsh Language Board.'[83] In other words, the Commission made the same voluntary bind as NS&I. In 2009 the Commission announced a change of practice with regard to translating 'y Cofnod', the Assembly equivalent of Hansard.[4] The Board intervened, stating that this was in breach of the Scheme, as was noted in the media at the time.[85] The Assembly was advised by Counsel that the Board, in fact, had no jurisdiction in this matter and that the Commission, as a Crown body, was not subject to the regulatory powers of the Board. In other words, the issue at hand bears a strong similarity to the case put by NS&I. In resisting being subject to the Measure and in bringing forward legislation (National Assembly for Wales (Official Languages) Act 2012) subsequent to which the Commission adopted its Official Languages Scheme, the Commission deliberately set itself apart.

It was argued in the Explanatory Memorandum to the 2012 Act that this was 'needed' so as to end 'uncertainties relating to the legal position of the Welsh Language Scheme and to the relationship between the Assembly, the Commission, the Welsh Language Board and Welsh Ministers'[86] and to place the Welsh language duties of the Assembly and the Commission 'on a sound statutory footing', and that 'In line with fundamental constitutional principles, neither the Assembly nor the Commission is subject to [the] new arrangements.'[87] It was explained by the Commission in the associated Scheme that these 'fundamental constitutional principles' are due to:

> [y] sefyllfa gyfansoddiadol arbennig yng Nghymru a'r egwyddor gyfansoddiadol sylfaenol y dylai Gweinidogion Cymru fod yn atebol i'r Cynulliad yn hytrach na'r gwrthwyneb[88]
>
> ['the particular constitutional situation in Wales and the basic constitutional principle that the Welsh Ministers ought to be accountable to the Assembly rather than the other way around']

In the Explanatory Memorandum it is further explained that bringing forward the Act and the Scheme

> will make it clear that accountability for the Assembly Commission's bilingual services will be directly to the National Assembly (and therefore to the public) rather than to the Welsh Language Commissioner and Welsh Ministers as in the case of public bodies on whom standards are imposed under the Welsh Language (Wales) Measure 2011.[89]

Briefly, there is no fundamental constitutional principle that elevates the Commission above Welsh Ministers – both enjoy Crown status and are therefore absolutely equivalent in that sense. Ministers are as accountable to the Assembly as is the Commission, yet the former are included within the scope of the Measure. Equally, the Commission could have been included in the Measure. If there was a fundamental constitutional principle causing that to be frustrated, which applied to the Commission as a Crown body and not to Ministers as a person acting on behalf of the Crown, then it is not clear what that principle was, or is. In fact, the argument given by the Commission in the Scheme on the specific constitutional point fails to differentiate between the Assembly, which is the sovereign legislature, and the Commission, which is not, and which is a distinct body with Crown status. As things now stand, the public may bring a complaint about the Commission's Scheme to the Public Services Ombudsman Wales (PSOW), yet the PSOW has no powers of enforcement, merely recommendation. In other words, Welsh citizens have no immediate statutorily binding or legal remedy with regard to the Commission breaching its Scheme. This seems rather anomalous, especially given the wishes of the Assembly to tighten the regulatory regime and also to bring 'the Crown' within the reach of the Commissioner, whether Welsh Ministers, Ministers of the Crown and Crown bodies generally. Indeed, even as a body with Crown status, the Commission would appear to be *sui generis*, set in its own unique Welsh language regulatory regime.

Returning specifically to the case of NS&I and the matter of binding the Crown, the question now arises as to how, through NS&I, the Crown is bound under the 2011 Measure. NS&I is a

Non-Ministerial Department (NMD) according to the UK government.[90] While the relationship between NMDs and Ministers is rather ambiguous, whereby while 'the Minister is responsible, and answerable to Parliament for what the NMD does [. . .] the NMD does not answer directly to a Government Minister'[91] and they have limited accountability to Parliament,[92] it remains the case that a ministerial department 'must' remain responsible for the body so that a Minister can account for that NMD to Parliament.[93] With regards its own relationship to government and Parliament, NS&I describe this as follows: it is 'accountable to HM Treasury', and the Chancellor of the Exchequer, no less, is 'answerable' to Parliament for its activities and so forth.[94] Thus, NS&I is an NMD that has 'a very clear Ministerial relationship and see[s] this as their principal accountability route to Parliament.'[95] The Institute for Government also notes that 'The Treasury [. . .] has two representatives on the board of NS&I – possibly as far removed from the notion of independence from departments as it's possible to manage'.[96] In addition, and more confusingly still, since 1996 NS&I has had executive agency status, implying close ministerial control and involvement. Such bodies are normatively regarded as being a part of a ministerial department, with the Minister being 'fully accountable'[97] for them. Seeing as a Minister of the Crown is responsible and accountable for NS&I, how then, does the ministerial 'veto' under the 2011 Measure not apply to NS&I? The same applies to other organisations named by the Commissioner in Round 3, such as HMRC, which is described by the Institute for Government as 'clearly [a] ministerial department in all but name'.[98] The Institute for Government rightly points to the confusion of accountability in relation to NMDs and other arm's length bodies, and this is inherent to the Measure. Thus, in the case of NS&I it would appear that the Commissioner is able to impose regulatory standards upon an organisation for which a Minister of the Crown is both responsible and accountable to Parliament without first obtaining the approval of the responsible Minister – in other words, the Commissioner may impose upon a Minister of the Crown in relation to some of his functions. Yet, according to the Measure the Commissioner cannot impose upon Ministers of the Crown but, rather, must obtain prior approval to do so.

Conclusions

The Welsh language regulatory regime is currently populated by a more diverse range of statutory instruments through which regulatory standards for Welsh language service delivery are set than was the case prior to the 2011 Measure. Many organisations, of course, are subject to Standards, and others will be brought within their scope. However, not only will some Schemes continue in operation – the Commissioner has also recognised as much[99] – but a wholly distinctive regulatory regime has been created for one organisation on its own. Specifically, the Wales Office confirmed in early 2015 that Welsh Language Schemes, as framed by the 1993 Act, form the basis for the delivery of Welsh language services for UK government departments[100] and will continue to do so as, 'The UK Government is committed to developing and enhancing its Welsh language provision by ensuring a more rigorous application of Welsh language schemes under the 1993 Act.'[101] Nowhere is it stated that the UK government is minded to consider that its Ministers approve that they be brought within the scope of the Measure and be subject to the authority of the Commissioner and Welsh Language Standards. Thus, the conclusion of the Bench with regards the case of NS&I that '*public bodies, including government departments and Crown bodies, must be able to change policy to fit changing circumstances, including changes in political priorities*'[102] (author's italics) will certainly hold. In addition, given the fact that Schemes are still in force, and many are likely to remain in force for some time yet, and given the doubt cast upon the content of the Board's statutory guidelines from 1996 by the Bench during the course of the judicial review, it would appear to be worth attending to their revision. The diversity of the regulatory regime is also reflected in the fact that the Commission of the National Assembly for Wales, despite its status as a Crown body, does not fall within the scope of the Measure, as do certain other 'Welsh' Crown bodies, neither may it be brought within the scope of the Measure with the consent of the Secretary of State, as with 'non-Welsh' Crown bodies. It has instead its own Official Languages Scheme. The Assembly could have determined that the Commission, as a body apart from the Assembly itself, fall within the scope of the Measure, but that it did not do so means that the Commission has a Welsh language regulatory regime which is unique. Complaints about the Commission's Scheme may only be dealt with by the PSOW. As regards 'the Crown' in particular and its relationship to the Welsh language in public life, as things currently stand it is sometimes subject to the Commissioner with particular powers under the 2011 Measure, sometimes subject to the Commissioner with other very different powers under the 1993 Act, and sometimes not subject to the Commissioner at all. In other cases it is subject to the powers of the PSOW. This variation suggests that the Welsh language regulatory regime comprises an ad hoc collection of mechanisms rather than a coherent system of administrative justice for Welsh speakers.[103] If there is a constitutional principle at stake here with regard to sovereignty, as argued by the Commission of the National Assembly for Wales, then the present inconsistent and unequal treatment of the Crown would appear to suggest that that principle is currently being frustrated.

Notes

1. For an authoritative list of UK Crown bodies see: http://www.nationalarchives.gov.uk/information-management/re-using-public-sector-information/copyright/uk-crown-bodies/#azl
2. Welsh Policy Paper 1, *Potential models and structures* (unpublished paper, June 2008), pp. 1 and 7.
3. Welsh Policy Paper 2, *Enforcement powers and remedies* (unpublished paper June 2008), p. 4.
4. Welsh Policy Paper 2, *Enforcement powers and remedies*, p. 4.
5. Welsh Policy Paper 2, *Enforcement powers and remedies*, p. 5.
6. Welsh Policy Paper 2, *Enforcement powers and remedies*, p. 5.
7. Welsh Policy Paper 2, *Enforcement powers and remedies*, p. 15.
8. Welsh Policy Paper 2, *Enforcement powers and remedies*, p. 20.
9. Welsh Policy Paper 8, *Future of the Welsh Language Act 1993* (unpublished paper July 2008), p. 3.
10. Welsh Policy Paper 8, *Future of the Welsh Language Act 1993*, p. 5.
11. Welsh Policy Paper 9, *Matters excluded from the LCO* (unpublished paper August 2008), p. 2.
12. Welsh Policy Paper 9, *Matters excluded from the LCO*, p. 2.
13. P. Ward, *The Proposed Welsh Language Legislative Competence Order. Standard Note SN/HA/4973* (London: House of Commons Library, 11 December 2009), p. 10.
14. Ward, *The Proposed Welsh Language Legislative Competence Order*, p. 10.
15. Welsh Assembly Government, *Memorandum from the Welsh Assembly Government. Constitutional Law : Devolution, Wales. The National Assembly for Wales (Legislative Competence) (Welsh*

Language) Order 2009. Proposal for a Legislative Competence Order on the Welsh Language (Cardiff: Welsh Assembly Government, 2009a [January]), pp. 10–11, and also, Welsh Assembly Government, *Memorandum from the Welsh Assembly Government. Constitutional Law: Devolution, Wales. The National Assembly for Wales (Legislative Competence) (Welsh Language) Order 2009. Draft Legislative Competence Order on the Welsh Language* (Cardiff: Welsh Assembly Government, 2009b [October]), pp. 24–6.

16 Welsh Policy Paper 15, *Policy instructions to legal services on the proposed Welsh Language Measure* (unpublished paper, April 2009), p. 27.
17 Welsh Policy Paper 15, p. 29.
18 Welsh Policy Paper 15, p. 35.
19 Welsh Policy Paper 15, p. 50.
20 Welsh Policy Paper 31, *Addition of National Assembly for Wales Commissioner to the Schedule 6 table* (unpublished paper 3 September 2010); Welsh Policy Paper 39, *Addition of National Assembly for Wales Commissioner to the Schedule 6 table* (unpublished paper, 18 November 2010).
21 Welsh Policy Paper 31, p. 1.
22 Welsh Policy Paper 31, p. 1.
23 Welsh Policy Paper 31, p. 2.
24 National Assembly for Wales, *Notice of Amendments. Tabled 5 October 2010. Proposed Welsh Language (Wales) Measure* (Cardiff: National Assembly for Wales, 2010c), p. 30.
25 Welsh Policy Paper 39.
26 Welsh Policy Paper 39, p. 1.
27 Welsh Policy Paper 39, p. 1.
28 Welsh Policy Paper 39, p. 2.
29 Welsh Policy Paper 39, p. 2.
30 Welsh Policy Paper 39, p. 2.
31 Welsh Policy Paper 39, p. 3.
32 Welsh Policy Paper 39, p. 5.
33 Welsh Policy Paper 39, p. 5.
34 Welsh Policy Paper 39, p. 5.
35 Welsh Policy Paper 39, p. 3.
36 Welsh Language Commissioner, *Adroddiad Blynyddol 2012–13. Annual Report 2012–13* (Cardiff: Welsh Language Commissioner, 2013b), p. 45.
37 Welsh Language Commissioner, *Adroddiad Blynyddol 2012–13. Annual Report 2012–13*, p. 45.
38 Welsh Language Commissioner, *Standards and the Welsh language: what are your views?* (Cardiff: Welsh Language Commissioner, 2012a), p. 7.

39 Welsh Language Commissioner, *Adroddiad Blynyddol 2013–14. Annual Report 2013–14* (Cardiff: Welsh Language Commissioner, 2014b), p. 7.
40 B. Thomas, 'Comisiynydd y Gymraeg v Llywodraeth Prydain', *Golwg*, 16 October (2014b), p. 4.
41 Welsh Language Commissioner, *Adroddiad Blynyddol 2013–14. Annual Report 2013–14*, p. 31.
42 Welsh Language Commissioner, *Adroddiad Blynyddol 2013–14. Annual Report 2013–14*, p. 33.
43 Welsh Language Commissioner, *Adroddiad Blynyddol 2013–14. Annual Report 2013–14*, p. 33.
44 Mr Justice G. Hickinbottom, *Neutral Citation Number [2014] EWHC 488 (Admin) Case No CO/9841/2013 in the High Court of Justice, Queen's Bench Division, Divisional Court, Mr Justice Hickinbottom & His Honour Judge Milwyn Jarman QC. Between The Queen on the application of the Welsh Language Commissioner and National Savings and Investments and the Welsh Ministers Hearing date 19 February 2014, Judgment date 6 March 2014*, pars 42–3.
45 Hickinbottom, *Neutral Citation Number [2014] EWHC 488 (Admin) Case No CO/9841/2013 in the High Court of Justice*, par. 55.
46 Hickinbottom, *Neutral Citation Number [2014] EWHC 488 (Admin) Case No CO/9841/2013 in the High Court of Justice*, par. 60.
47 Hickinbottom, *Neutral Citation Number [2014] EWHC 488 (Admin) Case No CO/9841/2013 in the High Court of Justice*, par. 62.
48 Hickinbottom, *Neutral Citation Number [2014] EWHC 488 (Admin) Case No CO/9841/2013 in the High Court of Justice*, par. 63.
49 Hickinbottom, *Neutral Citation Number [2014] EWHC 488 (Admin) Case No CO/9841/2013 in the High Court of Justice*, par. 62.
50 Hickinbottom, *Neutral Citation Number [2014] EWHC 488 (Admin) Case No CO/9841/2013 in the High Court of Justice*, par. 72.
51 See also: http://www.justice.gov.uk/courts/procedure-rules/civil/protocol/prot_jrv.
52 Hickinbottom, *Neutral Citation Number [2014] EWHC 488 (Admin) Case No CO/9841/2013 in the High Court of Justice*, par. 70.
53 Hickinbottom, *Neutral Citation Number [2014] EWHC 488 (Admin) Case No CO/9841/2013 in the High Court of Justice*, par. 84.
54 *Golwg*, 20 March (2014), 13, under the headline '1–0 i'r Comisiynydd'.
55 Welsh Language Commissioner, *Adroddiad Blynyddol 2013–14. Annual Report 2013–14*, p. 7.
56 J. N. E. Varuhas, 'Governmental rejections of Ombudsman findings: what role for the Courts?', *The Modern Law Review Limited*, 72/1 (2009), 91–115.

57 Such a decision may only be quashed if it is, to paraphrase Varuhas ('Governmental rejections of Ombudsman findings, p. 110), outrageous in its defiance of logic or absurd. See also the concept of *Wednesbury reasonableness* – Associated Provincial Picture Houses Ltd v Wednesbury Corporation [1948] 1 KB 223, 229; CCSU v Minister for the Civil Service [1985] AC 374, 410.

58 Welsh Language Board, *Welsh Language Schemes. Their preparation and approval in accordance with the Welsh Language Act 1993* (Cardiff: Welsh Language Board, 1996).

59 Welsh Language Board, *Welsh Language Schemes. Their preparation and approval in accordance with the Welsh Language Act 1993*, par. 1.22.

60 Welsh Language Board, *Welsh Language Schemes. Their preparation and approval in accordance with the Welsh Language Act 1993*, pars 1.36 and 1.37.

61 Welsh Language Board, *Welsh Language Schemes. Their preparation and approval in accordance with the Welsh Language Act 1993*, p. 20.

62 Hickinbottom, *Neutral Citation Number [2014] EWHC 488 (Admin) Case No CO/9841/2013 in the High Court of Justice*, par. 15. Since the judicial review, and despite the fact that it is noted in the Welsh Language Board document that, 'The Board's statutory guidelines issued under Section 9 of the Act are included in Part II of this document' (p. 7), the research team have garnered anecdotal evidence from a number of authoritative sources close to the case of NS&I and the now defunct Welsh Language Board asserting that they are not the statutory guidelines, as approved by the Secretary of State, and that the proper statutory guidelines comprise a single sheet, A4-sized document 'appended to the 1993 Act sometime during 1995'. The research team has been unable to uncover evidence of the latter. The sources asserted that this was how the Board was able to 'do things for the language' that would otherwise have been difficult; the implication is that the Board was engaged in regulatory activism.

63 Hickinbottom, *Neutral Citation Number [2014] EWHC 488 (Admin) Case No CO/9841/2013 in the High Court of Justice*, par. 14.

64 Hickinbottom, *Neutral Citation Number [2014] EWHC 488 (Admin) Case No CO/9841/2013 in the High Court of Justice*, par. 15.

65 Hickinbottom, *Neutral Citation Number [2014] EWHC 488 (Admin) Case No CO/9841/2013 in the High Court of Justice*, par. 15.

66 Welsh Policy Paper 45, *Sherwood & Co – Welsh Language Board – Note on interpretation of Welsh Language Act 1993* (unpublished paper, 1994), p. 5.

67 Pepper v Hart [1992] 3 WLR 0132 [1993], 1 All ER 42, HL (E).

68 Welsh Policy Paper 45, p. 5.
69 'It is now not only statutory codes and guidance to which the courts will have regard in applying and determining the meaning of legislative text. For many years, the range of material to which the courts are prepared to have regard has been expanding. Pepper v Hart (the decision by which the courts finally allowed themselves to have regard to Hansard in construing Acts), far from being a watershed as some predicted, can be seen as a mere pebble forming part of a general avalanche of new kinds of material which the courts will consider' (D. Greenberg, 'Welsh devolution. Legal information and aspects of devolution', *Legal Information Management*, 13 (2013), 134–8, p. 137).
70 Richard Commission, *Annex 1* (Richard Commission, 2002a). Published online at: *http://webarchive.nationalarchives.gov. uk/20090807221003/http://www.richardcommission.gov.uk/content/ evidence/written/jranderson/index.htm*; Richard Commission, *Evidence of Welsh Assembly Government Minister for Culture Jenny Randerson* (Richard Commission, 2002b). Published online at: *http://webarchive.nationalarchives.gov.uk/20090807221003/http:// www.richardcommission.gov.uk/content/evidence/oral/randersonj/ index-e.htm*.
71 Richard Commission, *Alan Pugh AM: Minister for Culture, Welsh Language and Sport* (Richard Commission, 2003a). Published online at: *http://webarchive.nationalarchives.gov. uk/20090807221003/http://www.richardcommission.gov.uk/content/ evidence/written/pugha/index-e.htm*.
72 Richard Commission, *Paper from the Welsh Language Board to the Commission on the Powers and Electoral Arrangements of the National Assembly for Wales – March 2003* (Richard Commission, 2003b). Published online at: *http://webarchive.nationalarchives.gov. uk/20090807221003/http://www.richardcommission.gov.uk/content/ evidence/written/wlb/index.htm*.
73 Welsh Language Board, *Annual Report 2004–5* (Cardiff: Welsh Language Board, 2005), p. 3.
74 Welsh Language Board, *The legislative position of the Welsh language. A position paper by the Welsh Language Board* (Cardiff: Welsh Language Board, 2006), pp. 8–9.
75 Welsh Language Board, *Annual Report 2006–7* (Cardiff: Welsh Language Board, 2007), p. 40.
76 Welsh Language Commissioner, *Schedule for carrying out standards investigations [January 2015]* (Cardiff: Welsh Language Commissioner, 2015c).
77 Office of the Parliamentary Counsel, *Crown Application* (London: Office of the Parliamentary Counsel, 2013a). Published

online at: *https://www.gov.uk/government/uploads/system/ uploads/attachment_data/file/193143/Crown_Application_ pamphlet_12-03-13.pdf.*

78 P. Leyland, *Constitution of the UK: A Contextual Analysis* (Oxford: Hart, 2012), p. 99.

79 'on the basis that legislation is made by the Sovereign in Parliament for the regulation of Her subjects and not Herself'; see: *http:// www.publications.parliament.uk/pa/cm200506/cmselect/ cmhaff/540/54014.htm#note242.*

80 *http://www.hse.gov.uk/enforce/enforcementguide/* (previously *http://www.hse.gov.uk/enforce/enforcementguide/investigations/ approving-enforcement.htm*); *http://www.pcs.org.uk/en/resources/ health_and_safety/health_and_safety_legal_summaries/crown_ immunity_and_health_and_safety.cfm.*

81 See p. 1 in M. Sunkin, 'Crown immunity from criminal liability in English law', *Public Law* (2003), 716–29.

82 *http://www.publications.parliament.uk/pa/cm200506/cmselect/ cmhaff/540/54014.htm.*

83 National Assembly for Wales, *Welsh Language Scheme* (Cardiff: National Assembly for Wales, 2007), par. 6.10.

84 The policy change appears to have been agreed at a meeting of the Assembly Commission on 7 July 2009, although the official minutes describe the matters discussed as budgetary issues rather than policy issues. See: *http://www.assemblywales.org/abthome/ abt-nafw/abt-commission/abt-commission-agendas.htm?act=dis&i d=145898&ds=9/2009*. The policy change appears to have become public knowledge by early August 2009. For example: *http://news.bbc.co.uk/welsh/hi/newsid_8180000/newsid_8187800/ 8187875.stm.*

85 *http://news.bbc.co.uk/welsh/hi/newsid_8190000/newsid_8197700/ 8197751.stm.*

86 National Assembly for Wales, *National Assembly for Wales (Official Languages) Bill Explanatory Memorandum* (Cardiff: National Assembly for Wales, 2012a), p. 5.

87 National Assembly for Wales, *National Assembly for Wales (Official Languages) Bill Explanatory Memorandum*, p. 6.

88 National Assembly for Wales, Assembly Commission, *Cynllun Ieithoedd Swyddogol Drafft* (Cardiff: National Assembly for Wales, 2012b), par. 16.

89 National Assembly for Wales, *National Assembly for Wales (Official Languages) Bill Explanatory Memorandum*, par. 12.5.

90 See Cabinet Office, *Categories of Public Bodies: A Guide for Departments* (London: Cabinet Office, 2012). See also: *https://www.gov.uk/government/organisations.*

91 Institute for Government, *The Strange Case of Non-Ministerial Departments* (London: Institute for Government, 2013), pp. 7–8.
92 HM Treasury, *Managing Public Money* (London: HM Treasury, 2013).
93 HM Treasury, *Managing Public Money*, 7.9.2. See also Institute for Government, T*he Strange Case of Non-Ministerial Departments*, p. 7.
94 HM Treasury, *Managing Public Money*, p. 10.
95 HM Treasury, *Managing Public Money*, p. 10.
96 HM Treasury, *Managing Public Money*, p. 11.
97 HM Treasury, *Managing Public Money*, p. 57.
98 HM Treasury, *Managing Public Money*, p. 14.
99 Welsh Language Commissioner, *Llythyr i Jocelyn Davies AC 'Ymchwiliad i ystyried pwerau Ombwdsmon Gwasanaethau Cyhoeddus Cymru'*, dated 20 February 2015 (2015d), p. 4.
100 HM Government, *Powers for a purpose: towards a lasting devolution settlement for Wales* (London: HMSO, 2015), p. 41, par. 2.10.4.
101 HM Government, *Powers for a purpose: towards a lasting devolution settlement for Wales*, par. 2.10.5.
102 Hickinbottom, *Neutral Citation Number [2014] EWHC 488 (Admin) Case No CO/9841/2013 in the High Court of Justice*, p. 62.
103 Bondy and Le Sueur ask this question of systemic coherence of the administrative justice system as a whole (2012, pp. 3–4).

7 | OFFICIAL LANGUAGE

Introduction
One of the key functions of the Welsh Language Commissioner is to 'raise awareness of the official status of the Welsh language in Wales'.[1] Under the Welsh Language (Wales) Measure 2011 (Part 2, § 3) this pertains directly to the 'principal aim of the Commissioner', which is to 'promote and facilitate the use of the Welsh language', and in doing so the Commissioner 'must have regard to the official status which the Welsh language has in Wales'. The official status of the Welsh language was subject to considerable debate during the passing of the Measure and creating the office of the Commissioner. The key question here is what is the meaning of this 'official status', how is it to be interpreted and applied? The purpose of this chapter, therefore, is to highlight a number of key issues arising from the analysis of the full range of research data with regard to (1) conceptions of the official status of language and the term 'official language', in particular to the extent that they are relevant to the Welsh Language (Wales) Measure 2011, and, to a lesser degree, (2) the notion of equality as it pertains to the official status of language.

Policy cycle discussion, recommendation and instruction (June 2008–April 2009)
The starting point for the policy cycle with regard to the matters at hand in this chapter is the *One Wales* governmental programme commitment 'to confirm official status for both Welsh and English'.[2]

Evidence from the early stages of the policy cycle suggests that some actors were of the view that it ought not be too fraught an issue. Welsh Policy Paper 6 noted, significantly, that 'If it is accepted that confirming official status, of itself, does not confer any specific duties or rights, the actual confirmation should not present too many difficulties.'[3] The content of the paper indicated that in reaching this view a number of case studies on official language status were considered, namely the Republic of Ireland, Canada (federal), New Brunswick (Canada), Catalonia (Spain) and the Basque Country (Spain).[4] In the light of these cases, potential examples of legal text confirming the official status of the Welsh language were proffered in the paper, as follows:

> 'Both Welsh and English are official languages of Wales';
>
> 'Welsh is the national language of Wales. English is also an official language of Wales.'

Further, it was argued that the first statement 'would be the easiest way of confirming that both languages have a particular legal status in Wales'.[5] With regard to the second statement, it was asserted that

> This would echo the approach adopted in the Republic of Ireland. The first clause emphasises that Welsh is the language that is distinct to the geographical entity of Wales (Priod iaith[6]) and Wales alone. The second sentence confirms that both Welsh and English are the official languages of Wales.[7]

The remainder of the policy discussion at this stage was with regard to giving effect to official status.

Another policy paper from this stage of the policy cycle noted that

> Consideration will need to be given as to whether the LCO will need to confer powers in relation to the English language. The LCO may need to confer such competence, but only to the extent that they are relevant to defining the position and status of the Welsh language.[8]

It was also noted in this paper that 'The LCO should aim to avoid making any references to issues such as official status [...] although this position might need to be revisited if discussions ensured that the LCO could apply [...] to Ministers of the Crown.'[9] Together, this implies three things: (1) that the status of the Welsh language is, in the minds of some actors related to the UK Parliament, in all likelihood, bound up with that of the English language; (2) that there is a connection of some delicacy between the official status of a language on the one hand and function of Ministers of the Crown on the other; and (3) that the actors based at Westminster are very likely to have a particular sensitivity to questions regarding the statutory recognition, or even declaration, of the official status of any given language.

As it transpired, the LCO did not make use of the term 'official language', but rather it reiterated the Welsh government's commitment to 'seek legislative competence to enable it to bring forward Assembly Measures to confirm official status for both Welsh and English',[10] a fact noted at Westminster.[11] In Ward's policy briefing note for the UK Parliament it was noted that

> arguably, the language has had 'official' recognition since the 1967 Act. However, the debate has been about practical application [...] the 1967 Act was deemed 'toothless' by some and the 1993 Act introduced a 'basis of equality' which means that Welsh has an official status but falls short of the principle of full bilingualism where everything produced by Government is available in both languages.[12]

Ward rightly noted that amendments were tabled during the passage of the Welsh Language Act 1993 aimed at declaring Welsh to be an official language but that these were refused by the government of the day. The government's position was articulated by Lord Ferrers, and it is worth quoting him fully, as follows:

> The Government understand the depth of feeling which many of your lordships have on this – a feeling which is a reflection of that which is prevalent in the Principality. We understand that because confirming the status of the Welsh language in Wales is a prime objective of this Bill. We think, though, that the Bill achieves this by establishing the principle of equality and by

> removing legislative obstacles which would prevent the Welsh language from enjoying equality of status with the English language [. . .] The Government's view is that the official status of the Welsh language should not be dependent upon any single piece of legislation. Its status should be – and is – a reflection of its general position in the statute book and because it has been the everyday language of public administration in many parts of Wales for many years. The whole philosophy behind the Bill has been that the provision of public services in Welsh should be seen as part and parcel of the provision of public services in Wales. The intention is not to establish Welsh as an official language, but to reflect our view that it already is. We are not, therefore, proposing that Welsh language schemes should be drawn up in order to emphasise the status of Welsh as an official language. They will be prepared because Welsh already enjoys official status, and they will simply illustrate how individual public bodies intend to reflect that fact.[13]

Ward noted that during the passage of the Welsh Language Bill some felt that such a declaration would have been useful, not least for courts in the interpretation of the practical meaning of the official status of Welsh:

> Adopting such a clause would have been an expression of the high constitutional status of the language. It would have given a firm purpose to the [1993] Act and provided guidance to the executive and to the courts, when in doubt, about the application of any of its provisions.[14]

During the passage of the LCO, a further policy paper was drafted, this time for the purpose of the anticipated Welsh Language (Wales) Measure 2011, in order to do the following:

> determine what is envisaged by the term 'official status' within the One Wales commitment; address the problems associated with handling the concept of official language within UK/ England and Wales law; and, consider whether the issue of official status for both languages should/could be handled identically within the Measure.[15]

It was noted in this paper that the LCO itself 'makes no direct reference to status',[16] while the accompanying Welsh government Explanatory Memorandum 'merely restates the One Wales commitment, [and] does not elaborate upon what is meant by "official" status'.[17] In other words, the matter having become more nuanced during the LCO process, policy actors now found themselves in the position of having to define the meaning of the official status of a given language for the purpose of the Measure. By now, the policy actors were of the view that a simple declaration in and of itself would be unlikely to have any practical impact on the status of the language, as was demonstrated by the case of the Irish language in the Republic of Ireland being declared the national and first official language under the Constitution of 1937 (Article 8: 1–3).[18] The policy actors read from this case that 'giving an indigenous language official status, without any duties or rights resulting from such status, can have little or no effect on the vitality of that particular language'.[19] They concluded in this paper that it was not until the implementation of the Official Languages Act 2003 that the provision of public services in the Irish language was made a practical and enforceable reality.

It was also argued in this policy paper that the nature of Common Law, as with the jurisdiction of England and Wales, renders making a declaration in and of itself that a language be official pointless. For example:

> General statements in legislation are essentially meaningless and unenforceable in the context of common law jurisdictions. Legislation is the primary source of law in civil law jurisdictions, and it is the responsibility of the Courts to apply abstract rights or principles, such as that of official language status, established in legislation. In common law jurisdictions, such as England and Wales, legislation effectively deals with rights, duties and responsibilities. Therefore, for any definition of official status to be meaningful, it needs to result in rights, duties or responsibilities being placed on individuals or bodies corporate.[20]

Being cognisant of the apparent exceptionality of the case of Scottish Gaelic, for which the stated purpose of the Gaelic Language (Scotland) Act 2005 is to secure 'the status of the Gaelic language as an official language of Scotland',[21] the policy actors asserted in the paper that the reason for this is to be found in the fact that the Scottish legal system is different. As it is 'grounded in un-codified civil law [with] features of common law',[22] therefore such a declaration carries a weight of statutory meaning derived from how Civil Law jurisdictions, generally speaking, function in contrast to Common Law jurisdictions. It was concluded in this paper that

> There is no precise definition [of official language/language status] in *One Wales* and therefore no clear expectation of how official status is to be expressed in the Measure. There is no clear pointer, nor a single/dominant approach to be found in other countries when it comes to designating a language as official. Common law does not appear accommodating and the wording of the LCO presents additional problems when seeking to include the English language within the designation. Consequently it would seem unlikely that a simple line in a measure such as, 'Both Welsh and English are official languages of Wales' would be acceptable in terms of legal drafting.[23]

Instead, it was recommended that 'the issue of official status be addressed by including wording in the Measure to explain how status would be secured through the exercising of functions by a Language Commissioner'.[24] These functions would include, specifically, the placing of duties upon organisations. In other words, by this stage of the policy cycle the matter of 'confirming' the official status of the Welsh language had become fraught with complexity and ambiguity.

By the final stage of the policy cycle official status was defined in the following rather convoluted terms:

> the concept of English and Welsh possessing 'official status' in Wales is intended to refer to the use of those languages in dealings with organisations providing public services of one sort or another, and where there is a distinct 'package' of rights established as a result of duties being placed on persons providing services that can be seen as underpinning the status of the language.[25]

It was also asserted that up until the point at which the paper was being written that a 'well understood legal definition of official status' had not yet been developed, although it was argued that it was possible to identify examples of 'activities' that are within the ambit of the 'general principle of official status', along with those which fall outside of that. It is explained that

> Activities which would typically be seen as reflecting official status include: being able to use the Welsh language in dealings with public authorities; the use of the Welsh language in the National Assembly for Wales; and the use of the Welsh language in the Courts.[26]

Significantly, with regard to the idea of the freedom to use the Welsh language, it was also asserted that 'Activities which fall outside the general principle include: individuals having a private conversation.'[27]

That said, it was asserted that in any case the Welsh language, as with English, already possessed official status despite that not being stated in law,[28] while it was also noted that this was the UK government's position in relation to the matter during the passing of the Welsh Language Act 1993.[29] In short, what this means is that the contentious matter that is at the heart of the official status of a language was conceived of as being to do with the practicalities of public service delivery rather than with legal status; thereby

> the use of the Welsh language in dealings with the state is not a matter which is dependent on specific legal provision. Rather, the practical difficulty which the concept of official status seeks to deal with surrounds the uncertainty which speakers of a minority language like Welsh can face in determining whether or not public organisations are able and willing to conduct business through the medium of Welsh.[30]

Thus, according to this approach to the matter, the resolution to this problem is to be found in attending to the language of the delivery of services rather than to the official status of the language in the statute book.

At the point of policy instruction, the approach taken under the proposed Measure was explained as follows: 'in a common law jurisdiction such as that which is in place in England and Wales an abstract concept such as official status will have practical meaning only if it is linked to specific rights and duties'.[31] In other words, a bald declaration, understood in legal drafting terms as a purpose clause, that the Welsh language is an official language was understood to carry no precise and unambiguous legal meaning on its own. Thus, it was explained at this stage that the duties to be placed upon organisations arising from the Measure will 'further confirm' the official status which the Welsh language already enjoys.[32] Moreover, given that the Measure would not, and indeed does not, include the use of Welsh in the courts, for example, it was also explained that the official status of the Welsh language is, in fact, understood to be broader than the provisions outlined in the Measure.[33]

Legislative cycle discussion and determination (March–December 2010)

The Measure as proposed incorporated the following article with regard to confirming the official status of the Welsh language:

1   Official status of the Welsh language

(1) This Measure makes further provision about the official status of the Welsh language in Wales, including –
   (a) provision establishing a Welsh Language Commissioner;
   (b) provision giving the Commissioner functions relating to the Welsh language, including functions of –
      (i) promoting and facilitating the use of the Welsh language and promoting equality between the Welsh and English language, and
      (ii) investigating interference with the freedom to use the Welsh language; and
   (c) provision for setting, and requiring compliance with, standards of conduct in relation to the Welsh language.
(2) The existing provision about the official status of the Welsh language in Wales includes –
   (a) in the Government of Wales Act 2006, sections 35(1), 78(1) and (2) and 156(1), and par. 8(3) of Schedule 2;
   (b) in the Welsh Language Act 1993, Part 2, and sections 22, 24, 25, 26 and 27(1) and (2).
(3) This Measure does not affect the status of the English language in Wales.

There was immediate and trenchant criticism of this in some quarters. Emyr Lewis, activist-lawyer, had an opinion piece published in which he specifically asked for the aforementioned article to be replaced as follows: 'gallwn ofyn am un diwygiad bach, sef Cymal 1 newydd syml: Y Gymraeg a'r Saesneg yw ieithoedd swyddogol Cymru, ac mae eu statws yn gyfartal' ('One small revision is asked for, namely a new and simple Article 1: Welsh and English are the official languages of Wales, and they are of equal status').[34] This was followed up with an open letter to the Minister, signed by '13 legal experts'[35] including Lewis,[36] asking for the same:

> Mae'r Mesur wedi'i lunio mewn modd sy'n cymryd yn ganiataol bod y Gymraeg eisoes yn meddu ar rywfaint o statws swyddogol. Credwn fod angen datganiad clir a diamwys mewn deddf gwlad fod y Gymraeg yn iaith swyddogol yng Nghymru [. . .]
>
> ['The Measure is drafted in a manner that takes for granted that the Welsh language already has some official status. We believe that a clear and unambiguous statement is needed in the law of the land that the Welsh language is an official language in Wales [. . .].']

In his written evidence to the Committee, Lewis argued that the Government of Wales Act 2006, under Schedule 5, matter 20(1), enables the Assembly to,

> make a formal and definitive statement with regards to the status of the Welsh language in a Measure. For example, it could be stated that the Welsh and English languages are official languages in Wales, and that they are equal. That would be consistent with the aim in the One Wales Agreement to confirm official status for both the Welsh and English languages.[37]

He argued that such a legal statement 'has psychological and social effect, as well as legal power'.[38] In elaborating on this point he asserted that he recognised that there were certain objections to setting the term 'official language' in statute, but he rejected as unreasonable any arguments that such a term when used in isolation is ambiguous and lacks precise legal meaning. For example,

There are some who argue that using the word 'official' without defining it in detail would create unacceptable legal ambiguity. This was, I believe, the nature of the United Kingdom Government's objection during deliberations on the 1993 Act. In my opinion, that is not reason enough not to include a definitive statement regarding the official nature of both languages in the Measure. Also, there is a precedent in British legislation for using such a statement to deal with a bilingual situation, namely the Canada Act 1982 which offers a useful starting point: 'English and French are the official languages of Canada and have equality of status and equal rights and privileges as to their use in all institutions of the Parliament and government of Canada.' There is another provision in the same Act that says the same thing about these languages with regards to the state of New Brunswick. I would therefore like to suggest this new Clause 1 for the proposed Measure: 'Welsh and English are the official languages of Wales, and have equality of status.'[39]

In his oral evidence Lewis rejected the wording of the Measure as proposed, arguing instead that

it would be far easier to state clearly that the Welsh and English languages – and it is important to mention both – are official languages in Wales, and that they have equal status. It is a very simple statement; it is transparent and people will understand it.[40]

With regard to understanding the meaning of the term 'official language', Lewis explained as follows: 'what does "official" mean? Put simply, it means the language or languages that government and official and public bodies operate in, and the languages in which they are willing to engage officially with the public.'[41] In his argument he asserts that 'there is no Act that says English is the official language and no court case that says so', yet in fact the contemporary de facto official status of the English language is subsequent to the following historical statutes conferring *de jure* official status upon that language during the course of the development of Common Law in the jurisdiction of England and Wales, namely the Proceedings in Courts of Justice Act 1730; An Act for turning the Books of the Law, and all Process and Proceedings in Courts of Justice, into the English Tongue 1650; Laws in Wales Act 1535 (§ 20); and, Pleading in English Act 1362. In elaborating upon his line of argument, Lewis asserted that

> to those who are nervous about the idea of declaring something is official without defining in detail what 'official' means, I say that there is a precedent for that within British legislation and within Commonwealth legislation [he has in mind here Canada and New Zealand] and this has not led to any kind of legal meltdown.[42]

The examples offered by Lewis and the issue of legal meltdown will be subject to analysis below.

Other actors echoed the position taken by Emyr Lewis with regard to making a 'simple' and 'transparent' declaration on the case of the Measure. For example, the Welsh Language Board asserted in their written evidence (29 April 2010):

> 5. So far as the status of the Welsh language is concerned, we ask: if the status of Welsh is already confirmed in several Acts, why can't its status be declared simply and unambiguously in this legislation? Why not use some such wording as 'The Welsh language is an official language in Wales'?[43]

Similarly, in their written evidence Cwmni Iaith asserted as follows (7 May 2010):

> We welcome the proposed Measure's intent to confirm the official status of the Welsh language. However, we feel that the current wording of the proposed Measure is a missed opportunity. We believe that a clear and unambiguous statement on the official status of the Welsh language is needed in the proposed Measure. This proposal has a key symbolic aim. A statement of this kind would send out a clear message that would have a positive impact on people's perceptions of the Welsh language, both in Wales and beyond.[44]

Also, in a letter to the Minister of 10 June 2010, fourteen language organisations, along with Colin H. Williams, asked for 'an unambiguous statement that the Welsh language is an official language in

Wales'.[45] Note that a spokesperson for the Welsh Language Society used this letter in order to assert that 'Erbyn hyn, mae yna gonsenws ymysg mudiadau, arbenigwyr ieithyddol ac arbenigwyr cyfreithiol' ('by now there is a consensus amongst groups, linguistic experts and legal experts') regarding the Measure and official status in particular.[46]

That the Welsh Language Society sought to corral other actors is clear from their evidence to the Committee, as is illustrated in the assertion of Catrin Dafydd of the Society as follows: 'Every lawyer and every piece of advice that we have received from language experts has said that the proposed Measure does not establish official status.'[47] In presenting their own case that

> The Measure has been drafted in a way which assumes that the Welsh language already has some status as an official language. We believe that there needs to be a clear and unambiguous statement in law that the Welsh language is an official language in Wales in order to realise the Government's objective,

they also deploy the argument used by the barrister Gwion Lewis of Landmark Chambers[48] in favour of declaring Welsh to be an official language, as follows:

> I have heard some politicians asking: what will this [official status] add to other measures? Is this not adding another layer of complication that we could well do without? I do not see things that way, for this would not be some symbolic declaration announcing that the Welsh language is an official language in Wales, and nothing more. There is a definite legal significance to the principle. If someone looks at legal cases where courts of law have agreed that it is reasonable and therefore lawful to take steps in order to promote one specific language, they will almost invariably have declared that the policy is a reasonable one because the language in question is the official language of that particular country.

Lewis elaborates upon this line of argument elsewhere[49] and, clearly, has in mind the potential for the ECHR to more generously interpret such a declaration than that given by the State of a 'particular country'.

The legal argument put forward by Lewis in his 2008 text seems to have been severely eroded, if not wholly undermined, by more recent, substantive scholarly tomes that argue, most convincingly, to the contrary. They variously assert that the relevant cases in international law almost entirely without exception assert the primacy and sovereignty of the State and its law in interpreting the meaning implied by 'official language'.[50] For a view from political theory further problematising this issue, while at the same time reinforcing the point, see Peled.[51] Revealingly, while rejecting Mowbray's thesis regarding linguistic justice and international human rights, de Varennes draws his review of her 2012 text to the conclusion that the fault in this state of affairs, as described by Mowbray, Paz, Peled and others, lies 'in a too-narrow interpretation of existing norms by a number of international bodies, but especially in the states still unwilling to have their sovereignty restricted by international human rights in language matters'.[52] The use of the term 'norms' by de Varennes is problematic. Whose norms? Arzoz and Woehrling penetrate to the heart of this when they variously assert that de Varennes is doing no more than articulating his own normative claim in his descriptions of language rights under international law. Arzoz states that de Varennes, in general terms, is 'isolated in the relevant legal literature and [his position] does not appear to correspond with current international law',[53] while Woehrling says that the interpretation of the case of Diergaardt v. Namibia[54] by de Varennes, from which he draws wider implications for language rights in international law, is similarly a minority view, for example: 'Cette position reste actuellement minoritaire et ne correspond pas au droit international positif'[55] ('This position is a minority view and does not correspond to positive international law'). In other words, to assert that international law is fertile ground for legal challenges by linguistic minorities against the State is to adopt a normative position regarding jurisprudence; it is not a positive statement in legal terms. Thus, normative claims regarding international law appear to be presented as positive statements and the idea that the creation of language rights solves language problems is taken as a self-evident proposition. Conflation, such as this, of positive and normative arguments in international law scholarship more generally has been subject to substantial criticism elsewhere.[56] Lewis is on much more secure ground when he argues that linguistic justice has to 'look homewards'[57] and engage with 'program', as Moyn puts it.[58] In other words, international law provides no panacea; rather, linguistic justice is to be found in the jurisdiction of the local polity.

Returning to the case of Welsh, in elaborating upon their case, the Welsh Language Society stated that such a declaration would be of use 'when employers try to prohibit members of staff from speaking Welsh', and they concurred with Emyr Lewis in that it would be an 'important psychological and social change'.[59] On giving evidence to the Committee in June, the Minister, Alun Ffred Jones (17 June 2010), noted that he had heard the arguments. As a result, the Measure was amended as follows by November 2010:[60]

4.1. Part 1: Official Status of the Welsh Language

Official Status of the Welsh Language (amendments 5 and 153):

Amendment 5, proposed by the Minister, was agreed by the Committee. The amendment leaves out the whole of subsections (1) and (2) in Section 1 and inserts completely new subsections relating to the official status of the Welsh Language. The full amendment is included below:

Page 12, line 13, leave out subsections (1) to (2) and insert –
'( ) The Welsh language has official status in Wales.
( ) The official status of the Welsh language is given legal effect by the enactments about –
(a) duties on bodies to use the Welsh language, and the rights which arise from the enforceability of those duties, which enable Welsh speakers to use the language in dealings with those bodies (such as the provision of services by those bodies);
(b) the treatment of the Welsh language no less favourably than the English language;
(c) the validity of the use of the Welsh language;
(d) the promotion and facilitation of the use of the Welsh language;
(e) the freedom of persons wishing to use the Welsh language to do so with one another;
(f) the creation of the Welsh Language Commissioner; and
(g) other matters relating to the Welsh language.

( ) Those enactments include (but are not limited to) the enactments which –
(a) require the Welsh and English languages to be treated on the basis of equality in the conduct of the proceedings of the National Assembly for Wales;
(b) confer a right to speak the Welsh language in legal proceedings in Wales;
(c) give equal standing to the Welsh and English texts of –
   (i) Measures and Acts of the National Assembly for Wales, and
   (ii) subordinate legislation;
(d) impose a duty on the Welsh Ministers to adopt a strategy setting out how they propose to promote and facilitate the use of the Welsh language;
(e) create standards of conduct that relate to the use of the Welsh language, or the treatment of the Welsh language no less favourably than the English language, in connection with –
   (i) delivering services,
   (ii) making policy, and
   (iii) exercising functions or conducting businesses and other undertakings;
(f) create standards of conduct in promoting and facilitating the use of the Welsh language;
(g) create standards of conduct for keeping records in connection with the Welsh language;
(h) impose a duty to comply with those standards of conduct that are created, and create remedies for failures to comply with them; and
   (i) create the Welsh Language Commissioner with functions that include –
   (ii) promoting the use of the Welsh language,
   (iii) facilitating the use of the Welsh language,
   (iv) working towards ensuring that the Welsh language is treated no less favourably than the English language
   (v) conducting inquiries into matters relating to the Commissioner's functions, and
   (vi) investigating interference with the freedom to use the Welsh language.'

This version of the Measure, agreed by the Committee,[61] was very warmly commended by the UK parliamentary legal drafter Daniel Greenberg when he gave oral evidence to the Constitutional Affairs Committee at the Assembly on 3 November 2010 (as recorded in the minutes, and noted elsewhere):[62]

> It is a question of fact and degree. If there is a later provision that makes it absolutely clear, in a black-letter[63] sense, by saying, 'Thou shalt not', then you are stuck. The purpose clause is not intended, and should not be allowed, to override that. However, while I think purpose clauses are particularly helpful, the reason why I started off by not agreeing is because I do not think they are there for people to judge the success of an Act, but to enable readers and courts to judge its application. However, if a statute gets to the courts, you have already failed because, by that time, you will have already driven the litigants, who may not have known what they were obliged to do, to all the expense and trouble of litigation. So, it should be about the readers, such as local authorities, who will pick up the Children Act, for example, with regard to a particular incident and say, 'On the face of it, we're not clear whether it requires us to do this or that'. There is clearly a welfare issue here, and if we look at it with regard to the welfare of the child, if there is no doubt about which way the legislation is pointing, you will not have to worry about the ambiguity or the slight lack of certainty of the law. So, black-letter law always takes precedence, but there should not be a clash. If there is a clash, the drafter has failed. However, all the uncertainties that are inherent to the legislative process can be assisted by having a well-drafted, clear purpose clause, and the clause last suggested in relation to the proposed Welsh language Measure is superb, because it states, 'This is about making the Welsh language an official language. But we're not sure what that means. We want to see that; it's a political statement that we need or want to see, but it won't be clear to everybody what that means, so here is a list of how we have given effect to that'. It is almost a definition of what it all means. That is a brilliant way to set out a proposed Measure.[64]

But, despite Greenberg's commendation, the Minister's amendment was not deemed sufficient by the critics. A further open letter to the Minister was published on 4 November 2010, this time signed by eighty 'prominent Welsh people' and calling for further change to the Measure in the form of an 'unconditional declaration'. In particular, they noted that despite the amendment:

> datganiad cyfyng a gafwyd: mewn cyd-destunau penodol yn unig y bydd yr iaith yn swyddogol. Pryderwn y gall fod canlyniadau andwyol i'r Gymraeg mewn cyd-destunau ehangach lle na fydd statws swyddogol ganddi. Mae datganiadau diamod o statws swyddogol yn gyffredin ledled y byd [. . .] Nid yw'n eglur pam na ellir cymryd y cam hwn er lles y Gymraeg yng Nghymru, yn unol â'r consensws trawsbleidiol yn y Pwyllgor Deddfwriaeth ym mis Gorffennaf. Hefyd, er bod sôn yn y gwelliannau am beidio â thrin y Gymraeg yn llai ffafriol na'r Saesneg, nid yw'r geiriad yn rhoi i'r Gymraeg na statws na dilysrwydd cyfartal â'r Saesneg [. . .][65]

['the resulting declaration is narrow: the language will be official only in certain contexts. We are concerned that there could be a negative impact upon the Welsh language in other contexts in which it does not have official status. Unconditional statements of official status are common throughout the world [. . .] It is not clear why this step cannot be taken in order to benefit the Welsh language in Wales, in accordance with the cross-party consensus in the Legislation Committee in July. Also, while it is noted in the amendments that the Welsh language will not be treated less favourably than English, the wording gives the Welsh language neither equal status nor equal validity with English [. . .]']

The Minister justified the government's amendment as follows:

> The Government has given careful consideration to its amendment in light of the strength of the views put forward during the committee's consideration of the proposed Measure at Stage 1 that section 1, as drafted, did not achieve the *One Wales* objective of confirming official status. The result is seen in amendment 5, which confirms the official status of the Welsh language

and provides certainty as to how the law gives legal effect to the concept of official status for the Welsh language. To this end, new subsection 1 states that the Welsh language has official status in Wales. New subsection 2 provides that legal effect is given to official status through legislation about the matters described in that part of the legislation. New subsection 3 provides examples of the types of enactments that give legal effect to the official status of the Welsh language. New subsection 4 states that the proposed Measure does not affect the status of the English language in Wales. In Wales, the English language already enjoys the status of being the language of default of the Governments of the UK. Therefore, it is important to stress that the rights of English speakers are not affected.[66]

An alternative amendment (153), proposed by the Liberal Democrat AM Jenny Randerson, was not agreed by the Committee.[67] This amendment sought to replace section 1 completely with a concise declaration on the official status of the Welsh language. Arguing for the amendment, Kirsty Williams, the leader of the Liberal Democrats in the Assembly, explained to the Committee that

we believe that the Minister's amendment is very complex. It sets out several areas where the official status of the language is guaranteed, such as in the proceedings of our own institution, the National Assembly, by setting standards for the use of Welsh. Nevertheless, we believe that there is a danger in this approach. By setting out in such detail the circumstances in which Welsh is equal, it inevitably implies that anything not included on the list does not have equal status. Our amendment is simple and clear. It is directly based on the committee's report and previous work, including a specific proposed amendment. We believe that the inclusion of a clear, unambiguous statement of official status is an important symbolic action. Without that, the whole proposed Measure is undermined.[68]

Paul Davies AM (Conservative), arguing for amendment 153, said:

I understand the Government's amendment, and that it endeavours to strengthen the proposed Measure, but it does not go far enough. If we want to create a truly bilingual Wales, it is crucial that Welsh and English are recognised as official languages of Wales and that they are treated equally.[69]

The Minister's explanation as to why amendment 153 was to be rejected was as follows:

> For the most part, critics of section 1 as drafted have advocated the insertion of a broad statement along the lines of amendment 153. However, an amendment such as is proposed is completely unpredictable and ambiguous in terms of its legal effect. It should be borne in mind that a key part of the Assembly's role as a democratically elected legislature is to produce clear and certain legislation, and what is proposed in amendment 153 represents the opposite of these aims and would result in lawyers challenging and, ultimately, courts of law determining the effect of this section. I cannot for the life of me believe that that is what Members of this Assembly would want.[70]

The Minister rejected amendment 153, along with the possibility of any general declaration, as suggested by Emyr Lewis, Gwion Lewis and others, in a public letter of his own in November. Here he states that:

> I have given a great deal of thought to the case for an open-ended statement on the status of the Welsh language. However, I have come to the conclusion that such a course of action could pose a serious risk of undermining the core principles which underpin this Measure namely that duties and rights established at law should be clearly set out in legislation; that establishing and securing an individual's right to a service through the medium of Welsh should not be the responsibility of, and a burden upon, that individual. I am not convinced that a Court should be given the primary responsibility of deciding the full nature and extent of duties in relation to the Welsh language. In my view, the creation and extent of duties in relation to the Welsh language should be a matter for the Welsh Assembly Government and the National Assembly to decide. For this reason, the declaration of the status of the Welsh language

contained in the Measure sets out how the declaration of status is given legal effect and that the declaration is something tangible and real. It would not be clear what effect on the law an open-ended statement of status would have [. . .] the only way of resolving the extent to which a statement required a person to act in a certain way in relation to the Welsh language would be to take the matter before a Court.[71]

Further ministerial explanation of this was set out in a definitive manner in the Revised Explanatory Memorandum published at the end of Stage 2 (30 November 2010): '3.11 The proposed Measure's first section makes provision about the official status of the Welsh language in Wales, and sets out how that status is given legal effect. The Measure does not affect the status of the English language in Wales.' The text of the Measure was described and explained in some detail in the Explanatory Memorandum:

Part 1: Official Status of the Welsh Language

This Part of the Measure makes provision about the official status of the Welsh language in Wales.

Section 1: Official Status of the Welsh Language

This section makes provision about the official status of the Welsh language in Wales.

Subsection (1) states that the Welsh language has official status in Wales.

Subsection (2) provides that legal effect is given to the official status of the Welsh language by the enactments about duties on bodies to use the Welsh language; the treatment of the Welsh language no less favourably than the English language; the validity of the use of the Welsh language; the promotion and facilitation of the use of the Welsh language; the freedom of persons wishing to use the Welsh language to do so with one another; the creation of the Welsh Language Commissioner and other matters relating to the Welsh language.

Subsection (3) refers to examples of the enactments which give legal effect to the official status of the Welsh language.

Subsection (4) states that the Measure does not affect the status of the English language in Wales.[72]

That said, in approaching the determining Plenary on 7 December 2010 the Welsh government were concerned at their position and the ability of Plaid Cymru, in particular, to secure the votes of all of its AMs on the matter of official status as it stood in the Measure. Indeed, Bethan Jenkins AM (Plaid Cymru) had tabled an amendment (amendment 70) in a very similar vein to Randerson's (at this stage, amendment 51) seeking, 'a clear statement in the proposed Measure that states that the Welsh and English languages are official languages in Wales and they should have equal validity' (Paul Davies AM (Conservative)).[73] As a result, a last-minute 'late amendment' (amendment 72) that was 'tabled in extraordinary circumstances'[74] was made to the Measure; in consequence, the Measure as passed reads as follows:

Version as passed, incorporating the amendment introduced by emergency resolution on 7 December 2010

1   Official status of the Welsh language

(1) The Welsh language has official status in Wales.

(2) *Without prejudice to the general principle of subsection (1),* [author's italics] the official status of the Welsh language is given legal effect by the enactments about –

   (a) duties on bodies to use the Welsh language, and the rights which arise from the enforceability of those duties, which enable Welsh speakers to use the language in dealings with those bodies (such as the provision of services by those bodies);
   (b) the treatment of the Welsh language no less favourably than the English language;
   (c) the validity of the use of the Welsh language;
   (d) the promotion and facilitation of the use of the Welsh language;
   (e) the freedom of persons wishing to use the Welsh language to do so with one another;
   (f) the creation of the Welsh Language Commissioner; and
   (g) other matters relating to the Welsh language.

This change was explained by the Minister as answering the concerns of the critics:

> Mae'r gwelliant yn mynd i'r afael gyda phryderon pobol a oedd yn gofidio bod Adran 1(2) y mesur yn tanseilio egwyddor cyffredinol statws swyddogol yr iaith. Mae'r gwelliant yma yn tawelu meddwl pobol nad ydi'r egwyddor cyffredinol bod gan y Gymraeg statws swyddogol yng Nghymru wedi ei gyfyngu. Mae Adran 1(2) yn ei gwneud hi'n glir bod gan y statws swyddogol rym cyfreithiol.[75]

> ['The amendment deals with the concerns of people that were worried about Section 1(2) of the Measure undermining the general principle of the official status of the language. This amendment will assure people that the general principle that the Welsh language has official status in Wales is not being restricted. Section 1(2) makes it clear that official status has legal weight.']

In coming to the aid of the Labour–Plaid Cymru coalition government, Rhodri Morgan AM (Labour) drew the attention of the Assembly to Daniel Greenberg's view on the Measure in relation to the matter of official status, suggesting that Greenberg's words carried special weight; it is necessary to quote Morgan at some length here:

> I was in the same place as Jenny Randerson during the committee stage, and I was therefore in favour of having the kind of clear, no-beating-around-the-bush sentence that she supports in her amendment. After that, I went to see the Minister, and he and his chief civil servant, John Howells, gave me strong reasons – along the same lines as Jenny Randerson's amendment – for drafting the proposed Measure in its current form. After that, even stronger evidence than that came to light, in the sense that it came from one of the Aztec high priests of the drafting world, namely Daniel Greenberg from the Berwin Leighton Paisner law firm. When he came to give evidence to the Constitutional Affairs Committee, he dealt with this issue and the standard of drafting of our legislation in the Assembly. I will quote his words on 3 November, which were overwhelmingly in favour of the current means of achieving

what Jenny seeks to achieve in her amendment: 'However, all the uncertainties that are inherent to the legislative process can be assisted by having a well-drafted, clear purpose clause.' That is the aim of Jenny Randerson's amendment. To continue with the quotation, 'and the clause last suggested in relation to the proposed Welsh language Measure is superb, because it states, "This is about making the Welsh language an official language. But we're not sure what that means. We want to see that; it's a political statement that we need or want to see, but it won't be clear to everybody what that means, so here is a list of how we have given effect to that". It is almost a definition of what it all means. That is a brilliant way to set out a proposed Measure.' When someone of Daniel Greenberg's calibre comes down from London, from a respected firm – and he is experienced, and is highly respected in the corridors of Westminster on how to draft a clear Bill – I am willing to accept his opinion, even if it is [sic] differs from mine. I have, therefore, changed my mind, although I agreed with Jenny Randerson before that. Do we want legislation that is made by judges in courts of law in the future, or do we want to accept the responsibility of doing our best to create legislation here that is as clear as possible, rather than legislation that will be defined in countless minor cases before the courts of Wales and in other places in future? Our function and our responsibility is to legislate as clearly as we can. We have received advice, and the Minister has received advice from his civil servants, his lawyers, and the people who draft legislation for the Assembly Government. We have heard a completely objective view – which took me by surprise – from Daniel Greenberg. I accept, therefore, that the way of solving this problem – and everyone accepts what the problem is – is the way that the Government has put before us, as we have heard from someone who is well placed to give us objective advice. That is the way to avoid having our legislation framed by judges in courts of law in the future.[76]

Gareth Jones AM (Plaid Cymru) seized upon Morgan's intervention as a means of supporting the Minister, noting that 'I have just heard Greenberg being mentioned. That is the first that I have heard about him or any reference to him [. . .] Support the Government's amendment.'[77] Jones also argued that the matter of granting 'full status' to the Welsh language was frustrated by 'constitutional circumstances' as follows:

> After publishing the committee report last July, it was revealed that the Assembly, through the language LCO, does not have the authority to legislate on full status. Further to that, owing to the restrictions here and our constitutional settlement, it was revealed that it will be the courts that adjudge and decide on the linguistic status of the language. Therefore, to my mind, it is not the Assembly Government or the Minister who will refuse to fulfil full status, but constitutional circumstances.[78]

Jones takes 'full status' to mean 'equal status to that of the English language'.[79] Similarly, Davies takes it to mean 'equal validity and status'.[80] Jones also noted at this point that the AMs on the Committee had the support of the 'advice from an expert adviser, who is an authority on the linguistic status of countries such as Canada, Catalonia, Scotland and Ireland among others'.[81]

The change was welcomed on the very same day by the aforementioned critics, activists and experts alike, as follows:

> Rydym yn croesawu'r ffaith fod y Llywodraeth wedi dwyn y gwelliant hwn gerbron. Mae'r datblygiad cyffrous hwn ar y munud olaf yn dangos bod gennym yng Nghymru Lywodraeth sy'n gwrando ar ei phobol ac yn ymateb yn gadarnhaol i farn ei hetholwyr [. . .] Bydd cenedlaethau'r dyfodol yn cydnabod yr hyn gyflawnwyd heddiw. Carem ddiolch i bawb sydd wedi bod yn llythyru, yn e-bostio, yn ffonio, ac yn cyfarfod â'r Aelodau Cynulliad er mwyn eu cymell i gefnogi'r egwyddor ganolog o statws swyddogol cyflawn i'r iaith Gymraeg. Bydd pawb yn gallu cysgu'n dawel heno.[82]

> ['We welcome the fact that the Government has tabled this amendment. This exciting last-minute development shows that we have in Wales a Government that listens to its people and responds positively to the opinions of its electors [. . .] Future generations will recognise that which has been achieved today. We would love to thank everyone who wrote letters, e-mails,

made phone calls, and who met with AMs in order to persuade them to support the central principle of complete official status for the Welsh language. Everyone will be able to sleep well tonight.']

That Plaid Cymru canvassed the support of these critics is clear, as two in particular, Emyr Lewis and Richard Wyn Jones, were named by Rhodri Glyn Thomas AM (Plaid Cymru) during the course of the Plenary:

'This is a historic step forward that will lay a strong foundation for the future.' Not my words, but those of Professor Richard Wyn Jones and Emyr Lewis in reference to amendment 72 that the Minister has moved. They go on to say that 'future generations will acknowledge what has been achieved today' on the assumption that everyone in this place will support amendment 72. They refer to the vision and leadership of the Minister, and welcome the fact that the Government has tabled this amendment. They refer to this exciting last-minute development, which shows that we have in Wales a Government that listens to its people and responds positively to its electorate. Therefore, there is a consensus among those who have contacted us; I accept that the message has not reached the opposition yet – after all, they have not had strong links with some of these people in the past, and perhaps it will take some time for them to accept this message, but the message has certainly reached us. There is a consensus among those who campaigned for unequivocal status for the Welsh language in Wales that amendment 72 proposed by the Minister will meet that requirement. I challenge the opposition parties to support that amendment and to recognise that the Minister has listened to the people of Wales.[83]

The emergency amendment was passed.

Analysis

The heat generated by the issue of official status is reflected, quite simply, in the fact that there were more policy and other advisory documents on this issue during the course of the policy and legislative cycles than on any other single issue. In addition, four documents on official status were redacted in their entirety.[84] In the matter of the weight given to the view of Daniel Greenberg on aspects of the wording of the Measure, there was certainly more heat than light. It is the case that during the course of the Plenary on 7 December 2010, AMs welcomed the fact that Greenberg appeared to be so approving of the wording of the Measure. But, the matter to hand in the Plenary was the emergency, last-minute amendment, upon which Greenberg had not, in fact, offered any comment whatsoever. Rather, Greenberg's comments were made on the amended version of the Measure as it stood in November 2010. Evidence of the same confusion arising amongst expert-activists was elicited during project fieldwork (Fieldwork Interview 56).

It would appear to be the case that some of the lawyer-activists seemed to be in pursuit of an agenda which they hoped would lead to the ECHR, which has a developing body of case law pertinent to the official status of language.[85] While the term official language is imprecise, according to de Varennes European case law suggests that there may be certain practical consequences arising from declaring a language to be an official language. His argument runs as follows:

> While there is no international consensus as to the consequences of having the status of an official language in terms of use of this language by authorities, the European Court of Human Rights suggested that there are clear consequences to the designation of an official language, indicating that by making a language its official language, the State undertakes in principle to guarantee its citizens the right to use that language both to impart and to receive information, without hindrance not only in their private lives, but also in their dealings with the public authorities [the case is that of Mentzen alias Mencina v. Latvia , application no. 71074/01, admissibility decision of 7 December 2004] there is therefore, in the absence of legislation to the contrary, at least a very strong implication that a government has an obligation to use such a language, and citizens the right to use it with government. The precise effect of an official language status, even whether or the extent it will be used for the purposes of government, will depend largely on a country's legislation and jurisprudence. There is at the very least

a strong implication that such status guarantees to citizens the right to use the official language with government authorities.[86]

Therefore, were the Welsh language to be declared an official language, in the style proposed by Emyr Lewis, Gwion Lewis and others, then it is very possible that the practical consequences or implications of such a declaration could, or indeed would, be tested in the ECHR and the resulting judgment be imposed upon the Welsh and UK governments. In actual fact, one of the simple, overarching outcomes of this process is that, contrary to that which is implied by Emyr Lewis and Jones in their statement of 7 December, the Measure as passed does not incorporate a declaration that the Welsh language is an official language in Wales. Instead, it declares that the Welsh language has official status in Wales. There is a significant difference between the two. Prima facie,[87] the statement in the Measure is not a declarative formulation sufficiently robust to the extent that it would require interpretative examination in the courts, such as the ECHR, where there is a developing body of pertinent case law.[88] Despite the modifying phrase 'without prejudice', the official status of the Welsh language is largely understood in relation to the Welsh Courts Act 1942, the Welsh Language Act 1993, the Government of Wales Act 2006, the Welsh Language Measure 2011 and the National Assembly for Wales (Official Languages) Act 2012.

Regarding certain aspects of the official status of language, certain authoritative voices appear to have forsaken their expert knowledge in favour of activist rhetoric. For example, while activists ask for an unambiguous declaration, in fact such a declaration in and of itself is ambiguous as there is no agreed definition of the meaning of official language.[89] Indeed, in approaching the matter described by Ruíz Vieytez[90] as the content of officiality, de Varennes[91] argues that any declaration asserting a language to be official requires clarification either in that piece of legislation itself or other statutory law, or in the courts. In asking for an unconditional declaration, these activists argued that such declarations are common throughout the world and that they have not resulted in legal contention. In fact, unconditional declarations are only made with regard to languages in contexts in which the said official language is wholly hegemonic, such as in the case of English in many of the states in the USA. Thus, the declaration of officiality merely reflects praxis.

The cases of Canada and New Zealand were both offered by expert-activists as illustrative examples. But, contrary to their arguments, the statutory declarations are in fact accompanied by statutes which set out in detail the precise meaning and implication of the official status of the languages to hand. In the very few cases where a constitutional declaration has been made with regard to the official status of a minority language without any accompanying, detailed statute, such as the case of the Irish language in the Republic of Ireland prior to 2003, there was indeed 'legal meltdown' as Irish-speakers sought to vindicate their constitutional rights through the courts.[92] Expert-activist evidence may also be challenged with regard to the 'constitution of Québec'[93] and the assertion that 'There is no declaration of official status for that language [Scottish Gaelic] in that Act [Gaelic Language (Scotland) Act 2005].'[94] In fact, Québec has no such constitution and instead the centrepiece of its statutory architecture with regard to language is the well-known Loi (or Bill) 101.

With regard to the status of Gaelic in Scotland, McLeod asserts that the Gaelic Language (Scotland) Act 2005 'grants official status to the language for the first time' and that

> The most significant formal statement of Gaelic's status as a national language is given in the preamble to the recently enacted Gaelic Language (Scotland) Act 2005, which declares Gaelic to be 'an official language of Scotland commanding equal respect with the English language'.[95]

Others, including authoritative bodies and commentators in the public record, have made similar such assertions.[96] Prior to that, the language enjoyed 'no official status in the United Kingdom or even within Scotland'.[97] That said, according to the Scottish government of 2003 during consultation on the Gaelic Language Bill, it would be incorrect to argue that Gaelic did not enjoy any form of official status prior to that. Rather, the Scottish government asserted that

> The Executive is clear that there is official recognition of Gaelic in Scotland, and that Gaelic is a language of Scotland. The evidence for this is that Gaelic is supported by a range of Executive programmes, there is a Cabinet portfolio which includes responsibility for Gaelic and Bòrd na Gàidhlig has been established

recently by Executive action. The Scottish Parliament also makes provision for the use of Gaelic in oral and written business [...] In addition, in June 2003, in response to a question in the House of Lords, Lord Evans of Temple Guiting said, 'the Gaelic language has [...] official status within the United Kingdom'.[98]

Returning to the difficulties regarding certain expert evidence upon the case of the Welsh language and its official status in Wales, the assertion that 'We cannot bestow official status upon the Welsh language without giving it to the English language as well' seems peculiar, given that legislative powers were delegated, via the LCO, to the Assembly with regard to the Welsh language alone.[99] No powers were delegated to the Assembly in relation to the English language. Hence, if the two languages are bound in the manner stated by Lewis, then it follows that the Assembly simply cannot do as Lewis asks of it. In actual fact, the Measure as passed does indeed distinguish between Welsh and English with regard to the matter of official status, contrary to Emyr Lewis's assertion that this could not be done. During the Plenary on 7 December 2010 Paul Davies AM (Conservative) returned to the evidence given by Lewis in challenging Rhodri Glyn Thomas AM (Plaid Cymru) to explain whether he agreed with Lewis or not: 'Do you also accept that Emyr Lewis said that we cannot give status to the Welsh language without also giving official status to the English language?' Put simply, Davies is saying that, on this particular matter, either the Measure as passed is wrong or Emyr Lewis is wrong.[100]

In a number of regards, many of the actors appear to do little more than revisit the debate regarding the official status of the Welsh language during the legislative process that gave rise to the Welsh Language Act 1993. It was also argued then by the government that the Welsh language already had official status.[101] Indeed, the same argument was deployed with regard to Scottish Gaelic during passage of the Gaelic Language Bill.[102] In the context of the LCO and of the Measure, several actors echo the words of Ferrers with regard to the problem Common Law has in accommodating the notion of official language:

> The concept of Welsh being an official language raises similar concepts of definition and uncertainty. It is the Government's view that, whatever uncertainty there may have been in the past concerning the official status of Welsh, it should be removed by

> the Bill [i.e. Welsh Language Act 1993]. I am afraid that that [un]certainty would be reintroduced should the language once again become dependent on a general declaration which could only be defined in individual cases by recourse to the courts.[103]

Also,

> If it were to incorporate the provision, we may [sic] find that we had a tiger by the tail. We simply do not know where it will take us other than almost certainly and inevitably into the labyrinths of the Courts. An important objective of the Bill is to keep the matter out of the Courts.[104]

It was explained elsewhere by the Prime Minister at that time, John Major, in response to a question by Dafydd Wigley MP (Plaid Cymru), that 'We [the UK government] believe that Welsh already enjoys official status in Wales. A general declaration in the Bill would have no practical effect and would probably only increase legal uncertainty.'[105]

It is possible that this tendency to revisit has resulted in a failure on the part of expert actors to robustly problematise the assertion that general declarations of official language are 'essentially meaningless and unenforceable' in Common Law jurisdictions, in contrast to Civil Law jurisdictions. Legal systems can be so categorised, of course.[106] Common Law derives from the model of England and Wales and was internationalised via the British Empire. Common Law jurisdictions include Australia, Barbados, Brunei, Canada, England and Wales, Hong Kong, India, Malaysia, New Zealand, Northern Ireland, Pakistan, Republic of Ireland, Scotland, Singapore, South Africa, Sri Lanka and the United States of America.[107] Civil Law has three basic European types: French, German and Scandinavian. Many states across the globe have Civil Law models (Figure 12).

However, the working assumption at the heart of much of the policy discussion that Civil Law easily allows for declarations that a language be an official language and that Common Law runs counter to that is falsely straightforward. For example, it is widely assumed that French was declared the official language for France from the inception of the First Republic in 1792, but in actual fact French was not recognised by statute as the official language of France until 1992.[108] One

French Civil Law	German Civil Law	Scandinavian Civil Law
Belgium	Austria	Denmark
France	Estonia	Iceland
Luxembourg	Germany	Finland
Netherlands	Latvia	Norway
Romania	Switzerland	Sweden
Spain	Greece	–
–	Portugal	–
–	Turkey	–
–	Japan	–

Figure 12. *Examples of Civil Law jurisdictions.*[146]

of the few states in the USA where English has not been declared an official language is Louisiana, which is a Civil Law jurisdiction, unlike most of the other states.[109] While it is very common indeed for sources to assert that German is the declared official language of Germany, in actual fact that is not stated in the constitution;[110] rather, it is asserted elsewhere that German is the language of administration (Administrative Procedure Act – Verwaltungsverfahrensgesetz, § 23, R5) and in the administration of justice (Court Constitution Act – Gerichtsverfassungsgesetz, § 184, R4). In a survey of the member states of the Council of Europe it was found that an official language is explicitly declared in the constitution of twenty-two out of those forty-eight states.[111] On the other hand, a wide range of jurisdictions that are understood to be, at least in part, Common Law jurisdictions have statutorily recognised official languages including, for example, French and English in Canada, Māori and New Zealand Sign Language in New Zealand, English and Irish in the Republic of Ireland, Chinese (in practice Cantonese) and English in Hong Kong, and English, Malay, Mandarin and Tamil in Singapore. In India Hindi is the official language at Union level and English is the 'subsidiary' official language, while several dozen languages are officially recognised at the level of the constituent states of the Union. In other words, 'Common Law' and 'official language' are not mutually exclusive notions. Moreover, it would appear that while clear distinctions may be drawn between Common Law and Civil Law types of jurisdiction there is, in fact, considerable overlap and hybridity. Tetley argues that the two are 'converging' in Europe,[112] while in the UK the Permanent Secretary for the Cabinet Office and the First Parliamentary Counsel has stated quite baldly that 'In truth, England and Wales is a hybrid jurisdiction – as, I might add, is Scotland.'[113]

Many of the activists, including expert-activists, argue for the making of a statutory declaration given the symbolic value of doing so. The work of Gusfield (1963 and 1967) on this subject, in which he identified the symbolic and the instrumental dimensions of law, is seminal.[114] Briefly, symbolic legislation serves to affirm some values and lifestyles, but does not depend on actual law enforcement for its effect, while instrumental law controls behaviour through law enforcement practices. Gusfield puts it as follows: 'The fact of public affirmation of a norm through law and government actions expresses the public worth of one sub-culture vis-à-vis others.'[115] A broad consensus exists amongst academic and practising lawyers that symbolic law undermines the credibility of the law. Simply, declarative statements are unnecessary if their purpose is to confirm that which already exists. In addition, the concept of official language lacks precision, as Greenberg made clear despite the fog of debate on the floor of the Welsh Assembly, and therefore requires explanation in the form of legislation if it is to be made justiciable or enforceable. Writing on the consequences of symbolic law, Tushnett and Yackle argue that symbolic statutes may be said to define or to express 'who we are as a society' but that they have 'undesirable effects', which they explain as follows,

> As real laws, they must be administered and integrated into a legal system with many instrumental laws as well [. . .] Judges have to make symbolic statutes compatible with the first-order instrumentalism of the rest of the law. In so doing, courts may produce some peculiar results [. . .] In the main, however, courts will reconcile symbolic laws with the prevailing order [. . .] some judges may not be inclined to do the interpretive work that would be necessary to integrate the statutes into a coherent body of law. Other judges may dismiss as insubstantial the constitutional concerns that we believe ought to influence interpretation. The result will be that the statutes will occasionally have essentially random adverse effects, serving no discernible public purpose.[116]

The authors imply that symbolic law, while not, 'undesirable in the abstract' is so in practice, as it has the potential to 'affect cases in an essentially random way' and 'such randomness is itself a constitutional concern'.[117] Dwyer puts it most succinctly: 'by enacting this type [symbolic] of statute, legislators reap the political benefits of voting for [the value] and successfully sidestep the difficult policy choices that must be made'.[118] In other words, symbolic statute is good politics but bad law.

Turning now to equality, the application, in the form of statute, of the notion of equality to the Welsh language has a history of being misunderstood. For example, Ager claimed that under the Welsh Language Act 1993 the Welsh language 'has equal validity with English'.[119] At a reading of the Welsh Language Bill in the House of Lords in 1993, Lord Elis-Thomas articulated the confused, and perhaps even misleading, view that the principle that the Welsh language 'be treated on a basis of equality' with the English language was not more restrictive at all, but in fact was 'more wide-ranging' than the principle of 'equal validity' (HL Deb 02 February 1993 vol. 542 cc 136–216). Of course, equal validity may be understood to have a clear legal meaning, namely laws in two official languages are held to be equally valid, or authentic, as with the case of French and English in Canada[120] or Chinese and English in Hong Kong,[121] both of which are Common Law jurisdictions at least in part. Equal validity and the potential declaration of Welsh as an official language were largely conflated at Westminster and seen as leading to 'statutory bilingualism', both in relation to the LCO[122] and also in relation to the Welsh Language Act 1993.[123] The meaning of this was clearly understood by policy actors in the UK Parliament to be as follows:

> in other words, that for official purposes everything must be done in both languages [. . .] every Act of Parliament that applies in any way to Wales would have to be printed in Welsh as well as in English, as would every statutory instrument, every decision of a government department and every copy of Hansard in both Houses. The statute books themselves might even have to be written in Welsh too. The task would be endless, as would be [. . .] the cost.[124]

This was resisted at Westminster both in 1993 and in relation to the LCO.

That said, the 2011 Measure does in fact accord the Welsh language equal validity in Wales, whereby 'the official status of the Welsh language is given legal effect by enactments about – the validity of the use of the Welsh language' (§ 1(2)(c)). This has since been further reinforced in relation to National Assembly for Wales legislation by the National Assembly for Wales (Official Languages) Act 2012. Under this Act, the Government of Wales Act 2006 is modified so that it is declared that 'the official languages of the Assembly are English and Welsh' (National Assembly for Wales (Official Languages) Act 2012, 1(1)(2)(1)). Prima facie, this action is ultra vires for the reason that the English language is not amongst the subjects over which the Assembly has legislative competence. Indeed, the Wales Office was minded to take the matter to the Supreme Court and after passing through the Assembly the Act underwent a period of intimation. The case is explained as follows:

> The Wales Office's referral was made on the premise that the Bill amends the Government of Wales Act 2006 to make Welsh and English the official languages of the Assembly. The Assembly has legislative competence to legislate in relation to the Welsh language, but not, according to the Wales Office, in relation to the English language. In this case, the position of the Assembly Commission is similar to that of the Counsel General in the Byelaws Case, that the reference to the English language is 'incidental' to the provision on the Welsh language.[125]

The Attorney General for England and Wales decided against taking the matter to the Supreme Court on 1 November 2012, having just lost the case regarding the Local Government (Byelaws) (Wales) Bill 2012.[126] In any case, taken together, these build upon the fact of the recognition that Welsh and English were of 'equal standing' in terms of law-making under the Government of Wales Act 2006.[127] With regard to equality, the 2011 Measure states that the Welsh language may be treated 'no less favourably than' (§ 1(2)(b)) the English language. While lacking the unambiguous simplicity of being of equal status, this wording allows for the Welsh language to be treated more favourably than English, as is clear from Welsh Policy Paper 19: 'The policy intention was not to leave open the possibility that English speakers in predominantly Welsh speaking areas could attempt to use the Measure to call for equal treatment of the English language with Welsh', but rather to ensure that the powers of the Commissioner are focused, 'on measures aimed at working towards parity of treatment for the Welsh language with the English language and not vice versa'.[128] Thereby, the policy intention to 'focus the Commissioner's powers (etc.) on aspiring to ensure that the Welsh language is treated no less favourably than the English language'[129] results in the notion of equality being framed as it is in the Measure as passed.

Thus, during the legislative cycle there is a shift from the notion of 'promoting equality between the Welsh and English languages' in the Measure as introduced, a wording understood by policy actors to be of a piece with the principle of equality as understood by the Welsh Language Act 1993[130] to a wording that is, with regard to intended application, more assertive. De Varennes seems to miss this point when he asserts that both the Welsh Language Act 1993 and the Measure 'indicate' that the Welsh and English languages 'should be treated on a basis of equality'.[131] Conceiving of equality in relation to a minority not being subjected to conditions or treatment 'no less favourable' is central to the Disability Discrimination Act 1995, where there is a duty not to treat people less favourably than others. There is evidence from the project fieldwork that the wording of legislation in this area may well have informed the wording pertaining to the notion of equality in the Measure. Also, the term is used in the Irish context, where it formed a crucial part of certain Supreme Court determinations, including Ó Beoláin v. Fahy 2001 IESC 26, 4 April 2001; Ó Murchú v. Registrar of Companies and the Minister for Industry & Commerce [1988] IRSR 42; and Ó Murchú v. The Taoiseach et al. SC No. 91 of 2005, 6 May 2010, whereby it was found as follows: 'Nor can it [the Irish language] be treated less favourably in these contexts than the second official language.'[132] More to the point, this wording directly informs the Irish government's Irish Language Scheme Guidelines.[133] Despite the apparent commonalities, there does not appear to be any evidence that Welsh actors were informed by Irish practice in this regard.

One final point may be made on the matter of equality in relation to the Welsh language and that arises from the so-called 'Silk Commission'.[134] This body, properly entitled the Commission on

Devolution in Wales, began its work of examining the current financial and constitutional arrangements in Wales in 2011. It reported in 2012 on the matter of fiscal powers and in 2014 on the wider powers of the Assembly. Amongst the matters of consideration was the place of the Welsh language in UK legislation.[135] Most interestingly, amongst the recommendations of the Commission was that the UK government ought to review and amend the law 'to give equal status to the Welsh language',[136] following evidence given by the Commissioner requesting that the Commission review UK legislation 'which currently treats the Welsh language less favourably than the English language'.[137] More quixotically, the Commissioner also expressed her opinion that 'any further amendments to the Welsh constitution should contain a clear statement on the face of legislation, confirming that Welsh is one of the official languages in Wales, and that it has official status'.[138] The former point was subsequently taken up by the UK government in the shape of the Wales Office. In that office's 'Command Paper' of 2015[139] it is asserted that there was a consensus with regard to accepting the Silk Commission recommendation, as follows:

> The UK Government and Welsh Government should systematically assess and keep under review the way in which the Welsh language is used across government, in particular with a view to amending any United Kingdom legislation that does not give equal status to the Welsh language in Wales [;][140]

and that 'The UK Government further accepts the principle that legislation which does not give equal status to the Welsh language in Wales should be amended.'[141] A very precise parsing of the notion of equality as framed by this Command Paper on the one hand and the Measure on the other would invite the reader to conclude that the two documents approach the concept of equality in contrasting, even contradictory, ways. The former takes the 1993 Act as its substantive point of reference, and in particular the principle set in that Act that 'the Welsh and English languages should be treated on the basis of equality',[142] while under the Measure the notion of equality is noticeable only by its absence. Thus, the UK government and the Welsh government would appear to be in different directions of travel.

Conclusions

The Minister was right to, largely, resist calls for an unconditional declaration that the Welsh language is an official language in Wales, along with resisting those who urged him to do so despite any concerns regarding any legal ambiguity, and to listen to those who concurred with the evidence of the Law Society to the Welsh Assembly that 'Signalling the law is not what we need. We need clear legislation. We need to be clear that problems that can be foreseen are dealt with at the time of law making and that we do not leave any queries and issues as grey areas.'[143] Noting in particular the demographic position of the Welsh language in Wales, it would appear that unconditional declarations regarding minority languages are almost unheard of. Where they exist they inevitably give rise to legal challenges, as was the case with the Irish language in the Republic of Ireland. The cases of both Canada and the Republic of Ireland demonstrate that a constitutional declaration regarding an official language does not in itself entail practical consequences or implications, but that this requires enabling legislation. It is this, and not the declarative statement, which makes real to citizens the commitment of the State to the implied status of the language. Some argue that what government does in practice is more important than any declarative statement. According to Revenga Sánchez, for example,

> From a 'constitutional culture' point of view, what central government officials do on language issues turns out to be more significant than producing statutory definitions laden with ambivalence. This is particularly true in the case of Article 3 of the Spanish Constitution, a dense arrangement of statements that fails to explain exactly what 'official character' means.[144]

Activists appear to be rather misguided on a number of lines of argument, or ill-informed on a number of issues, and merely revisit the debate of 1993. In this regard in particular it is most unfortunate that many experts appear to have been co-opted by certain activist interests and their expert knowledge somehow dissipated. As a result, an opportunity was lost to problematise the notion that Common Law is unaccommodating of official languages. Some argue that it may be useful to draw a distinction, in the context of the matters to hand in this chapter, between Common Law and Civic or Statutory Law and to categorise legal jurisdictions as either one of the other, and that is instructive to a degree – however, the jurisdiction of England and Wales features both. Indeed, very many jurisdictions are, in fact, hybrid. Some argue that the absence of a written constitution is also significant. Yet, neither New Zealand nor Israel has written constitutions but they do have de jure official languages. Canada has two de jure official languages even though it declares its constitution to be 'similar in principle to that of the UK', and while it has a Constitution Act, significant parts of the constitutional system are uncodified. In short, there does not appear to be a universal constitutional or legal principle that causes it to be necessarily unhelpful to declare a de jure official language in Common Law jurisdictions or in the context of an uncodified constitution. Rather, opposition to doing so is merely a matter of political judgement and practical consideration. A more robust interrogation of that empirical fact ought to have been possible during the course of the Measure, and were that to have happened, the results of that would have been most instructive. The problem with the LCO, in a nutshell, is that while it delegates power to the National Assembly for Wales with regard to the Welsh language, it does not do so for the English language.[145] Thus, any formulation regarding the official status of the Welsh language that also includes the English language would, quite simply, be beyond the legislative competence of the Assembly. In other words, for the Assembly to declare in statutory form that Welsh and English are the official languages of Wales and that they are of equal validity and status would be of doubtful vires, and very possibly ultra vires. Equally, it would be appear to be entirely intra vires to declare that the Welsh language is an official language of Wales while at the same time defining the meaning of that term, as per Greenberg, and also asserting that such a declaration does not affect the status of the English language.

Notes

1. http://www.comisiynyddygymraeg.org/English/Commissioner/Pages/Aim.aspx.
2. Labour Party and Plaid Cymru, *One Wales. A progressive agenda for the government of Wales. An agreement between the Labour and Plaid Cymru Groups in the National Assembly 27 June 2007*.
3. Welsh Policy Paper 6, *Official status* (unpublished paper, August 2008), p. 4.

4   Welsh Policy Paper 6, *Official status*, pp. 8–10.
5   Welsh Policy Paper 6, *Official status*, p. 4.
6   For a fuller articulation of the term see P. Carlin, 'Priod iaith', in S. Brooks (ed.), *Pa beth yr aethoch allan i'w achub? Ysgrifau i gynorthwyo'r gwrthsafiad yn erbyn dadfeiliad y Gymru Gymraeg* (Llanrwst: Gwasg Carreg Gwalch, 2013), pp. 130–54.
7   Welsh Policy Paper 6, p. 4.
8   Welsh Policy Paper 9, *Matters excluded from the LCO* (unpublished paper, 2008), p. 2.
9   Welsh Policy Paper 9, p. 3.
10 Welsh Assembly Government, *Memorandum from the Welsh Assembly Government. Constitutional Law: Devolution, Wales. The National Assembly for Wales (Legislative Competence) (Welsh Language) Order 2009. Proposal for a Legislative Competence Order on the Welsh Language* (Cardiff: Welsh Assembly Government, 2009a [January]), p. 5, and Welsh Assembly Government, *Memorandum from the Welsh Assembly Government. Constitutional Law: Devolution, Wales. The National Assembly for Wales (Legislative Competence) (Welsh Language) Order 2009. Draft Legislative Competence Order on the Welsh Language* (Cardiff: Welsh Assembly Government, 2009b [October]), p. 7.
11 P. Ward, *The Proposed Welsh Language Legislative Competence Order. Standard Note SN/HA/4973* (London: House of Commons Library, 11 December 2009), p. 8.
12 Ward, *The Proposed Welsh Language Legislative Competence Order*, p. 8.
13 Ferrers, quoted in Ward, *The Proposed Welsh Language Legislative Competence Order*, pp. 8–9.
14 Gwilym Prys Davies, quoted in Ward, *The Proposed Welsh Language Legislative Competence Order*, p. 9.
15 Welsh Policy Paper 13, *Official status* (unpublished paper, 2009), p. 1.
16 Welsh Policy Paper 13, *Official status*, p. 1.
17 Welsh Policy Paper 13, *Official status*, p. 1.
18 *http://www.irishstatutebook.ie/en/constitution/*.
19 Welsh Policy Paper 13, par. 9.
20 Welsh Policy Paper 13, par. 13.
21 *http://www.legislation.gov.uk/asp/2005/7/contents*.
22 Welsh Policy Paper 13, p. 3.
23 Welsh Policy Paper 13, p. 5.
24 Welsh Policy Paper 13, par. 28.
25 Welsh Policy Paper 15, *Policy instructions to legal services on the proposed Welsh Language Measure* (unpublished paper, April 2009), p. 41.
26 Welsh Policy Paper 15, par. 4.3.
27 Welsh Policy Paper 15, par. 4.4.

28 Welsh Policy Paper 15, p. 42.
29 Welsh Policy Paper 15, p. 42.
30 Welsh Policy Paper 15, par. 4.6.
31 Welsh Policy Paper 15, par. 4.8.
32 Welsh Policy Paper 15, p. 43.
33 Welsh Policy Paper 15, par. 4.9.
34 E. Lewis, 'Angen rhoi statws swyddogol a chyfartal i'r Gymraeg', *Golwg*, 11 Mawrth (2010a).
35 'Lawyers seek to expose flaws in new Welsh language laws', *Daily Post*, 18 March 2010.
36 E. Lewis et al., 'Cyfreithwyr yn ymateb i'r Mesur Iaith', *Golwg*, 18 Mawrth (2010).
37 Emyr Lewis, *Written Evidence, The proposed Welsh Language (Wales) Measure – Evidence Session 22 April 2010, Legislative Committee 2, the National Assembly for Wales* (2010).
38 Emyr Lewis, *Written Evidence*.
39 Emyr Lewis, *Written Evidence*.
40 Emyr Lewis, *Oral Evidence*.
41 Emyr Lewis, *Oral Evidence*.
42 Emyr Lewis, *Oral Evidence*.
43 Welsh Language Board, *Written Evidence. Response to the proposed Welsh Language (Wales) Measure 2010, National Assembly for Wales Legislative Committee No. 2. Paper 1. 29 April 2010* (2010).
44 Cwmni Iaith, *Written Evidence. Response to the proposed Welsh Language (Wales) Measure 2010, National Assembly for Wales Legislative Committee No. 2, 7 May 2010 MI 54*.
45 http://cymdeithas.org/2010/06/10/mudiadau_yn_gofyn_ir_llywodraeth_newid_y_mesur_iaith.html; http://bbc.co.uk/news/10279845; http://www.walesonline.co.uk/news/wales-news/plea-made-changes-welsh-language-1912609.
46 http://cymdeithas.org/2010/06/10/mudiadau_yn_gofyn_ir_llywodraeth_newid_y_mesur_iaith.html.
47 Welsh Language Society, *Oral & Written Evidence*, The Proposed Welsh Language (Wales) Measure – Evidence Session 27 May 2010, Legislative Committee 2, the National Assembly for Wales.
48 http://www.landmarkchambers.co.uk/gwion_lewis.
49 G. Lewis, *Hawl i'r Gymraeg* (Tal-y-bont: Y Lolfa, 2008).
50 J. Mowbray, 'Linguistic justice in international law: an evaluation of the discursive framework', *International Journal for the Semiotics of Law – Revue International de sémiotique juridque*, 24/1 (2011), 79–95; J. Mowbray, *Linguistic Justice. International Law and Language Policy* (Oxford: Oxford University Press, 2012); M. Paz, 'The failed promise of language rights: a critique of the international language rights regime', *Harvard International Law Journal*, 54/1

(2013), 195–218; V. Pupavac, 'Language rights in conflict and the denial of language as communication', *International Journal of Human Rights*, 10/1 (2006), 61–78; V. Pupavac, *Language Rights: From Free Speech to Linguistic Governance* (Basingstoke: Palgrave Macmillan, 2012).

51 Y. Peled, 'Language, rights and the language of language rights: the need for a new conceptual framework in the political theory of language policy', *Journal of Language and Politics*, 10/3 (2011), 436–56; Y. Peled, 'Normative language policy: interface and inferences', *Language Policy*, 13 (2014), 301–15.

52 F. de Varennes, 'Review of Linguistic justice: international law and language policy by Jacqueline Mowbray, Oxford: Oxford University Press', *American Anthropologist*, 116/4 (2014), 884–5.

53 X. Arzoz, 'The nature of language rights', *Journal of Ethnopolitics and Minority Issues in Europe*, 6/2 (2007), 1–35.

54 Case name and number: Diergaardt et al. v. Namibia. Co. Nr. 760/1997. Parties: Cpt. Diergaardt of the Rehoboth Baster Community et all, vs. State of Namibia. Published online as a 'case brief' by the University of Oslo at: *http://www.unio.no*; see also *http://www.uio.no/studier/emner/jus/humanrights/HUMR5508/v12/undervisningsmateriale/Diergaardt%20v.%20Namibia-CCPR.pdf* Alternatively, see J.G.A. Diergaardt (late Captain of the Rehoboth Baster Community) et al. v. Namibia, Communication No. 760/1997, U.N. Doc. CCPR/C/69/D/760/1997 (2000). Published online at University of Minnesota Human Rights Library: *http://www1.umn.edu/humanrts/undocs/session69/view760.htm*

55 See p. 314 in J. Woehrling, 'L'évolution du cadre juridique et conceptuel de la legislation linguistique du Québec', in A. Stefanescu and P. Georgeault (eds), *Le français au Québec: les nouveaux défis* (Québec: Conseil supérieur de la langue française, 2005), pp. 253–356.

56 See, for example, J. L. Goldsmith and E. A. Posner, *The Limits of International Law* (Oxford: Oxford University Press, 2005).

57 Lewis, *Hawl i'r Gymraeg*, p. 110.

58 S. Moyn, *The Last Utopia: Human Rights in History* (Cambridge, MA: Belknap, Harvard University Press).

59 Welsh Language Society, *Oral & Written Evidence*.

60 Amendments tabled 5 October 2010: *http://www.assemblywales.org/wl_stage2_101005-v2.pdf*; see also the accompanying Explanatory Memorandum at: *http://www.assemblywales.org/summary_of_amendments_wl.pdf*.

61 Section 4.1 on page 9 of the Summary of Amendments; see: *http://www.assembly.wales/NAfW%20Documents/summary_of_amendments_WL.pdf%20-%2017112010/summary_of_amendments_WL-English.pdf*.

62 National Assembly for Wales, Constitutional Affairs Committee, *Inquiry into the drafting of Welsh Government Measures: lessons from the first three years. February 2011* (Cardiff: National Assembly for Wales, 2011).

63 See also O. Lando, 'On legislative style and structure', *Juridica International Law Review*, XI (2006), 13–19, for example, on the meaning and function of 'black-letter law'.

64 National Assembly for Wales, Constitutional Affairs Committee, *Inquiry into the drafting of Welsh Government Measures: lessons from the first three years. February 2011*, pars 29 and 30.

65 *http://news.bbc.co.uk/welsh/hi/newsid_9150000/newsid_9155800/9155821.stm.*

66 At a meeting of the Committee on 14 October 2010; see Section 4.1, p. 10 of Summary of Amendments at: *http://www.assembly.wales/NAfW%20Documents/summary_of_amendments_WL.pdf%20-%2017112010/summary_of_amendments_WL-English.pdf.*

67 At a meeting of the Committee on 14 October 2010; see pp. 6–9 of Minutes of Meeting at: *http://www.assembly.wales/Committee%20Documents/LC2(3)-18-10%20%20Transcript%20(PDF,%20744KB)-14102010-201344/lc220101014fv_lc2-18-10-English.pdf; http://www.assembly.wales/NAfW%20Documents/summary_of_amendments_WL.pdf%20-%2017112010/summary_of_amendments_WL-English.pdf.*

68 At a meeting of the Committee on 14 October 2010; see pp. 6–9 of Minutes of Meeting at: *http://www.assembly.wales/Committee%20Documents/LC2(3)-18-10%20%20Transcript%20(PDF,%20744KB)-14102010-201344/lc220101014fv_lc2-18-10-English.pdf; http://www.assembly.wales/NAfW%20Documents/summary_of_amendments_WL.pdf%20-%2017112010/summary_of_amendments_WL-English.pdf.*

69 At a meeting of the Committee on 14 October 2010; see pp. 6–9 of Minutes of Meeting at: *http://www.assembly.wales/Committee%20Documents/LC2(3)-18-10%20%20Transcript%20(PDF,%20744KB)-14102010-201344/lc220101014fv_lc2-18-10-English.pdf; http://www.assembly.wales/NAfW%20Documents/summary_of_amendments_WL.pdf%20-%2017112010/summary_of_amendments_WL-English.pdf.*

70 At a meeting of the Committee on 14 October 2010; see pp. 6–9 of Minutes of Meeting at: *http://www.assembly.wales/Committee%20Documents/LC2(3)-18-10%20%20Transcript%20(PDF,%20744KB)-14102010-201344/lc220101014fv_lc2-18-10-English.pdf; http://www.assembly.wales/NAfW%20Documents/summary_of_amendments_WL.pdf%20-%2017112010/summary_of_amendments_WL-English.pdf.*

71 A. Ff. Jones, *Welsh language policy and legislation update – November 2010. Open response letter from the Heritage Minister to correspondents on the proposed Welsh Language Measure* (Cardiff: Welsh Assembly Government, 2010b).
72 Welsh Assembly Government, *The Proposed Welsh Language (Wales) Measure 2010. Explanatory Memorandum to the Proposed Welsh Language Wales Measure 2010 30 November 2010* (Cardiff: Welsh Assembly Government, 2010b), p. 47.
73 National Assembly for Wales, *The Record of Proceedings 7 December 2010* (Cardiff: National Assembly for Wales, 2010b), p. 28.
74 National Assembly for Wales, *The Record of Proceedings 7 December 2010*, p. 24.
75 http://www.golwg360.com/archif/30441-mesur-iaith-croesawu-gwelliant-munud-olaf.
76 National Assembly for Wales, *The Record of Proceedings 7 December 2010*, pp. 26–7.
77 National Assembly for Wales, *The Record of Proceedings 7 December 2010*, p. 29.
78 National Assembly for Wales, *The Record of Proceedings 7 December 2010*, p. 29.
79 National Assembly for Wales, *The Record of Proceedings 7 December 2010*, p. 28.
80 National Assembly for Wales, *The Record of Proceedings 7 December 2010*, p. 28.
81 National Assembly for Wales, *The Record of Proceedings 7 December 2010*, p. 29.
82 http://www.golwg360.com/archif/30441-mesur-iaith-croesawu-gwelliant-munud-olaf.
83 National Assembly for Wales, *The Record of Proceedings 7 December 2010*, p. 31.
84 Welsh Policy Paper 17, *Official status* (unpublished paper, 2010); Welsh Policy Paper 34, *Official status* (unpublished paper, 2010); Welsh Policy Paper 35, *Letter from Parliamentary Counsel regarding official status* (unpublished paper, 2010); Welsh Policy Paper 40, *Official status of the Welsh language: legal advice* (unpublished paper, 2010).
85 European Court of Human Rights [ECHR], Research Division, *Cultural Rights in the Case-law of the European Court of Human Rights* (Strasbourg: Council of Europe, 2011).
86 F. de Varennes, *International and Comparative Perspectives in the Use of Official Languages. Models and Approaches for South Africa* (Afrikaanse Taalraad, 2012a), p. 4, and F. de Varennes, *International and Comparative Perspectives in the Use of Official Languages. Models and Approaches for South Africa. Brief Report. Legal Opinion* (Afrikaanse Taalraad, 2012b), p. 4.

87 The author consulted with a number of legal scholars on this matter in particular.
88 ECHR, *Cultural rights*.
89 De Varennes, *International and Comparative Perspectives in the Use of Official Languages. Models and Approaches for South Africa*.
90 E. J. Ruíz Vieytez, *Official Languages and Minority Languages: Issues about their Legal Status through Comparative Law* (II Simposio Internacional Mercator: Europa 2004: Un nou marc per a totes les llengües? Tarragona – Catalunya, 27–8 February, 2004).
91 De Varennes, *International and Comparative Perspectives in the Use of Official Languages. Models and Approaches for South Africa*, pp. 4–7.
92 S. Ó Conaill, 'The Irish language and the Irish legal system, 1922 to present' (unpublished PhD thesis, Cardiff University, 2013), and T. Ó Máille, *Stádas na Gaeilge – Dearcadh Dlíthiúil / The Status of Irish – A Legal Perspective* (Dublin: Bord na Gaeilge, 1990).
93 Ó Máille, *Stádas na Gaeilge – Dearcadh Dlíthiúil / The Status of Irish – A Legal Perspective*, pars 17–19.
94 Ó Máille, *Stádas na Gaeilge – Dearcadh Dlíthiúil / The Status of Irish – A Legal Perspective*, par. 32.
95 W. McLeod, 'Gaelic in contemporary Scotland: contradictions, challenges and strategies' (unpublished research paper, University of Edinburgh, January 2006), 1 and 6. Published online at: *http://www.poileasaidh.celtscot.ed.ac.uk*.
96 See Bòrd na Gàidhlig, *Draft Guidance on the Development of Gaelic Language Plans* (Inverness: Bòrd na Gàidhlig, 2014), p. 9, and Bòrd na Gàidhlig, *National Gaelic Language Plan 2012–2017. Growth and Improvement* (Isle of Skye: Bòrd na Gàidhlig, 2012), p. 7. For other similar such assertions see the following: *http://www.educationscotland.gov.uk/newsandevents/educationnews/2013/pressreleases/august/news_tcm4811070.asp*; *http://news.bbc.co.uk/local/northeastscotlandnorthernisles/hi/people_and_places/newsid_8790000/8790315.stm*; *https://www.scotreferendum.com/questions/will-gaelic-be-recognised-as-an-official-language-in-an-independent-scotland/*; *http://www.express.co.uk/news/uk/397171/Police-website-has-70-languages-but-not-Scots-Gaelic*; *http://www.visitscotland.com/about/arts-culture/uniquely-scottish/gaelic/*.
97 See p. 5 in W. McLeod, 'Official status for Gaelic: prospects and problems', *Scottish Affairs*, 21 (1997), 95–118. Published online at: *http://www.papers.celtscot.ed.ac.uk/officialstatus.html*.
98 Scottish Government, *The Gaelic Language Bill consultation paper* (Edinburgh: Scottish Executive, 2003), section 4.
99 Emyr Lewis, *Oral Evidence*, par. 29.
100 National Assembly for Wales, *The Record of Proceedings 7 December 2010*.

101 W. Wilson, *The Welsh Language Bill [HL] [Bill 146 of session 1992–93] Research paper 93/32. 17 March 1993* (London: House of Commons Library, 1993).
102 Wilson, *The Welsh Language Bill [HL] [Bill 146 of session 1992–93] Research paper 93/32. 17 March 1993.*
103 Ferrers quoted in Wilson, *The Welsh Language Bill*, p. 2.
104 Wilson, *The Welsh Language Bill*, p. 4.
105 http://www.publications.parliament.uk/pa/cm199293/cmhansrd/1993-07-13/Orals-2-html.
106 Excepting Sharia Law and Chinese Law.
107 http://socialsciences.exeter.ac.uk/law/undergraduate/commonlawcountries/.
108 Loi constitutionnelle no. 92-554 du 25 juin 1992 ajoutant à la Constitution un titre: 'Des communautés européennes et de l'Union européenne'.
109 W. Tetley, *Mixed Jurisdictions: Common Law vs Civil Law (Codified and Uncodified)* (2000). Published online at: http://www.cisg.law.pace.edu/cisg/biblio/tetley.html.
110 http://www.dw.de/constitution-should-protect-german-language-says-politician/a-5994684. For the Constitution see 'Basic Law of the Federal Republic of Germany'.
111 Ruíz Vieytez, *Official languages and minority languages*, p. 6.
112 Tetley, *Mixed Jurisdictions*, p. 4.
113 R. Heaton, 'Making the law easier for users: the role of statutes' (speech 14 October 2013). Published in 2014 online at: https://www.gov.uk/government/speeches/making-the-law-easier-for-users-the-role-of-statutes--2.
114 J. Gusfield, *Symbolic Crusade: Status Politics and the American Temperance Movement* (Chicago: University of Illinois Press, 1963), and J. Gusfield, 'Moral passage: the symbolic process in public designations of deviance', *Social Problems*, 15/2 (1967), 175–88.
115 Gusfield, 'Moral passage, 175.
116 See 84–5 in M. Tushnett and L. Yackle, 'Symbolic statutes and real laws: the pathologies of the Antiterrorism and Effective Death Penalty Act and the Prison Litigation Reform Act', *Duke Law Journal*, 47/1 October (1997), 1–85.
117 Tushnett and Yackle, 'Symbolic statutes and real laws', 85–6.
118 J. P. Dwyer, 'The pathology of symbolic legislation', *Ecology Law Quarterly*, 17/2 (1990), 233.
119 D. Ager, *Language Policy in Britain and France* (London: Cassell, 1996), p. 169.
120 R. M. Beaupré, *Interpreting Bilingual Legislation* (Toronto: Carswell, 1986); M. Bastarche, N. Metallic, R. Morris and C. Essert, *The Law of Bilingual Interpretation* (Markham, ON: LexisNexis, 2008).

121　Official Languages Ordinance Cap.1, Part IIA, § 10B(10).
122　Ward, *The Proposed Welsh Language Legislative Competence Order*.
123　Wilson, *The Welsh Language Bill*.
124　Ferrers, quoted in Wilson, *The Welsh Language Bill*, pp. 5–6. See also HL Deb 18.2.93 cc.1265–1267.
125　M. George, 'Supreme Court dictates pace of Welsh devolution', *Clickonwales*, 15 October 2012. Published online at: http://www.clickonwales.org/2012/10/supreme-court-dictates-direction-of-welsh-devolution-journey/.
126　See, for example, D. Dixon, 'David defeats Goliath', *The Law Society Gazette*, 14 January 2013. Published online at: http://www.lawgazette.co.uk/analysis/david-defeats-goliath/68959.fullarticle.
127　Welsh Policy Paper 6, p. 3.
128　Welsh Policy Paper 19, *Commissioner – equal treatment of Welsh and English* (unpublished paper, 2010), p. 1.
129　Welsh Policy Paper 19, *Commissioner – equal treatment of Welsh and English*, p. 2.
130　Welsh Policy Paper 6, p. 5.
131　De Varennes, *International and Comparative Perspectives in the Use of Official Languages. Models and Approaches for South Africa*, pp. 52–6.
132　See, for example: http://supremecourt.ie/supremecourt/sclibrary3.nsf/(WebFiles)/61352BDAC878CC728025771B005AF6E2/$FILE/O%20Murchu%20v%20Clerigh%20an%20Dail%20and%20Irila%20(Final)%20Web%20Version.pdf.
133　Department of Community, Rural and Gaeltacht Affairs, *Guidelines under Section 12 of the Official Languages Act 2003* (Dublin: Department of Community, Rural and Gaeltacht Affairs, 2004), p. 3.
134　http://webarchive.nationalarchives.gov.uk/20140605075122/http://commissionondevolutioninwales.independent.gov.uk/.
135　See chapter 12, 'Further matters', 12.2 'Welsh language', pp. 133–4, in Commission on Devolution in Wales, *Empowerment and Responsibility: Legislative Powers to Strengthen Wales* (Cardiff: Commission on Devolution in Wales, 2014).
136　Chapter 12, 'Further matters', 12.2 'Welsh language', p. 134.
137　Chapter 12, 'Further matters', 12.2 'Welsh language', p. 133.
138　Chapter 12, 'Further matters', 12.2 'Welsh language', p. 133.
139　HM Government, *Powers for a Purpose: Towards a Lasting Devolution Settlement for Wales* (London: HMSO, 2015).
140　HM Government, *Powers for a Purpose: Towards a Lasting Devolution Settlement for Wales*, p. 41, para. 2.10.1.
141　HM Government, *Powers for a Purpose: Towards a Lasting Devolution Settlement for Wales*, p. 41, para. 2.10.7.

142 HM Government, *Powers for a Purpose: Towards a Lasting Devolution Settlement for Wales*, p. 41, para. 2.10.3.
143 Law Society, quoted in National Assembly for Wales, Legislation Committee No. 2, *Proposed Welsh Language (Wales) Measure Stage 1 Committee Report July 2010* (Cardiff: National Assembly for Wales, 2010), pp. 61–2.
144 See p. 143 in M. Revenga Sánchez, 'Notas sobre oficialidad lingüística y cultura constitucional', *Revista de Llengua i Dret*, 43 (2005), 129–43.
145 The Welsh language is listed as 'Subject 20'. See, for example, *https://www.gov.uk/devolution-settlement-wales*.
146 The former colonies of the states listed above may, in almost all cases, be added under the respective categories.

8 | CONCLUSIONS: TOO COMPLEX A REGIME?

While one of the policy goals behind the 2011 Measure was to create a framework for the delivery of Welsh language services that would be more readily understood by the public, the First Minister has been obliged to defend the new Welsh language regulatory regime from the charge of being too complicated: 'Mae Carwyn Jones yn wfftio'r pryderon bod y drefn newydd [. . .] yn gymhleth ac aneglur'[1] ('Carwyn Jones dismisses concerns that the new regime [. . .] is complex and unclear'). That said, it is also the case that the Welsh government previously rejected the Commissioner's draft Standards as being 'too complex'.[2] Subsequent to this the Commissioner complained publicly that the Measure was poorly drafted due to its architects having 'no real experience of real life'.[3] During the passage of the Measure many commentators asserted that the Measure itself was very complex.[4] Some others asserted that the process as a whole, including the LCO process, was 'hugely complex', as noted by the Welsh Affairs Committee.[5] Some interviewees claimed that the complicating factor of the LCO was the main reason for the inherent complexity of the Measure and therefore of the Welsh language regulatory framework (Fieldwork Interview 66). Elsewhere, David Lambert of the Wales Governance Centre asserted in a BBC Radio Wales interview of 5 February 2009 that 'the current Welsh language LCO is likely to take some years before it finally sees an outcome in terms of a Measure passed'.

Yet, there is some expert praise for standards of drafting of legislation in Wales in general,[6] despite initial confusion with regard to

Year	Number of Acts	Total number of pages	Average number of pages
1951	59	628	11
1961	61	938	15
Welsh Language Act 1967			3 [total length of Act]
1971	66	1,300	20
1981	56	1,490	27
1991	58	1,492	26
Welsh Language Act 1993			21 [total length of Act]
2001	21	1,363	65
2011	22	2,121	96
Welsh Language Measure 2011			152 [total length of Measure]

Figure 13. *Length of the Welsh language legislation in the context of UK government primary legislation based upon data derived in part from House of Lords, 2013: 3–4.*

'the distinction between the legislative role of a parliament and the administrative and executive roles of a government'[7] and the concerns expressed by other experts that 'the Measures do not always contain clear language or provide legal clarity'.[8] In addition, some interviewees were most decidedly of the view that they were in fact familiar with other much more complex legislation (Fieldwork Interview 61). The Measure itself is certainly a lengthy piece of legislation. Set in the context of UK legislation, the Measure is well above average length, even allowing for the historical growth in the average length of primary legislation (Figure 13). But shorter does not necessarily mean less complicated, especially if the legislation requires substantial and complex delegated legislation, or regulations, for it to be implemented. How, therefore, might this question of complexity be approached; how is overly complex legislation identified?

The Office of the Parliamentary Counsel has formulated a set of questions through which one can address the matter of legislative complexity in an authoritative and objective manner[9] (Figure 14). Usefully in this regard, also, is the Hansard Society text on how to improve the quality of legislation.[10] Legislatures elsewhere have developed similar such texts, manuals or guidelines.[11] Very briefly, the Welsh language regulatory regime appears to be relevant as follows to some of the questions posed here. In particular, the regime does not achieve some of its intended policy outcomes (Standards are no less complex to the Welsh-speaking citizen than Schemes; Welsh is an official language in the Assembly but not in Wales); implementation has been fragmented and idiosyncratic (the Commissioner's non-statutory consultation of draft Standards; the conflict on interest arising from the connections between the Welsh Language Tribunal and the Minister holding the Welsh language policy portfolio); there are overlapping regulation mechanisms and there are over-complicated commencement provisions (the coexistence of Standards and several types of Schemes; more than one complaint-handling body operates in the Welsh language regulatory regime, namely the PSOW and the Commissioner); there are ambiguous provisions (the application of the regulatory regime to the Crown, Ministers of the Crown, and Crown bodies).

The next set of questions to ask is: when, where and why does complexity arise in Welsh language regulatory regime? This appears to be at various 'upstream' points including, to various degrees, in (1) policy development, (2) instructions and drafting, and (3) introduction (Figure 15). With regard to policy development, certain political contingencies had a direct impact. These include the prior manifesto commitments by Plaid Cymru to create a commissioner, establish language rights and confirm Welsh as an official language. None of these appears to have been subject to serious scrutiny during the course of their being adopted in the manifesto. Nor do they appear to have been subjected to any such scrutiny prior to their being adopted as features of the programme of government for the new Welsh government. Contrary to the case put forward by the Counsel General on Measures in general to the Assembly's inquiry into the drafting of legislation,[12] it is simply not the case that policy issues relating to the 2011 Measure were 'fully thought through before legislative proposals are brought forward', as it is demonstrably the case that policy was in actual fact adapted as the 2011 Measure was in the process of being scrutinised in the Assembly. Once these commitments had been made, then pressure from Welsh language interest groups and their co-opted experts closed down much

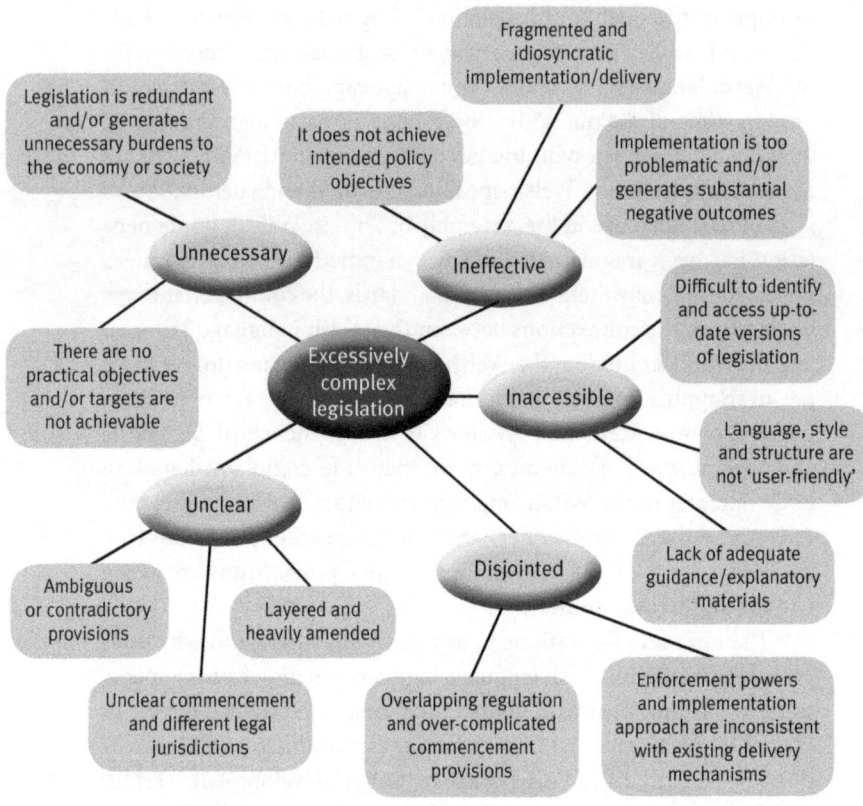

Figure 14. *Identifying excessively complex legislation (source: Office of the Parliamentary Counsel, 2013: 13).*

of the space for the reasoned examination of the policy options. During the legislative cycle in particular the quality and dependability of the expert evidence in some important cases is compromised by conflation with activism. In certain regards, the motivations for policy change, and in particular the decision to create a Commissioner as opposed to a corporate aggregate, were driven by presentational motivations, rather than the most appropriate model for the purpose of the office being identified and adopted. The most obvious weakness in relation to the policy instructions and drafting stage pertains to the lack of clarity regarding 'the Crown' with regard to the Measure and also uncertainty surrounding the legal significance of the term 'official language'.

As regards the former, the difficulty here lies in the wholly ambiguous nature of the constitutional position of 'the Crown' in UK law in and of itself; this is not a fault of the authors of the Measure. It may be instructive to note that in the case of OCOL in Canada there is no such ambiguity; the Crown is subject to the Commissioner and that is that. No constitutional or legal difficulties have arisen from the particular arrangement made there. Regarding the latter, casting the evidence-gathering net more widely would have generated much more certainty as to whether Common Law can accommodate an official language along with the implications of statutory declarations on official language status. With regard to the final 'upstream' point, namely introduction, the dialogue between the Commissioner and the government in the opening part of the implementation stage appears to have been inadequate. For example, the Framework Agreement was not signed until September 2012 nor, indeed, did the prospective Commissioner attend a crucial pre-commencement briefing. In particular, there would appear not to have been a shared understanding between the Commissioner and the Government of the precise nature of the independence of the office of the Commissioner from the government.

Complexity also arises from the simple fact that the Welsh government commitments created an extremely tight timetable for achieving too much. While contributing to the overall timetable,[13] the LCO process in itself is not a cause of unnecessary complexity. In the UK parliamentary review of the LCO process as a whole it was concluded that the Welsh language LCO in particular, 'provides an example of successful working with the Assembly'.[14] Indeed, during the course of this review, in a very lively exchange between Alun Michael MP and Professor Richard Wyn Jones, it was agreed that many of the critics of the LCO process in academia and amongst journalists had quite simply got their facts wrong.[15] Under the Measure alone the government created the office of the Commissioner, a Tribunal, a mechanism for the creation of Standards, made a declaration on the official status of Welsh, gave statutory protection to the freedom to use the Welsh language, provided for enforcement and remedies, made provision for 'the Crown', created an Advisory Panel and provided for ministerial direction to be applied to the Commissioner (Figure 16). As a result of the timetable, the policy development stage is very truncated and there

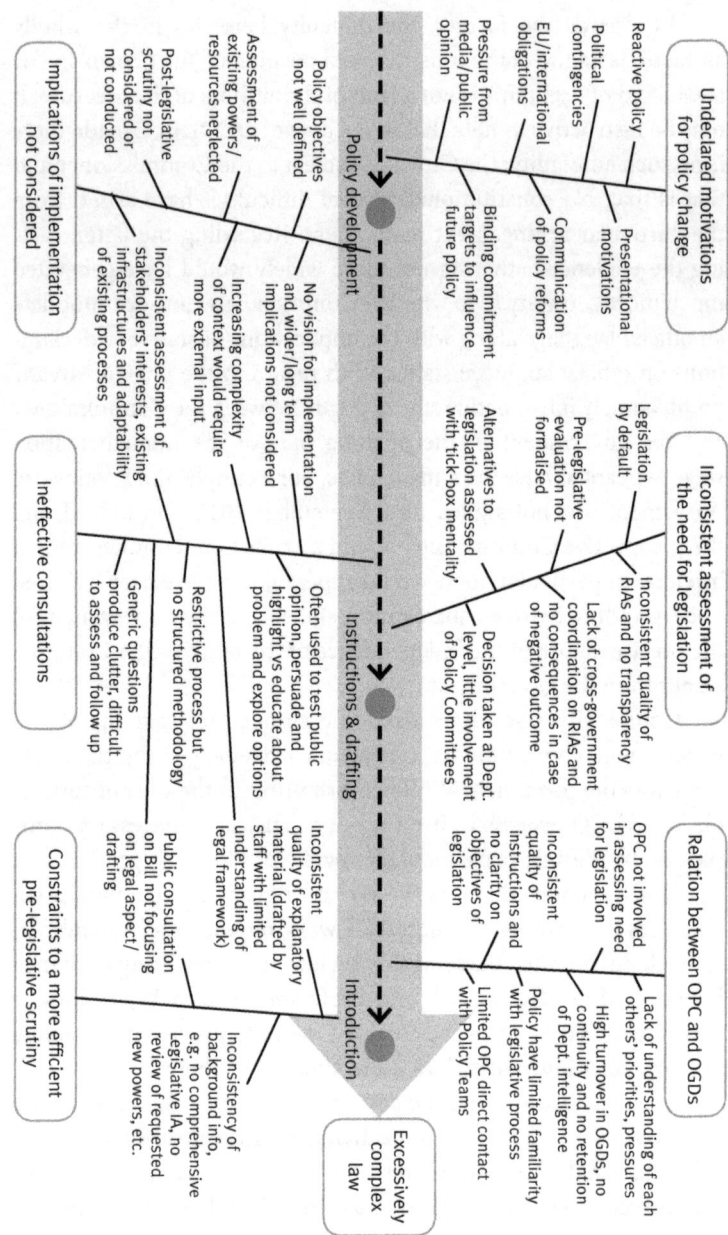

Figure 15. *From policy to Bill – a summary of upstream causes of excessively complex legislation (source: Office of the Parliamentary Counsel, 2013b: 25).*

Conclusions: too complex a regime?   213

are significant shifts in policy aim with little analysis of the effects (e.g. the shift from minimum Standards, and the erosion of the policy-based distinction between statutory and non-statutory promotion). While some of the complexity is necessary to the effective implementation of the Measure and the realisation of policy aims, the multi-purpose nature of the Measure confirms that it is, as the Office of the Parliamentary Counsel puts it, a 'Christmas tree' law.[16] That is, it has had hung upon it all the decorations which attracted the attention of the principal actors in the government at that time. Some aspects to the Measure would have merited being separated out, such as those parts relating to freedom to use Welsh and the clauses regarding the official status of the language. The Measure can be said to be a 'Christmas tree' law, in the sense of the term as understood in the law-making circles in the USA,[17] in that it attracted a very considerable number of amendments, including some proposed by the Welsh government itself.[18] In addition, the Measure has given rise to several other instruments (Figure 17), both directly (e.g. in relation to Standards) and indirectly (e.g. in

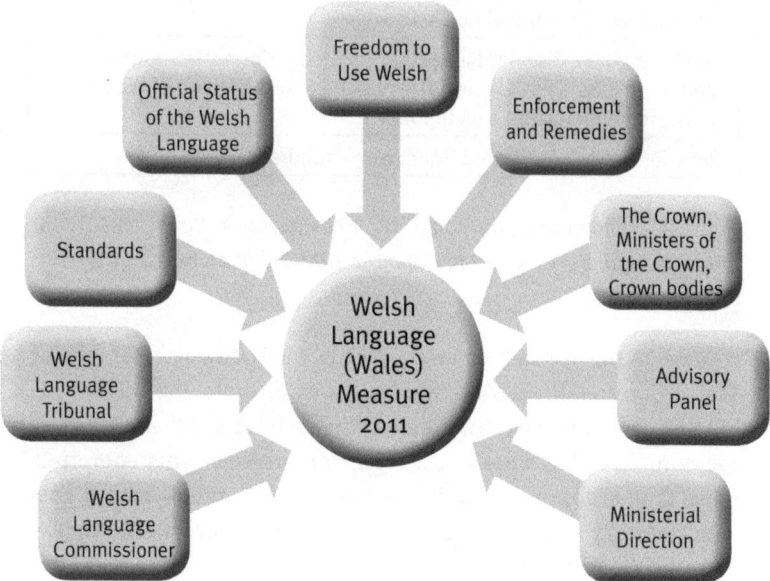

Figure 16. *Identifying the potential for complexity arising from the main content and purpose of the Measure.*

Welsh Language Act 1993
Welsh Language Schemes Statutory Guidelines 1996
Welsh Language Schemes (inherited from Welsh Language Act 1993 – 550 in 2011)
Government of Wales Act 2006
National Assembly for Wales Commission (Crown Status) (No.2) Order 2007
Welsh Language (Wales) Measure 2011
Welsh Language Commissioner (Appointment) Regulations 2012
Advisory Panel to the Welsh Language Commissioner (Appointment) Regulations 2012
Welsh Statutory Instruments 2012 No.752 (W.102) Welsh Language, Wales. The Welsh Language Board (Transfer of Staff, Property, Rights and Liabilities) Order 2012
National Assembly for Wales (Official Languages) Act 2012
Welsh Language Tribunal (Appointment) Regulations 2013
National Assembly for Wales Assembly Commission Official Languages Scheme 2013
Welsh Language Tribunal Rules 2015
Welsh Language Standards: Regulations 2015 (County Boroughs and County Councils in Wales, National Park Authorities and Welsh Ministers) (with further sets to follow)
Compliance Notices (issued from 2015 – hundreds?)

Figure 17. *Quantifying the potential for complexity in the current Welsh language regulatory regime: pertinent statute and instruments with statutory force.*

relation to the Welsh language policy of the National Assembly for Wales Commission). Moreover, taken as a whole, the Measure is but one constituent part of the statutory architecture that comprises the complete Welsh language regulatory regime. This comprises more than a dozen distinctive pieces of law or other instruments with statutory force; it is inarguable that certain layers of complexity result from this, too.

Finally, to what extent can it be said that a regime based upon Standards is more complex than one based upon Schemes? During the passage of the Measure through the Assembly the Wales

Governance Centre stated that 'It is impossible to decide whether the Measure provides greater clarity and consistency for Welsh speakers in terms of the services they can expect to receive in Welsh without seeing the draft of the Standards proposed [under the Measure].'[19] A crude quantification of the volume of individual commitments made under Schemes indicates that they are complex in that regard. There were around 550 Schemes in operation in 2011. Given that the average number of separate commitments, or individual regulatory standards, embodied in a Scheme is 94, then the Welsh language regulatory regime as was under Schemes alone comprised something in the order of 51,700 individual regulatory standards (Figure 18). The simplicity of Schemes, however, is that each individual organisation is only governed by its own Scheme. Also, this simplicity is reinforced by the fact that most of the routine interaction of the individual citizen is with a very discrete set of public bodies, most of which are local to them.

Under the previous regime, therefore, complexity was at the level of regulatory oversight, in other words only the regulator was required to be familiar with all 550 Schemes and their contents. For the individual citizen some complexity could arise upon their moving between different public bodies similar in function to avail themselves of their services, but being confronted by the contrasting

---

'By the end of 2011, some 550 Welsh Language Schemes were in operation.'

Average length of sample of Schemes – 33 pages.

Average number of service delivery commitments of sample of Schemes – 94.

550 x 33 = 18,150 pages of regulatory standards as per body of Schemes.

550 x 94 = 51,700 individual regulatory standards as per body of Schemes.

Figure 18. *Quantifying the potential for complexity in Welsh Language Schemes: volume and length of Schemes.*

commitments of those bodies to the Welsh language under their own unique Schemes. Such movement is likely to be sector sensitive; that is to say, not very important for individual citizens with regard to services provided by the local council, but potentially very important in domains such as the health sector, where there exist myriad actors providing services to the public and where the individual is likely to travel outside the locality in order to make use of a certain specialism. The simplicity of Standards is that the regulator does not have to negotiate the detail of the regulatory standards with hundreds of bodies. The greater simplicity is more clearly perceived by the institutional actors rather than the citizen.

It can be concluded with considerable confidence, therefore, that the Welsh language regulatory regime is complex. Some of that complexity is necessary, but some features of the regime are overly complex. Given the complications outlined briefly here, along with the various issues interrogated in some detail in the substantive chapters of this book, there is scope for reshaping the architecture of the Welsh language regulatory regime, including the office of the Commissioner itself.

Notes

1. G. Pennant, 'Amddiffyn y safonau', *Golwg*, 13 November (2014), 5.
2. L. Andrews, *Written statement – the Welsh Ministers' response to the Welsh Language Commissioner's proposals for Welsh Language standards*, 25 February 2013. Published online at: http//wales.gov.uk/about/cabinet/cabinet statements/2013/welshlanguagestandards/?lang=en.
3. Fieldnotes taken during the Commissioner's address to the International Conference of Language Commissioners in Dublin on 24 May 2013.
4. For example, Wales Governance Centre, *Response to the proposed Welsh Language (Wales) Measure MI 27 Written evidence submitted to National Assembly for Wales, Legislation Committee No. 2* (2010b).
5. Welsh Affairs Committee, *Fifth report – Review of the LCO process* (2010a). Published online at: *http://www.publications.parliament.uk/pa/cm200910/cmselect/cmwelaf/155/15502.htm*; Welsh Affairs Committee, *Wales and Whitehall. Minutes of evidence. Examination of witnesses. Professor Tim Jones, Professor Richard Wyn Jones, Ms Christina Palko, Ms Tessa Shellens & Mr Huw Williams 2 February*

2010 (2010b). Published online at: *http://www.publications. parliament.uk/pa/cm200910/cmselect/cmwelaf/246/10020203.htm.*

6   National Assembly for Wales, Constitutional Affairs Committee, *Inquiry into the drafting of Welsh Government Measures: lessons from the first three years. February 2011* (Cardiff: National Assembly for Wales, 2011).

7   D. Greenberg, 'Welsh devolution. Legal information and aspects of devolution', *Legal Information Management*, 13 (2013), 134–8, p. 135.

8   See p. 1. in Wales Governance Centre, *Drafting Welsh Measures: lessons from the first three years' evidence presented to the Constitutional Affairs Committee, National Assembly for Wales*, CA DM 5 (2010a). Published online at: *http://www.assembly.wales/ NAfW%20Documents/ca_5_-_cardiff_law_school.pdf%20-%20 28092010/ca_5_-_cardiff_law_school-English.pdf.*

9   Office of the Parliamentary Counsel, *When laws become too complex. A review into the causes of complex legislation* (London: Office of the Parliamentary Counsel, Cabinet Office, 2013b), p. 13.

10   R. Fox and M. Korris, *Making Better Law. Reform of the Legislative Process from Policy to Act* (London: Hansard Society, 2010).

11   For example, A. Seidman, R. Seidman and N. Abeysekere, *Assessing Legislation – A Manual for Legislators* (Boston, MA, 2003). Published online at: *http://iknowpolitics.org/sites/default/files/ assessing20legislation20-2001.200320-20en20-20pi.pdf.*

12   National Assembly for Wales, Constitutional Affairs Committee, *Inquiry into the drafting of Welsh Government Measures: lessons from the first three years. February 2011*, p. 12.

13   According to D. Miers, *Law Making in Wales: A Measure of Devolution* (London: Study of Parliament Group, 2011), p. 9, f.44, it took eighty-eight weeks to reach the Welsh Affairs Select Committee, due to negotiations between the governments of the UK Parliament and Welsh Assembly on agreeing upon a text. Other LCOs took different times, ranging from one week up to 104. The average was forty-five.

14   Welsh Affairs Committee, *Fifth report – Review of the LCO process* (2010a), section 3.

15   Welsh Affairs Committee, *Wales and Whitehall. Minutes of evidence. Examination of witnesses. Professor Tim Jones, Professor Richard Wyn Jones, Ms Christina Palko, Ms Tessa Shellens & Mr Huw Williams 2 February 2010* (2010b). See especially Q395 & Q396.

16   Office of the Parliamentary Counsel, *When laws become too complex*, p. 6.

17   *http://www.senate.gov/reference/glossary_term/christmas_tree_bill. htm.*

18 Miers states that the total number of proposed amendments was 'well over 100'; see Miers, *Law Making in Wales*, p. 24.
19 Wales Governance Centre, *Response to the proposed Welsh Language (Wales) Measure 2010 MI 27 Written evidence submitted to National Assembly for Wales, Legislation Committee No. 2* (2010b), point 1.
20 Welsh Language Board, *Review 1993–2012* (Cardiff: Welsh Language Board, 2012), p. 17.

BIBLIOGRAPHY

Admiral, *Admiral news update: Admiral apologise for language complaint*, 19 August 2013. Published online at: http://www.customerservicecontact.co.uk.

Ager, D., *Language Policy in Britain and France* (London: Cassell, 1996).

Andrews, L., *Written statement – the Welsh Ministers' response to the Welsh Language Commissioner's proposals for Welsh language standards*, 25 February 2013. Published online at: http://wales.gov.uk/about/cabinet/cabinetstatements/2013/welshlanguagestandards/?lang=en.

Arfon-Jones, E., *The tribunal system in Wales: Map and Update on Jurisdictions* (2012). Published online at: http://www.publiclawproject.org.uk/resources/129/the-tribunal-system-in-wales-map-and-update-on-jurisdictions.

Arzoz, X., 'The nature of language rights', *Journal of Ethnopolitics and Minority Issues in Europe*, 6/2 (2007), 1–35.

Baldwin, R., Cave, M., and Lodge, M. (eds), *The Oxford Handbook of Regulation* (Oxford: Oxford University Press, 2010).

Baldwin, R., Cave, M., and Lodge, M., *Understanding Regulation. Theory, Strategy, and Practice* (Oxford: Oxford University Press, 2011).

Bastarache, M., Metallic, N., Morris, R., and Essert, C., *The Law of Bilingual Interpretation* (Markham, ON: LexisNexis, 2008).

Bastiat, F., *The Law* (Auburn, AL: Ludwig von Mises Institute, 2007 repr.; original text 1850). Published online at: https://mises.org/sites/default/files/thelaw.pdf.

Beaupré, R. M., *Interpreting Bilingual Legislation* (Toronto: Carswell, 1986).

Becker, G. S., 'A theory of competition among pressure groups for political influence', *Quarterly Journal of Economics*, 98/3 (1983), 371–400.

Beiner, R., 'National self-determination: some cautionary remarks concerning the rhetoric of rights', in M. Moore (ed.), *National Self-Determination and Secession* (Oxford: Oxford University Press, 1998), pp. 158–80.

Berry, J. M., *The Interest Group Society* (Glenview, IL: Addison Wesley Publishing Company, 1989, 2nd edn).

Biaggini, G., 'Sprachenfreiheit und territorialitätsprinzip – Entwicklungstendenzen in der höchstrichterlichen rechtsprechung zum sprachenverfassungsrecht', *Recht. Zeitschrift für juristische Ausbildung und Praxis*, 15/3 (1997), 112–24.

Blodgett, J. G., Hill, D. J., and Tax, S. S., 'The effects of distributive, procedural and interactional justice on post-complaint behavior', *Journal of Retailing*, 73/2 (1997), 185–210.

Blommaert, J., 'The Asmara Declaration as a sociolinguistic problem: reflections on scholarship and linguistic rights', *Journal of Sociolinguistics*, 5/1 (2001), 131–55.

Boileau, F., *Special Report on French Language Health Services Planning in Ontario* (Toronto: Office of the French Language Services Commissioner, 2009). Published online at: http://csfontario.ca/wp-content/uploads/2009/05/FLSC_report_french_health_planning_2009.pdf.

Bondy, V., and Le Sueur, A., *Designing Redress: A Study about Grievances against Public Bodies*. Queen Mary University of London, School of Law, Legal Studies Research Paper no. 121/2012 (London: Public Law Project, 2012).

Bòrd na Gàidhlig, *Draft Guidance on the Development of Gaelic Language Plans* (Inverness: Bòrd na Gàidhlig, 2014).

Bòrd na Gàidhlig, *National Gaelic Language Plan 2012-2017. Growth and Improvement* (Isle of Skye: Bòrd na Gàidhlig, 2012).

Braithwaite, J., and Braithwaite, V., 'The politics of legalism: rules versus standards in nursing-home regulation', *Social and Legal Studies*, 4 (1995), 307–41.

British and Irish Ombudsman Association [BIOA], *Guide to Principles of Good Complaint Handling. Firm on Principles, Flexible on Process* (Twickenham: BIOA, 2007).

Buck, T., Kirkham, R., and Thompson, B., *The Ombudsman Enterprise and Administrative Justice* (Farnham: Ashgate Publishing, 2011).

Cabinet Office, *Categories of Public Bodies: A Guide for Departments* (London: Cabinet Office, 2012).
Cahn, M., 'Institutional and non-institutional actors in the policy process', in S. Z. Theodoulu and M. A. Cahn (eds), *Public Policy: The Essential Readings* (Upper Saddle River, NJ: Pearson, 2012), pp. 199–206.
Carl, S., 'Toward a definition and taxonomy of public sector ombudsmen', *Canadian Public Administration*, 55/2 (June 2012), 203–22.
Carlin, P., 'Priod iaith', in S. Brooks (ed.), *Pa beth yr aethoch allan i'w achub? Ysgrifau i gynorthwyo'r gwrthsafiad yn erbyn dadfeiliad y Gymru Gymraeg* (Llanrwst: Gwasg Carreg Gwalch, 2013), pp. 130–54.
Carpenter, D., and Moss, D. A., *Preventing Regulatory Capture. Special Interest Influence and How to Limit It* (New York: Cambridge University Press, 2014).
Children's Commissioner for Wales and Welsh Government, *Memorandum of Understanding: operational working arrangements between the Children's Commissioner for Wales and the Welsh Government* (Children's Commissioner for Wales and Welsh Government, 2012).
Christensen, T., and Lægreid, P. (eds), *Autonomy and Regulation: Coping with Agencies in the Modern State* (Cheltenham: Edward Elgar, 2006).
Commission on Devolution in Wales, *Empowerment and Responsibility: Legislative Powers to Strengthen Wales* (Cardiff: Commission on Devolution in Wales, 2014).
Cwmni Iaith, *Written Evidence. Response to the proposed Welsh Language (Wales) Measure 2010, National Assembly for Wales Legislation Committee No. 2, 7 May 2010 MI 54*.
Cymdeithas yr Iaith Gymraeg [Welsh Language Society], *Y Llyfr Du* (Cymdeithas yr Iaith Gymraeg, 2012).
Cymdeithas yr Iaith Gymraeg [Welsh Language Society], *Polisi Gorfodi Comisiynydd y Gymraeg* (Cymdeithas yr Iaith Gymraeg, 2014).
Dal Bó, E., 'Regulatory capture: a review', *Oxford Review of Economic Policy*, 22/2 (2006), 203–25.
Denzin, N. K. (ed.), *Sociological Methods* (New Jersey: Aldine Transaction Publishers, 2006).
Department for Business, Innovation & Skills/Welsh Government, *Mapping the Regulatory Landscape in Wales* (London: Department for Business, Innovation & Skills, 2013).

Department for Business, Innovation & Skills, *Regulators' Code* (London: Department for Business, Innovation & Skills, 2014).

Department of Community, Rural and Gaeltacht Affairs, *Guidelines under Section 12 of the Official Languages Act 2003* (Dublin: Department of Community, Rural and Gaeltacht Affairs, 2004).

de Varennes, F., 'Language and freedom of expression in international law', *Human Rights Quarterly*, 15 (1993), 163–86.

de Varennes, F., *International and Comparative Perspectives in the Use of Official Languages. Models and Approaches for South Africa* (Afrikaanse Taalraad, 2012a).

de Varennes, F., *International and Comparative Perspectives in the Use of Official Languages. Models and Approaches for South Africa. Brief Report. Legal Opinion* (Afrikaanse Taalraad, 2012b).

de Varennes, F., 'Review of Linguistic justice: international law and language policy by Jacqueline Mowbray, Oxford: Oxford University Press', *American Anthropologist*, 116/4 (2014), 884–5.

Diver, C., 'The optimal precision of administrative rules', *Yale Law Journal*, 93 (1983), 65–109.

Dixon, D., 'David defeats Goliath', *The Law Society Gazette*, 14 January 2013. Published online at: *http://www.lawgazette.co.uk/analysis/david-defeats-goliath/68959.fullarticle*.

Douglas, K., and Holmes, N., 'Funding Officers of Parliament', *Canadian Parliamentary Review*, 28/3 (2010), 38–42. Published online at: *http://www.revparl.ca/English/issue.asp?param=171=1152*.

Drakeford, M., *Written statement – Welsh Government response to My Language, My Health. The Welsh Language Commissioner's inquiry into the Welsh language in primary care*, 10 December 2014. Published online at: *http://gov.wales/about/cabinet/cabinetstatements/2014/9453684/?lang=en*.

Dwyer, J. P., 'The pathology of symbolic legislation', *Ecology Law Quarterly*, 17/2 (1990), 233.

Eleftheriadis, P., *Legal Rights* (Oxford: Oxford University Press, 2008).

Elis-Thomas, D., 'Dafydd Êl: "rheoleiddio'r Gymraeg yn y gors"', *Golwg*, 30 January (2014), 4–5.

Ellis, A., 'Minority rights and the preservation of languages', *Philosophy*, 80/2 (2005), 199–217.

European Court of Human Rights [ECHR], Research Division, *Cultural Rights in the Case-law of the European Court of Human Rights* (Strasbourg: Council of Europe, 2011).

Feaver, D,. and Sheehy, B., 'The political division of regulatory labour: a legal theory of agency selection', *Oxford Journal of Legal Studies*, 35/1 (2015), 153–77.

Fleiner, T., 'Die sprachenfreiheit', in D. Merten and H-J. Papier (eds), *Handbuch der grundrechte in Deutschland und Europa* (Heidelberg: Müller, 2007), pp. 405–43.

Fox, R., and Korris, M., *Making Better Law. Reform of the Legislative Process from Policy to Act* (London: Hansard Society, 2010).

Fraser, G., *Statement to Standing Committee on Official Languages, House of Commons, Parliament of Canada, Evidence Meeting 23, 2nd session, 41st Parliament 8 May 2014.* Published online at: http://openparliament.ca/committees/official-languages/41-2/23/graham-fraser-1/only/.

Freeman, J., and Langbein, L. I., 'Regulatory negotiation and the legitimacy benefit', *New York University Environmental Law Journal*, 9/6 (2000), 543–675.

Gay, O., *Officers of Parliament – A Comparative Perspective. Research paper 03/77 20 October 2003* (London: House of Commons Library, 2003).

Gay, O., *Officers of Parliament: Recent Developments SN/PC/04720 29 August 2013* (London: House of Commons Library, 2013).

Gay, O., and Winetrobe, B. K., *Officers of Parliament – Transforming the Role* (London: UK Study of Parliament Group, the Constitution Unit, UCL, 2003).

George, M., 'Supreme Court dictates pace of Welsh devolution', *Clickonwales*, 15 October 2012. Published online at: http://www.clickonwales.org/2012/10/supreme-court-dictates-direction-of-welsh-devolution-journey/.

George, M., Graham, C., and Lennard, L., *Complaint Handling: Principles and Best Practice. Report for Energywatch* (Centre for Utility Consumer Law, University of Leicester/Gas and Electricity Consumer Council [energywatch], 2007).

Giddings, P., 'The ombudsman as advocate', in M. Nijhoff (ed.), *European yearbook of minority issues* (Leiden, Boston: Matrinus Nijhoff Publishers, 2005), pp. 207–19.

Giddings, P., 'The Parliamentary Ombudsman: A classical watchdog', in O. Gay and B. K. Wintrobe (eds), *Parliamentary watchdogs: at the crossroads* (London: The Constitution Unit, UCL, 2008), pp. 93–103.

Gill, C., Williams, J., Brennan, C., and Hirst, C., *Models of Alternative Dispute Resolution (ADR). A Report for the Legal Ombudsman*

(Edinburgh: Queen Margaret University, Consumer Insight Centre, 2014).

Goldsmith, J. L., and Posner, E. A., *The Limits of International Law* (Oxford: Oxford University Press, 2005).

Gregory, R., 'Building an ombudsman scheme: statutory provisions and operating practices', *The Ombudsman Journal*, 12 (1994), 83–116.

Green, L., 'Freedom of expression and choice of language', *Law & Policy*, 13/3 (1991), 215–29.

Greenberg, D., 'Welsh devolution. Legal information and aspects of devolution', *Legal Information Management*, 13 (2013), 134–8.

Gusfield, J., *Symbolic Crusade: Status Politics and the American Temperance Movement* (Chicago: University of Illinois Press, 1963).

Gusfield, J., 'Moral passage: the symbolic process in public designations of deviance', *Social Problems*, 15/2 (1967), 175–88.

Hajer, M., 'Policy without polity? Policy analysis and the institutional void', *Policy Sciences*, 36 (2003), 175–95.

Hampton, P., *Reducing Administrative Burdens: Effective Inspection and Enforcement* (London: HM Treasury, 2005)

Hansard Society, *Hansard Society briefing paper. Issues in Law Making 3: Delegated Fegislation* (London: Hansard Society, 2003).

Health Care Human Resource Sector Council, *Directory of French speaking Primary health care providers in Nova Scotia. Réseau santé. Réseau pour les services de santé en français – Nouvelle-Écosse* (Nova Scotia: Health Care Human Resource Sector Council, 2006).

Heaton, R., 'Making the law easier for users: the role of statutes' (speech 14 October 2013). Published in 2014 online at: https://www.gov.uk/government/speeches/making-the-law-easier-for-users-the-role-of-statutes--2.

Hickinbottom, G. [The Hon Sir], 'Administrative justice in Wales: a new dawn?' (lecture to Legal Wales conference, Cardiff, 8 October 2009).

Hickinbottom, G. [Mr Justice], *Neutral Citation Number [2014] EWHC 488 (Admin) Case No CO/9841/2013 in the High Court of Justice, Queen's Bench Division, Divisional Court, Mr Justice Hickinbottom & His Honour Judge Milwyn Jarman QC. Between The Queen on the application of the Welsh*

Language Commissioner and National Savings and Investments and the Welsh Ministers Hearing date 19 February 2014, Judgment date 6 March 2014.

HM Government, *Powers for a purpose: towards a lasting devolution settlement for Wales* (London: HMSO, 2015).

HM Treasury, *Managing Public Money* (London: HM Treasury, 2013).

Hohfeld, W., *Fundamental Legal Conceptions* (New Haven: Yale University Press, 1919).

Holmes, S., and Sunstein, S., *The Costs of Rights* (New York: W. W. Norton, 1990).

Hood, C., Rothstein, H., and Baldwin, R., *The Government of Risk: Understanding Risk Regulation Regimes* (Oxford: Oxford University Press, 2001).

House of Lords, Select Committee on the Constitution, *The Regulatory State: Ensuring its Accountability. Volume 1: Report* (London: The Stationery Office Limited, 2004a).

House of Lords, Select Committee on the Constitution, *The Regulatory State: Ensuring its Accountability: The Government's Response. Report* (London: The Stationery Office Limited, 2004b).

House of Lords, Select Committee on Regulators, *UK Economic Regulators. Volume I: Report* (London: The Stationery Office Limited, 2007a).

House of Lords, Select Committee on Regulators, *UK Economic Regulators. Volume I: The Evidence* (London: The Stationery Office Limited, 2007b).

House of Lords Library Note, *Volume of legislation, 10 May 2013*, LLN 2013/008.

Hrbek, R., 'The role of expert advisors in the formulation of policy: brief report on the Federal Republic of Germany', in N. Verrelli (ed.), *The Role of the Policy Advisor: An Insider's Look* (Kingston: Institute of Intergovernmental Relations, Queen's University, 2008), pp. 27–33.

Hutchison, B., Levesque, J.-F., Strumpf, E., and Coyle, N., 'Primary health care in Canada: systems in motion', *The Millbank Quarterly*, June 89/2 (2011), 256–88. Published online at: http://www.ncbi.nlm.nih.gov/pmc/articles/PMC3142339/.

Huws, M., 'Comisiynydd y Gymraeg a'r ymgynghoriad', *Golwg*, 6 March (2014a).

Huws, M., 'Beth wnaeth yr Arsyllfa?', *Golwg*, 1 May (2014b), 15.

IFF Research, *NHS Governance of Complaints Handling. Prepared for the Parliamentary and Health Service Ombudsman by IFF Research* (London: IFF Research Ltd, 2013).

Institute for Government, *Read Before Burning. Arm's Length Government for a New Administration* (London: Institute for Government, 2010).

Institute for Government, *The Strange Case of Non-Ministerial Departments* (London: Institute for Government, 2013).

Institute for Welsh Affairs [IWA], *Putting Wales in the Driving Seat* (Cardiff: IWA, 2009).

Irish Language Commissioner, *Annual Report Irish 2005–6* (An Spidéal: An Coimisinéir Teanga, 2006).

Irish Language Commissioner, *Annual Report 2006–7* (An Spidéal: An Coimisinéir Teanga, 2007).

Irish Language Commissioner, *Annual Report 2011–12* (An Spidéal: An Coimisinéir Teanga, 2012).

James, O., Moseley, A., Petrovsky, N., and Goyne, G., 'United Kingdom', in K. Verhoest, S. Van Thiel, G. Bouckaert and P. Lægreid (eds), *Government Agencies. Practices and Lessons from 30 Countries* (Houndmills: Palgrave Macmillan, 2012), pp. 57–68.

John, P., *Local Governance in Western Europe* (London: Sage, 2001).

Jones, A. Ff., *Letter from Alun Ffred Jones AM, Minister for Heritage to Val Lloyd AM, Chair of Legislation Committee No. 2 National Assembly for Wales, 14 June 2010a*.

Jones, A. Ff., *Welsh language policy and legislation update – November 2010. Open response letter from the Heritage Minister to correspondents on the proposed Welsh Language Measure* (Cardiff: Welsh Assembly Government, 2010b).

Jones, C., *Written statement – timetable for the first set of Welsh Language Standards 21 October 2013*. Published online at: http://wales.gov.uk/about/cabinet/cabinetstatements/2013/welshlangstandards/?lang=en.

Jones, J. Elfed, *Dyfroedd dyfnion. Hunangofiant John Elfed* (Talybont: Y Lolfa, 2013).

Jones, M. Prys, 'Neb yno i hyrwyddo'r iaith', *Golwg*, 14 November (2013), 4.

Kincaid, J. 'Role of expert advisor', in N. Verrelli (ed.), *The Role of the Policy Advisor: An Insider's Look* (Kingston: Institute of Intergovernmental Relations, Queen's University, 2008), pp. 35–8.

Kingdon, J. W., *Agenda, Alternatives and Public Policies* (New York: HarperCollins, 1995).
Kirkham, R., Thompson, B., and Buck, T., 'Putting the ombudsman in constitutional context', *Parliamentary Affairs*, 62/4 (2009), 600–17.
Kloegman, L., 'A democratic defence of the Court Challenges Program', *Constitutional Forum constitutionnel*, 16/3 (2007), 107–15.
Kloss, H., 'Language rights of immigrant groups', *International Migration Review*, 5/2 (1971), 250–68.
Kloss, H., *The American Bilingual Tradition* (Rowley, MA: Newbury House, 1977).
Labour Party and Plaid Cymru, *One Wales. A progressive agenda for the government of Wales. An agreement between the Labour and Plaid Cymru Groups in the National Assembly 27 June 2007*.
Laffont, J.-J., and Tirole, J., *The Politics of Government Decision-Making: A Theory of Regulatory Capture* (Cambridge, MA: MIT, 1988).
Lando, O., 'On legislative style and structure', *Juridica International Law Review*, XI (2006), 13–19.
Leith, J. C., 'The design of policy frameworks and the role of the policy advisor' (conference paper, 'Rationality in public policy: Retrospect and prospect', University of Toronto, November 1998).
Lewis, E., 'Angen rhoi statws swyddogol a chyfartal i'r Gymraeg', *Golwg*, 11 March (2010a).
Lewis, E., *Written Evidence*, The Proposed Welsh Language (Wales) Measure – Evidence Session 22 April 2010, Legislative Committee 2, the National Assembly for Wales (2010b).
Lewis, E., et al., 'Cyfreithwyr yn ymateb i'r Mesur Iaith', *Golwg*, 18 March (2010).
Lewis, G., *Hawl i'r Gymraeg* (Tal-y-bont: Y Lolfa, 2008).
Leyland, P., *Constitution of the UK: A Contextual Analysis* (Oxford: Hart, 2012).
Lodge, M., and Hood, C., 'Regulation inside government: retro-theory vindicated', in R. Baldwin, M. Cave and M. Lodge (eds), *The Oxford Handbook of Regulation* (Oxford: Oxford University Press, 2010), pp. 590–612.
Lodge, M., and Stirton, L., 'Accountability in the regulatory state', in R. Baldwin, M. Cave and M. Lodge (eds), *The Oxford*

Handbook of Regulation (Oxford: Oxford University Press, 2010), pp. 349–70.

Lortie, L., and Lalonde, A. L., *Consortium national de formation en santé. Reference framework. Training for active offer of French-language services* (Ottawa: Consortium national de formation en santé, 2012).

Lyons, D., 'The correlativity of rights and duties', *Noûs*, 4 (1970), 45–57.

McDougal, M. S., Chen, L., and Lasswell, H. D., 'Freedom from discrimination in choice of language and international human rights', *Faculty Scholarship Series. Paper 2650* (1976). Published online at: *http://digitalcommons.law.yale.edu/fss_papers/2650*.

McLeod, W., 'Official status for Gaelic: prospects and problems', *Scottish Affairs*, 21 (1997), 95–118. Published online at: *http://www.papers.celtscot.ed.ac.uk/officialstatus.html*.

McLeod, W., 'Gaelic in contemporary Scotland: contradictions, challenges and strategies' (unpublished research paper, University of Edinburgh, January 2006). Published online at: *http://www.poileasaidh.celtscot.ed.ac.uk*.

Macmillan, C. M., 'Active conscience or administrative vanguard? The Commissioner of Official Languages as an agent of change', *Canadian Public Administration*, 49/2 (2006), 161–79.

Mader, L., 'Der verfassungsrechtliche rahman des sprachenrechts des bundes', *Babylonia*, 4/01 (2001), 15–22.

Majone, G., 'The regulatory state and its legitimacy problems', *West European Politics*, 22/1 (1999), 1–24.

Maxham III, J. G., and Netemeyer, R. G., 'Modeling customer perceptions of complaint handling over time: the effects of perceived justice on satisfaction and intent', *Journal of Retailing*, 78 (2002), 239–52.

Miers, D., *Law Making in Wales: A Measure of Devolution* (London: Study of Parliament Group, 2011).

Ministry of Justice and Attorney General's Office, *The Dispute Resolution Commitment. Guidance for Government Departments and Agencies* (London: Ministry of Justice, 2014).

Ministry of Justice and Information Commissioner's Office, *Framework Agreement* (London: Ministry of Justice and Information Commissioner's Office, 2011).

Misstear, R., 'Warning that Welsh Government's Planning Bill will only centralise decisions', *Walesonline*, 6 October 2014.

Published online at: *http://www.walesonline.co.uk/news/wales-news/warning-welsh-governments-planning-bill-7890683*.

Moran, M., 'Review article: Understanding the regulatory state', *British Journal of Political Science*, 32/2 (2002), 391–413.

Mowbray, J., 'Linguistic justice in international law: an evaluation of the discursive framework', *International Journal for the Semiotics of Law – Revue International de sémiotique juridque*, 24/1 (2011), 79–95.

Mowbray, J., *Linguistic Justice. International Law and Language Policy* (Oxford: Oxford University Press, 2012).

Moyn, S., *The Last Utopia: Human Rights in History* (Cambridge, MA: Belknap, Harvard University Press, 2010).

Moyn, S., 'Review of *The International Human Rights Movement: A History*, by Aryeh Neier, Princeton University Press, 2012', *Ethics and International Affairs*, 26/3 (2012), 392–5.

Narveson, J., *The Libertarian Idea* (Peterborough, ON: Broadview, 2001).

National Assembly for Wales, *Welsh Language Scheme* (Cardiff: National Assembly for Wales, 2007).

National Assembly for Wales, Legislation Committee No. 5, *National Assembly for Wales (Legislative Competence) (Welsh Language) Order 2009. Committee Report. June 2009* (Cardiff: National Assembly for Wales, 2009).

National Assembly for Wales, Legislation Committee No. 2, *Proposed Welsh Language (Wales) Measure Stage 1 Committee Report July 2010* (Cardiff: National Assembly for Wales, 2010).

National Assembly for Wales, *The Record of Proceedings 7 December 2010 Standing Orders of the National Assembly for Wales May 2010* (Cardiff: National Assembly for Wales, 2010a).

National Assembly for Wales, *The Record of Proceedings 7 December 2010* (Cardiff: National Assembly for Wales, 2010b).

National Assembly for Wales, *Notice of Amendments. Tabled 5 October 2010. Proposed Welsh Language (Wales) Measure* (Cardiff: National Assembly for Wales, 2010c).

National Assembly for Wales, Constitutional Affairs Committee, *Inquiry into the drafting of Welsh Government Measures: lessons from the first three years. February 2011* (Cardiff: National Assembly for Wales, 2011).

National Assembly for Wales, *National Assembly for Wales (Official Languages) Bill Explanatory Memorandum* (Cardiff: National Assembly for Wales, 2012a).

National Assembly for Wales, Assembly Commission, *Cynllun Ieithoedd Swyddogol Drafft* (Cardiff: National Assembly for Wales, 2012b).

National Assembly for Wales, Research Service, *Social Services and Well-being (Wales) Bill Summary of Changes at Stage 2* (Cardiff: National Assembly for Wales, 2013).

National Consumer Council, *A-Z of Ombudsmen. A Guide to Ombudsman Schemes in Britain and Ireland* (London: National Consumer Council, 1997).

Northern Ireland Ombudsman, *Memorandum – House of Lords – Constitution – Written evidence*, March (2003). Published online at: *http://www.publications.parliament.uk/pa/ld200304/ldselect/ldconst/68/68we52.htm*.

Northwest Territories Government, *Strategic Plan on French Language Communications and Services* (Government of the Northwest Territories, 2012).

Nova Scotia, Public Service Commission, *French Language Services Plan* (Nova Scotia, Public Service Commission, 2013).

Ó Conaill, S., 'The Irish language and the Irish legal system, 1922 to present' (unpublished PhD thesis, Cardiff University, 2013).

Ó Flatharta, P., Sandberg, S., and Williams, C. H., *From Act to Action. Implementing Language Legislation in Finland, Ireland and Wales* (2013). Published online at: *http://doras.dcu.ie/19655/1/From_Act_to_Action_2014.pdf*.

Ó Máille, T., *Stádas na Gaeilge – Dearcadh Dlíthiúil/The Status of Irish – A Legal Perspective* (Dublin: Bord na Gaeilge, 1990).

OCOL, *Annual Report 2004–05 Volume 2* (Ottawa: Minister of the Public Works and Government Services Canada, 2005).

OCOL, *Two official languages. One Common Space. Annual Report 2008–2009. 40th Anniversary of the Official Languages Act* (Ottawa: Minister of the Public Works and Government Services Canada, 2009).

OECD, *Principles for the Governance of Regulators. Public Consultation Draft* (OECD Publishing, 2013).

OECD, *The Governance of Regulators, OECD Best Practice Principles for Regulatory Policy* (OECD Publishing, 2014). Published online at: *http://www.oecd-ilibrary.org/governance/the-governance-of-regulators_9789264209015-en*.

Office of the Parliamentary Counsel, *Crown Application* (London: Office of the Parliamentary Counsel, 2013a). Published online at: *https://www.gov.uk/government/uploads/system/ uploads/attachment_data/file/193143/Crown_Application_ pamphlet_12-03-13.pdf.*

Office of the Parliamentary Counsel, *When laws become too complex. A review into the causes of complex legislation* (London: Office of the Parliamentary Counsel, Cabinet Office, 2013b).

Ombudsman and Child and Youth Advocate, *Report of the Ombudsman into the Minister of Education's decision to modify the French Second Language Curriculum* (n.p., June 2008).

Patten, A., 'Survey article: the justification of minority language rights', *Journal of Political Philosophy*, 17/1 (2009), 102–28.

Paz, M., 'The failed promise of language rights: a critique of the international language rights regime', *Harvard International Law Journal*, 54/1 (2013), 195–218.

Peled, Y., 'Language, rights and the language of language rights: the need for a new conceptual framework in the political theory of language policy', *Journal of Language and Politics*, 10/3 (2011), 436–56.

Peled, Y., 'Normative language policy: interface and inferences', *Language Policy*, 13 (2014), 301–15.

Pennant, G., 'Amddiffyn y safonau', *Golwg*, 13 November (2014), 5.

Pond, W., 'Restraining regulatory activism: the proper scope of public utility regulation', *Administrative Law Review*, 35/4 (1983), 423–50.

Pupavac, V., 'Language rights in conflict and the denial of language as communication', *International Journal of Human Rights*, 10/1 (2006), 61–78.

Pupavac, V., *Language Rights: from Free Speech to Linguistic Governance* (Basingstoke: Palgrave Macmillan, 2012).

Revenga Sánchez, M., 'Notas sobre oficialidad lingüística y cultura constitucional', *Revista de Llengua i Dret*, 43 (2005), 129–43.

Richard Commission, *Annex 1* (Richard Commission, 2002a). Published online at: *http://webarchive.nationalarchives.gov. uk/20090807221003/http://www.richardcommission.gov.uk/ content/evidence/written/jranderson/index.htm.*

Richard Commission, *Evidence of Welsh Assembly Government Minister for Culture Jenny Randerson* (Richard Commission, 2002b). Published online at: *http://webarchive.nationalarchives. gov.uk/20090807221003/http://www.richardcommission.gov.uk/ content/evidence/oral/randersonj/index-e.htm.*

Richard Commission, *Alan Pugh AM: Minister for Culture, Welsh Language and Sport* (Richard Commission, 2003a). Published online at: http://webarchive.nationalarchives.gov.uk/20090807221003/http://www.richardcommission.gov.uk/content/evidence/written/pugha/index-e.htm.

Richard Commission, *Paper from the Welsh Language Board to the Commission on the Powers and Electoral Arrangements of the National Assembly for Wales – March 2003* (Richard Commission, 2003b). Published online at: http://webarchive.nationalarchives.gov.uk/20090807221003/http://www.richardcommission.gov.uk/content/evidence/written/wlb/index.htm.

Richter, D., *Sprachenordnung und minderheitenschutz im schweizerischen bundesstaat. Relativität des sprachenrechts und sicherung des sprachfriedens* (Heidelberg: Springer, 2005).

Rothbauer, P. M., 'Triangulation', in L. Given (ed.), *The SAGE Encyclopedia of Qualitative Research Methods* (Thousand Oaks, CA: SAGE, 2008), pp. 893–5.

Ruíz Vieytez, E. J., *Official Languages and Minority Languages: Issues about their Legal Status through Comparative Law* (II Simposi Internacional Mercator: Europa 2004: Un nou marc per a totes les llengües? Tarragona – Catalunya, 27–8 February, 2004).

Sabatier, P. A., and Jenkins-Smith, H. C., *Policy Change and Learning: An Advocacy Coalition Approach* (Westview Press, 1993).

Sargeant, C., *Written statement – Technical Advice Note 20: Planning and the Welsh Language*, 9 October 2013. Published online at: http://wales.gov.uk/about/cabinet/cabinetstatements/2013/tan20/?lang=en.

Schilling, T., 'Language rights in the European Union', *German Law Journal*, 9 (2008), 1219–42.

Schmidt, R., *Language Policy and Identity Politics in the United States* (Philadelphia: Temple University Press, 2000).

Scott, C., 'Accountability in the regulatory state', *Journal of Law and Society*, 27/1 (2000), 38–60.

Scott, C., 'Standard-setting in regulatory regimes', in R. Baldwin, M. Cave and M. Lodge (eds), *The Oxford Handbook of Regulation* (Oxford: Oxford University Press, 2010), pp. 104–19.

Scottish Government, *The Gaelic Language Bill consultation paper* (Edinburgh: Scottish Executive, 2003).

Secretary of State for Constitutional Affairs and Lord Chancellor, *Transforming Public Services: Complaints, Redress and Tribunals* (London: HMSO, 2004).

Seidman, A., Seidman, R., and Abeysekere, N., *Assessing Legislation – A Manual for Legislators* (Boston, MA: 2003). Published online at: *http://iknowpolitics.org/sites/default/files/ assessing20legislation20-2001.200320-20en20-20pi.pdf.*

Shooter, M., *An Independent Review of the Role and Functions of the Children's Commissioner for Wales* (2014).

Shue, H., *Basic Rights: Subsistence, Affluence and U.S. Foreign Policy* (Princeton: Princeton University Press, 1996).

Siu, B., 'Book review: Nadia Verrelli (ed.), *The Role of the Policy Advisor: An Insider's Look*, Kingston: Institute of Intergovernmental Relations, Queen's University, 2008', *Journal of Public Policy, Administration and Law*, 1, November (2009), 10.

Stauss, B., and Seidel, W., *Complaint Management: The Heart of CRM* (Nashville, TN: South-western Publishing Group, 2004).

Steiner, H., *An Essay on Rights* (Oxford: Blackwell, 1994).

Stigler, G., 'The theory of economic regulation', *Bell Journal of Economics and Management Science*, 2 (1971), 3–21.

Stilborn, J., 'Funding the Officers of Parliament: Canada's experiment', *Canadian Parliamentary Review*, Summer (2010), 38–42.

Sumner, L., *The Moral Foundations of Rights* (Oxford: Oxford University Press, 1987).

Sunkin, M., 'Crown immunity from criminal liability in English law', *Public Law* (2003), 716–29.

Tetley, W., *Mixed Jurisdictions: Common Law vs Civil Law (Codified and Uncodified)* (2000). Published online at: *http://www.cisg.law.pace.edu/cisg/biblio/tetley.html.*

Thomas, A., '"Parliamentary Officers" in Wales: Evolving roles', in O. Gay and B. K. Winetrobe (eds), *Parliament's Watchdogs: At the Crossroads* (London: UK Study of Parliament Group, the Constitution Unit, UCL, 2008), pp. 47–57.

Thomas, B., '"Dryswch" safonau'r Gymraeg', *Golwg*, 15 May (2014a), 4.

Thomas, B., 'Comisiynydd y Gymraeg v Llywodraeth Prydain', *Golwg*, 16 October (2014b), 4.

Thomas, P. G., 'The past, present and future of officers of Parliament', *Canadian Public Administration*, 46/3 (2003), 287–314.

Thomson, J., *The Realm of Rights* (Oxford: Oxford University Press, 1990).

Thürer, D., and Burri, T., 'Zum sprachenrecht der Schweiz', in C. Pan and B. S. Pfeil (eds), *Zur entstehung des modernen minderheitenschutzes in Europa. Handbuch der europäischen volksgruppen* (Vienna: Springer, 2006), pp. 242–66.

Turner, C., *Letter to Meri Huws, the Welsh Language Commissioner* (17 December 2012).

Tushnett, M., and Yackle, L., 'Symbolic statutes and real laws: the pathologies of the Antiterrorism and Effective Death Penalty Act and the Prison Litigation Reform Act', *Duke Law Journal*, 47/1 October (1997), 1–85.

Varuhas, J. N. E., 'Governmental rejections of Ombudsman findings: what role for the Courts?', *The Modern Law Review Limited*, 72/1 (2009), 91–115.

Vašàk, K., 'A 30-year struggle: The sustained efforts to give force of law to the United Nations Declaration of Human Rights', *UNESCO Courier*, 3/11 (1977).

Verhoest, K., Van Thiel, S., Bouckaert, G., and Lægreid, P. (eds), *Government Agencies. Practices and Lessons from 30 Countries* (Houndmills: Palgrave Macmillan, 2012).

Verrelli, N. 'The role of experts in policy making', in N. Verrelli (ed.), *The Role of the Policy Advisor: An Insider's Look* (Kingston: Institute of Intergovernmental Relations, Queen's University, 2008), pp. 3–13.

Wales Governance Centre, *Drafting Welsh Measures: lessons from the first three years' evidence presented to the Constitutional Affairs Committee, National Assembly for Wales*, CA DM 5 (2010a). Published online at: *http://www.assembly.wales/ NAfW%20Documents/ca_5_-_cardiff_law_school.pdf%20-%20 28092010/ca_5_-_cardiff_law_school-English.pdf.*

Wales Governance Centre, *Response to the proposed Welsh Language (Wales) Measure 2010 MI 27 Written evidence submitted to National Assembly for Wales, Legislation Committee No. 2* (2010b).

Ward, P., *The Proposed Welsh Language Legislative Competence Order. Standard Note SN/HA/4973* (London: House of Commons Library, 11 December 2009).

Weible, C. M., Sabatier, P. A., Jenkins-Smith, H. C., Nohrstedt, D., Henry, A. D., and deLeon, P., 'A Quarter Century of the Advocacy Coalition Framework: An Introduction to the Special Issue', *The Policy Studies Journal*, 39/3 (2011), 349–60.

Welsh Affairs Committee, *Fifth report – Review of the LCO process* (2010a). Published online at: http://www.publications. parliament.uk/pa/cm200910/cmselect/cmwelaf/155/15502.htm.
Welsh Affairs Committee, *Wales and Whitehall. Minutes of evidence. Examination of witnesses. Professor Tim Jones, Professor Richard Wyn Jones, Ms Christina Palko, Ms Tessa Shellens & Mr Huw Williams 2 February 2010* (2010b). Published online at: http://www.publications.parliament.uk/ pa/cm200910/cmselect/cmwelaf/246/10020203.htm
Welsh Assembly Government, *Memorandum from the Welsh Assembly Government. Constitutional Law: Devolution, Wales. The National Assembly for Wales (Legislative Competence) (Welsh Language) Order 2009. Proposal for a Legislative Competence Order on the Welsh Language* (Cardiff: Welsh Assembly Government, 2009a [January]).
Welsh Assembly Government, *Memorandum from the Welsh Assembly Government. Constitutional Law: Devolution, Wales. The National Assembly for Wales (Legislative Competence) (Welsh Language) Order 2009. Draft Legislative Competence Order on the Welsh Language* (Cardiff: Welsh Assembly Government, 2009b [October]).
Welsh Assembly Government, *The Proposed Welsh Language (Wales) Measure 2010. Explanatory Memorandum to the Proposed Welsh Language Wales Measure 2010 4 March 2010* (Cardiff: Welsh Assembly Government, 2010a).
Welsh Assembly Government, *The Proposed Welsh Language (Wales) Measure 2010. Explanatory Memorandum to the Proposed Welsh Language Wales Measure 2010 30 November 2010* (Cardiff: Welsh Assembly Government, 2010b).
Welsh Committee of the Administrative Justice & Tribunals Council, *Review of Tribunals Operating in Wales* (London: HMSO, 2010).
Welsh Committee of the Administrative Justice & Tribunals Council, *Annual Report 2011/2012* (London: HMSO, 2012).
Welsh Committee of the Administrative Justice & Tribunals Council, *The Silk Commission on Devolution in Wales. Response of the Welsh Committee of the Administrative Justice & Tribunals Council (WCAJTC) to the Commission's second call for evidence* (2013). Published online at: http://commissionondevolutioninwales.independent.gov.uk/ files/2013/03/Welsh-Committee-of-the-Administrative-Justice- and-Tribunals-Council.pdf.

Welsh Government, *Cyflwyniad i'r Bwrdd am y Mesur Iaith 13 Rhagfyr 2011* (Cardiff: Welsh Government, 2011).

Welsh Government, *Welsh Statutory Instruments. 2012 No. 752 (W.102) Welsh language, Wales. The Welsh Language Board (Transfer of Staff, Property, Rights and Liabilities) Order 2012 Explanatory Note* (Cardiff: Welsh Government, 2012a).

Welsh Government, *More than just words… strategic framework for Welsh language services in health, social services and social care* (Cardiff: Welsh Government, 2012b).

Welsh Government, *Social Services and Well-being (Wales) Bill Explanatory Memorandum incorporating the Regulatory Impact Assessment and Explanatory Notes January 2013* (Cardiff: Welsh Government, 2013).

Welsh Government, *Consultation document. Proposed standards relating to the Welsh language* (Cardiff: Welsh Government, 2014a).

Welsh Government, *Consultation document. Welsh Language Standards: Regulations. Improving services for Welsh speakers* (Cardiff: Welsh Government, 2014b).

Welsh Government, Welsh Language Tribunal, Welsh Language Division, *The Welsh Language Tribunal Consultation Document. The Welsh Language Tribunal Rules* (Cardiff: Welsh Government, 2014c).

Welsh Government, *Social Services and Well-being (Wales) Bill Explanatory Memorandum incorporating the Regulatory Impact Assessment and Explanatory Notes January 2014* (Cardiff: Welsh Government, 2014d).

Welsh Language Board, *Welsh Language Schemes. Their preparation and approval in accordance with the Welsh Language Act 1993* (Cardiff: Welsh Language Board, 1996).

Welsh Language Board, *Annual Report 2004–05* (Cardiff: Welsh Language Board, 2005).

Welsh Language Board, *The legislative position of the Welsh language. A position paper by the Welsh Language Board* (Cardiff: Welsh Language Board, 2006).

Welsh Language Board, *Annual Report 2006–07* (Cardiff: Welsh Language Board, 2007).

Welsh Language Board, *Annual Report 2008–09* (Cardiff: Welsh Language Board, 2009).

Welsh Language Board, *Annual Report 2009–10* (Cardiff: Welsh Language Board, 2010a).

Welsh Language Board, *Written Evidence. Response to the proposed Welsh Language (Wales) Measure 2010, National Assembly for Wales Legislation Committee No. 2. Paper 1. 29 April 2010* (2010b).

Welsh Language Board, *Review 1993–2012* (Cardiff: Welsh Language Board, 2012).

Welsh Language Commissioner, *Polisi Gorfodi Comisiynydd y Gymraeg [Drafft]* (Cardiff: Welsh Language Commissioner, n.d.).

Welsh Language Commissioner, *Standards and the Welsh language: what are your views?* (Cardiff: Welsh Language Commissioner, 2012a).

Welsh Language Commissioner, *Complaints to the Welsh Language Commissioner* (Cardiff: Welsh Language Commissioner, 2012b).

Welsh Language Commissioner, *Governance Statement* (Cardiff: Welsh Language Commissioner, 2013a).

Welsh Language Commissioner, *Adroddiad Blynyddol 2012–13. Annual Report 2012–13* (Cardiff: Welsh Language Commissioner, 2013b).

Welsh Language Commissioner, *The Welsh Language Commissioner Strategic Plan 2013–15* (Cardiff: Welsh Language Commissioner, 2013c).

Welsh Language Commissioner, *The Welsh Language Commissioner's Evidence to the Commission on Devolution in Wales* (Cardiff: Welsh Language Commissioner, 2013d).

Welsh Language Commissioner, *Remit of Management Team* (Cardiff: Welsh Language Commissioner, 2014a).

Welsh Language Commissioner, *Adroddiad Blynyddol 2013–14. Annual Report 2013–14* (Cardiff: Welsh Language Commissioner, 2014b).

Welsh Language Commissioner, *Part 6 of the Welsh Language (Wales) Measure 2011: Freedom to Use Welsh. The Welsh Language Commissioner's determination and report on an investigation into an application under section 111 of the Welsh Language (Wales) Measure 2011* (Cardiff: Welsh Language Commissioner, 2014c).

Welsh Language Commissioner, *The Welsh language and Lidl UK. Press release 11 November 2014* (2014d). Published online at: http://www.comisiynyddygymraeg.org/english/news/Pages/The-Welsh-language-and-Lidl-UK-.aspx.

Welsh Language Commissioner, *Advice under Section 4, Welsh Language (Wales) Measure 2011. Standards relating to the Welsh language* (Cardiff: Welsh Language Commissioner, 2014e).

Welsh Language Commissioner, *Welsh Language Commissioner's Standards Report – Section 64 Welsh Language (Wales) Measure 2011 County councils and county borough councils in Wales* (Cardiff: Welsh Language Commissioner, 2014f).

Welsh Language Commissioner, *Welsh Language Commissioner's Standards Report – Section 64 Welsh Language (Wales) Measure 2011 National Park Authorities* (Cardiff: Welsh Language Commissioner, 2014g).

Welsh Language Commissioner, *Welsh Language Commissioner's Standards Report – Section 64 Welsh Language (Wales) Measure 2011 Welsh Ministers* (Cardiff: Welsh Language Commissioner, 2014h).

Welsh Language Commissioner, *My language, my health: the Welsh Language Commissioner's inquiry into the Welsh language in primary care* (Cardiff: Welsh Language Commissioner, 2014i).

Welsh Language Commissioner, *Enforcement Policy. Welsh Language Commissioner. Consultation: overview of responses* (Cardiff: Welsh Language Commissioner, 2015a).

Welsh Language Commissioner, *Statutory review of the Welsh language services of high street banks in Wales* (Cardiff: Welsh Language Commissioner, 2015b).

Welsh Language Commissioner, *Schedule for carrying out standards investigations [January 2015]* (Cardiff: Welsh Language Commissioner, 2015c).

Welsh Language Commissioner, *Llythyr i Jocelyn Davies AC 'Ymchwiliad i ystyried pwerau Ombwdsmon Gwasanaethau Cyhoeddus Cymru'*, 20 February 2015 (2015d).

Welsh Language Society [Cymdeithas yr Iaith Gymraeg], *Y Gymraeg yn goroesi globaleiddio. Maniffesto Cymdeithas yr Iaith Gymraeg 2002* (Aberystwyth: Cymdeithas yr Iaith Gymraeg, 2002).

Welsh Language Society [Cymdeithas yr Iaith Gymraeg], *Welsh Language Measure 2007* (Tal-y-Bont: Y Lolfa, 2007).

Welsh Policy Paper 1, *Potential models and structures* (unpublished paper, June 2008).

Welsh Policy Paper 2, *Enforcement powers and remedies* (unpublished paper, 2008).

Welsh Policy Paper 3, *Commission/Commissioner* (unpublished paper, July 2008).

Welsh Policy Paper 4, *Linguistic Rights* (unpublished paper, 2008).
Welsh Policy Paper 5, *Language Schemes/Policies* (unpublished paper, 2008).
Welsh Policy Paper 6, *Official status* (unpublished paper, 2008).
Welsh Policy Paper 7, *The Right to Speak Welsh* (unpublished paper, July 2008).
Welsh Policy Paper 8, *Future of the Welsh Language Act 1993* (unpublished paper, 2008).
Welsh Policy Paper 9, *Matters excluded from the LCO* (unpublished paper, 2008).
Welsh Policy Paper 10, *The Freedom to Speak Welsh* (unpublished paper, June 2008).
Welsh Policy Paper 11, *Welsh Language Commission/er and Welsh Language Schemes* (unpublished paper, 2009).
Welsh Policy Paper 12, *Supplementary Paper. Welsh Language Commission/er and Welsh Language Schemes* (unpublished paper, March 2009).
Welsh Policy Paper 13, *Official status* (unpublished paper, 2009).
Welsh Policy Paper 15, *Policy instructions to legal services on the proposed Welsh Language Measure* (unpublished paper, April 2009).
Welsh Policy Paper 17, *Official status* (unpublished paper, 2010).
Welsh Policy Paper 18, *Welsh Language Commissioner – Appointment* (unpublished paper, 2010).
Welsh Policy Paper 19, *Commissioner – equal treatment of Welsh and English* (unpublished paper, 2010).
Welsh Policy Paper 20, *Welsh Language Commissioner – Independence* (unpublished paper, 2010).
Welsh Policy Paper 23, *Freedom to Use Welsh* (unpublished paper, 2010).
Welsh Policy Paper 27, *Proposed Welsh Language (Wales) Measure: Government Amendments – Doc. 1 Appointment of the Welsh Language Tribunal* (unpublished paper, 2010).
Welsh Policy Paper 31, *Addition of National Assembly for Wales Commissioner to the Schedule 6 table* (unpublished paper, 3 September 2010).
Welsh Policy Paper 32, *Supplemental advice in relation to the appointment of the Welsh Language Tribunal* (unpublished paper, 2010).
Welsh Policy Paper 34, *Official status* (unpublished paper, 2010).

Welsh Policy Paper 35, *Letter from Parliamentary Counsel regarding official status* (unpublished paper, 2010).
Welsh Policy Paper 37, *Options for appointing members of the Welsh Language Tribunal* (unpublished paper, 2010).
Welsh Policy Paper 39, *Addition of National Assembly for Wales Commissioner to the Schedule 6 table* (unpublished paper, 18 November 2010).
Welsh Policy Paper 40, *Official status of the Welsh language: legal advice* (unpublished paper, 2010).
Welsh Policy Paper 45, *Sherwood & Co – Welsh Language Board – Note on interpretation of Welsh Language Act 1993* (unpublished paper, 1994).
Williams, Colin H., *Written Evidence*, The Proposed Welsh Language (Wales) Measure – Evidence Session 22 April 2010, Legislative Committee 2, the National Assembly for Wales.
Wilson, W., *The Welsh Language Bill [HL] [Bill 146 of session 1992–3] Research paper 93/32. 17 March 1993* (London: House of Commons Library, 1993).
Woehrling, J. , 'L'évolution du cadre juridique et conceptual de la legislation linguistique du Québec', in A. Stefanescu and P. Georgeault (eds), *Le français au Québec: les nouveaux défis* (Québec: Conseil supérieur de la langue française, 2005), pp. 253–356.
Wotton, J., 'Jurisdiction and the practice of law in Wales' (lecture to the Public Law Project Wales conference, Cardiff, 4 April 2012). Published online at: *https://www.lawsociety.org.uk/news/speeches/jurisdiction-and-the-practice-of-law-in-wales/*.
Yeung, K., 'The regulatory state', in R. Baldwin, M. Cave and M. Lodge (eds), *The Oxford Handbook of Regulation* (Oxford: Oxford University Press, 2010), pp. 64–86.
Yukon Government, French Language Services, *Chronology of Events and Accomplishments* (Yukon Government, French Language Services, 2014).

INDEX

accountability, accountable 3, 4, 7–10, 13–18, 20–3, 25, 27–30, 40, 81, 84, 86, 106, 145, 147, 148, 149
active offer 4, 71, 77, 78, 79, 80, 81, 86, 87, 88
activism, activist 4, 5, 15, 33, 59, 60, 120, 154, 167, 185–6, 195, 210
advocacy 8, 37, 115
advocate 12, 33
appointment 8, 9, 10, 12–8, 20, 22, 26, 27, 29, 30, 31, 40, 214
Auditor General for Wales 9, 14, 22

Basque Country 9, 55, 102, 160
budget 4, 9, 15, 20, 21, 31, 105

Canada 2, 9, 14, 20, 21,22, 32, 36, 55, 77, 78, 80, 81, 87, 95, 98, 101, 108, 110, 160, 168, 169, 182, 186, 188, 189, 195, 196, 211
Catalonia 9, 55, 102, 160, 182
Children's Commissioner for Wales 8, 10, 12, 14, 20, 22, 32, 104, 130

Civil Law 42, 163–4, 188–9
Common Law 4, 42, 163–5, 168, 187–9, 191, 195–6, 211
complaint, complaint-handling 3, 5, 8, 9, 42, 51, 58, 97, 98, 105, 108, 109, 115, 122, 148, 209
constitution, constitutional, unconstitutional 4, 16, 18, 21, 22, 35, 36, 54, 105, 120, 136, 146, 146–8, 151, 162, 163, 174, 180, 182, 186, 189–91, 194–6, 211
corporation aggregate 7, 26, 30
corporation sole 7, 26, 29, 30, 121
Crown 3, 5, 104, 133–57, 161, 209–11, 213, 214

direction (ministerial) 4, 14, 17, 18, 20, 25, 30–1, 211, 213
Dyfodol i'r Iaith 18

enforcement 8, 9, 17, 26, 43, 47, 89, 115, 134, 136, 142, 146, 148, 190, 210, 211, 213
equal, equality (linguistic) 44, 99, 101, 111, 159, 161, 162, 166–8, 173, 175–7, 179, 182, 186, 191–4, 196

expert 3, 4, 13, 15, 41, 55, 63, 74, 75, 81, 115, 116, 121, 126, 182, 184–8, 190, 195, 207, 210

freedom (to use Welsh, to use a language) 3, 4, 5, 17, 26, 41–69, 165–6, 172–3, 178–9, 211, 213

impartial, impartiality 8, 11, 12, 16, 26, 28, 79
independence, independent 3, 4, 7–11, 14–18, 20–3, 27, 28, 30–1, 101, 103, 105, 114, 115, 149, 211
interest (groups) 2, 5, 9, 23, 59, 85, 86, 115, 209
investigation (standards) 19, 80, 85–6, 146
investigation (statutory) 56–8, 105–9, 115, 136, 140, 146
Ireland 2, 9, 14, 55, 81, 101, 105, 108, 110, 160, 163, 182, 186, 188, 189, 195

judicial review 5, 26, 60–1, 140–4, 150, 154
jurisdiction 51, 87, 147, 163, 165, 168, 172, 189, 190, 196
justice (administrative) 3, 27, 39, 40, 151, 189
justice (linguistic) 3, 88, 157, 171, 172

language commissioner (Irish) 10, 47, 102, 108–9
language commissioner (Canadian, OCOL) 21–2, 35–6, 95, 101, 109–10, 211
Legislative Competence Order (LCO) 43, 134–5, 160–4, 182, 187, 191, 196, 207, 211, 217
legislature 2, 16, 20, 23, 86, 120, 148, 177, 209

lobby (groups), lobbyist 11, 18, 115, 121

New Brunswick 9, 32, 33, 55, 160, 168
Non-Ministerial Department (NMD) 149

official (language) 3, 4, 17, 43, 46, 47, 55, 56, 67, 78
official (status of language) 92, 101–2, 111, 128, 159–205, 209–11, 213
Older People's Commissioner for Wales 8, 12, 14, 22, 32, 130, 132
ombudsman, ombudsmen 2, 9, 14, 22, 105, 106, 115, 148, 150, 151, 209
Ontario 78, 79, 81, 87, 95

Parliament 14, 15, 21, 43, 78, 82, 105, 143–5, 149, 156, 161, 168, 187, 191, 208
Presiding Officer 16, 17, 22, 138
promotion (language) 3, 47, 77, 97–105, 106, 120, 122, 123–4, 139, 159, 170, 172–3, 178, 179, 213
Public Services Ombudsman Wales (PSOW) 9, 22, 148, 150, 151, 209

Québec 9, 55, 102, 186

regulation, regulations 1, 17, 19, 23, 24, 26–7, 53, 59, 71, 80, 84, 86, 88–9, 92, 97, 98, 101, 105, 106, 115, 117, 122, 139, 208–9, 210, 214
regulator 1, 4, 13, 14, 22–4, 26, 30–1, 84, 86, 89, 98, 115–16, 120–3, 130–1, 146, 215–16

remedy 43, 46, 51, 89, 106, 136, 146, 148, 173, 211, 213
rights (language) 2, 3, 4, 17, 41–51, 54-6, 58, 60-1, 63, 72, 75-6, 78–9, 89, 142, 160, 163–5, 168, 171–3, 176–7, 179, 184–6, 195, 209
risk 10, 11, 12, 13, 25, 26, 30, 59, 72, 97, 100, 123, 177

schemes [language] 4, 43, 46–7, 50, 61, 71–7, 79–82, 84, 88–90, 99, 108, 135–48, 150, 162, 193, 209, 214–16
Scotland 9, 163, 182, 186, 188, 190
scrutiny (of draft legislation, pubic policy) 7, 16, 20, 23, 37, 86, 103, 106, 110, 138, 143, 209, 212
Secretary of State 134, 135, 136, 139, 140, 143, 144, 150, 154

standards (language) 3, 4, 12, 16–19, 22, 24, 26, 30, 31, 41, 42–51, 61, 63, 71–95, 99, 104, 120, 135–7, 139, 140, 146, 148, 149, 150, 166, 173, 176, 207, 209, 211, 213–16

voice 8, 10, 11, 90

Welsh Language Board 5, 13, 14, 19, 30, 42, 45, 65, 73, 75–7, 79, 82, 83, 89, 90, 98, 99, 100, 101, 102, 103, 104, 106, 107, 108, 109, 117, 122, 133, 135, 143, 144, 145, 146, 147, 150, 154, 169, 214
Welsh Language Society (Cymdeithas yr Iaith Gymraeg) 82, 112–14, 119–21, 170, 172
Welsh Ministers 10, 14, 16, 17, 53, 80, 81, 83, 85, 86, 104, 118, 135, 136, 143, 147, 148